Sport in the Global Society

General Editors: J.A. Mangan and Boria Majumdar

BODY AND MIND

Sport in the global society
Series Editors: J. A. Mangan and Boria Majumdar

The interest in sports studies around the world is growing and will continue to do so. This unique series combines aspects of the expanding study of *sport in the global society*, providing comprehensiveness and comparison under one editorial umbrella. It is particularly timely, as studies in the multiple elements of sport proliferate in institutions of higher education.

Eric Hobsbawm once called sport one of the most significant practices of the late nineteenth century. Its significance was even more marked in the late twentieth century and will continue to grow in importance in the new millennium as the world develops into a 'global village' sharing the English language, technology and sport.

Other titles in the series

Body and Mind

Between the physical culture of ancient Greece and the development of our modern European and North American sports lie the 'forgotten centuries' of sport. *Body and Mind: Sport in Europe from the Roman Empire to the Renaissance* traces the evolution of sport in Western Europe from the arenas and chariot races of the Roman Empire, via the chivalric pursuits of the Middle Ages and the court games of the early modern period, to the triumph of personal decorum and scientific rationalism in the seventeenth century.

Drawing on primary sources, the book examines the ways in which political structures, educational systems, religious institutions, warfare, technology and medicine shaped sport over the long course of Europe's history. In doing so, it considers key themes and recurrent patterns in the development of physical cultures, as well as the wider significance of sport in the lives and societies of the time.

Offering a new and original perspective on the relationship between sport and society, this unique study will be of great interest to all historians of sport and culture.

John McClelland is Professor Emeritus of French Literature and former Associated Professor of Sports History at the University of Toronto.

Body and Mind

Sport in Europe from the Roman Empire to the Renaissance

John McClelland

Routledge
Taylor & Francis Group

LONDON AND NEW YORK

First published 2007
by Routledge
2 Park Square, Milton Park, Abingdon, Oxon OX14 4RN

Simultaneously published in the USA and Canada
by Routledge
270 Madison Ave, New York, NY 10016

Routledge is an imprint of the Taylor & Francis Group, an informa business

© 2007 John McClelland

Typeset in Baskerville by
HWA Text and Data Management, Tunbridge Wells
Printed and bound in Great Britain by
Antony Rowe Ltd, Chippenham, Wiltshire

British Library Cataloguing in Publication Data
A catalogue record for this book is available from the British Library

Library of Congress Cataloging-in-Publication Data
A catalog record for this book has been requested

ISBN10: 0–7146–5357–8 (hbk)
ISBN10: 0–203–96773–9 (ebk)

ISBN13: 978–0–7146–5357–0 (hbk)
ISBN13: 978–0–203–96773–7 (ebk)

To my beloved wife Laura and our daughters Claire
and Jacqueline

Contents

Illustrations

The illustrations are located following page 92

Series editors' foreword

Sport in the Global Society was launched in the late 1990s. It now has over 100 volumes. Until recently an odd myopia characterised academia with regard to sport. The global *groves of academe* remained essentially Cartesian in inclination. They favoured a mind/body dichotomy: thus the study of ideas was acceptable; the study of sport was not. All that has now changed. Sport is now incorporated, intelligently, within debate about *inter alia* ideologies, power, stratification, mobility and inequality. The reason is simple. In the modern world sport is everywhere: it is as ubiquitous as war. E.J. Hobsbawm, the Marxist historian, once called it one of the most significant of the new manifestations of late nineteenth-century Europe. Today it is one of the most significant manifestations of the twenty-first century world. Such is its power, politically, culturally, economically, spiritually and aesthetically, that sport beckons the academic more persuasively than ever – to borrow, and refocus, an expression of the radical historian Peter Gay – 'to explore its familiar terrain and to wrest new interpretations from its inexhaustible materials'. As a subject for inquiry, it is replete, as he remarked of history, with profound 'questions unanswered and for that matter questions unasked'.

Sport seduces the teeming 'global village'; it is the new opiate of the masses; it is one of the great modern experiences; its attraction astonishes only the recluse; its appeal spans the globe. Without exaggeration, sport is a mirror in which nations, communities, men and women now see themselves. That reflection is sometimes bright, sometimes dark, sometimes distorted, sometimes magnified. This metaphorical mirror is a source of mass exhilaration and depression, security and insecurity, pride and humiliation, bonding and alienation. Sport for many has replaced religion as a source of emotional catharsis and spiritual passion, and for many, since it is among the earliest of memorable childhood experiences, it infiltrates memory, shapes enthusiasms, serves fantasies. To co-opt Gay again: it blends memory and desire. Sport, in addition, can be a lens through which to scrutinise major themes in the political and social sciences: democracy and despotism and the great associated movements of socialism, fascism, communism and capitalism, as well as political cohesion and confrontation, social reform and social stability.

The story of modern sport is the story of the modern world in microcosm; a modern global tapestry permanently being woven. Furthermore, nationalist and imperialist, philosopher and politician, radical and conservative have all sought in sport a manifestation of national identity, status and superiority.

Finally, for countless millions sport is the personal pursuit of ambition, assertion, well-being and enjoyment.

For all the above reasons, sport demands the attention of the academic. *Sport in the Global Society* is a response.

J.A. Mangan
Boria Majumdar
Series editors
Sport in the Global Society

Preface

This book is addressed primarily to sports historians. It deals with athletics between the two historical periods and places that have tended to occupy their research, ancient Greece and modern Europe and North America. It is also addressed to the cultural historians of the early modern period, who have tended to overlook the role of sports and physical activities in the lives and social structures of individuals and political entities. It began life as a commissioned 40-page introduction, in French, to a facsimile reprint of Arcangelo Tuccaro's *Trois dialogues de l'exercice de sauter et voltiger en l'air* of 1599. For commercial reasons the reprint never saw the light of day, but the research I did on that project led to conference papers, contacts with colleagues working in related areas, and to the discovery of many more sixteenth-century books that taught the principles and practice of one or another of the varieties of athletics.

I had then thought to write a monograph on sport in the Renaissance, but was encouraged by J.A. Mangan to extend my scope back to include the Middle Ages, starting with the fall of the western Roman Empire in 476. Preliminary research convinced me that that date was as artificial for sports history as it was for social and political history, and that ancient sport underwent its real qualitative change in the years following Augustus's accession to the principate in 31–27 BC. On the other hand, to write a book that would treat Roman and Early Modern sport as if there was some continuity between the two flies in the face of what has seemed an irrefutable fact to all historians: the 'awful revolution', to use F. W. Walbank's term, that put an end to ancient civilisation. Sport was no more continuous through the Dark Ages than was any other form of Roman culture, but, I shall argue, recurrent cycles can be observed.

The starting point of my research, once I expanded it beyond the Renaissance, was naturally the general histories that had already been published, beginning with the work of Dennis Brailsford, Roland Auguet, HA. Harris, and Gerhard Lukas, and later with that of J.-P. Thuillier and Bernard Merdrignac. Although I have, as much as possible, gone back to the primary sources that they indicated to me, this book owes them a debt that is not always acknowledged. Similarly, other books and writers influenced my thinking about ancient and early modern sport in ways that are both concrete and intangible, hence more difficult to specify than any of the customary scholarly formats allow: Jacques Ulmann, Allen Guttmann, David Sansone, Nigel Crowther and Donald Kyle among those who have written directly on sport; James Ackerman, Alfred Crosby, Michel Foucault, Robert Klein, Bernard Weinberg, John White, and Sheldon Zitner among those whose subject lay elsewhere.

Along the way the project encountered a number of hurdles, the most significant of which has been the burgeoning of interest in the sports of ancient Rome and the concomitant appearance of a number of important books that revealed primary and secondary sources I had heretofore been unaware of. Gladiators, in particular, have been the object of recent studies almost too numerous to mention. In the early modern period, Fleckenstein's (1985) and Barber and Barker's (1989) work on the tournament, Heiner Gillmeister's history of tennis (1997), and Sydney Anglo's study of Renaissance martial arts (2000) have also obviated the necessity of covering those two subjects in the detail I had planned (and rendered superfluous some of the things I had already written). Ultimately, it became clear that it no longer made any sense simply to chronicle the evolution of sport during the 16 centuries in which, as several people have commented, sport seemed to drop off the historiographical radar. What is offered here then is a set of thematically based essays that each trace a particular dimension of sport and athletics in general over the *longue durée*. For this reason, the book is repetitious in places and at times it tells readers in some detail things they already know. The chapters may be read independently of each other and in almost any order, although the last three chapters should, I think, be read as a group.

In a book of this scope there are inevitably some imbalances. For the Early Modern period French and Italian sources are especially prominent because these have over the years been the major fields of my research. There are also, undoubtedly, materials that have been overlooked or given less prominence than some may think they deserve. In particular, I have not felt comfortable writing on horsemanship, and so there is nothing here on that subject. Fortunately the forthcoming work of Serge Vaucelle will palliate that neglect. Physical education generated a copious body of literature in the fifteenth and sixteenth centuries, but it belongs properly to another kind of study, except to the extent it impinges on sport. Beyond these, no other omission has been intentional and to the best of my knowledge I have not purposefully left out any primary or secondary text that might invalidate an argument I wish to make.

Some components of these chapters have been published elsewhere, as will be indicated in the notes, but only one is reprinted verbatim from a previous publication. Other elements have been drawn from papers and lectures given at the conferences and meetings of the North American Society for Sport History, the Society for the Study of Play, the Collège Européen de Sport Histoire, the France Seminar (Toronto), the Toronto Renaissance and Reformation Colloquium, the UCLA Center for Medieval and Renaissance Studies, the North Plains Conference on Early British Literature, the Convegni di Studi Umanistichi at Montepulciano, the Université de Paris IV-Sorbonne, the Université de Paris

V, the Ecole des Hautes Etudes en Sciences Sociales (Paris), the Centre d'Etudes Supérieures de la Renaissance (Tours), the Université de Montpellier, the Institut für Sportwissenschaften at the Georg-August Universität (Göttingen), and conferences and meetings organized by the Centre for Reformation and Renaissance Studies in Victoria University at the University of Toronto. On these occasions I received many helpful comments for which I wish to express my thanks.

Over time, many colleagues and friends have made contributions big and small, intellectual and material, to the realization of the project. Michael Flannery, David Hamilton, Jill Levenson, Greg Malszecki, Fik Meijer, Joachim Rühl, and Zahra Newby gave me access to their research before it was publicly available or not to be found in Toronto libraries. Joan Bigwood, Bill Edwards, Jim Estes, Michael Dewar, and Alison Keith were always willing to help me over the hurdles posed by languages with which I was less familiar. Nigel Crowther, Don Kyle, Stephen Miller, and J.-P. Thuillier provided helpful, off-the-record insight into aspects of ancient sport. Paul Denis, Teresa González Aja, Corey Keeble, Paul-Hervé Parsy, Manuel Terrón Bermúdez, and Nicola Woods assisted me in putting together the book's illustrations. Other, more intangible debts, are owed for their help, friendship and encouragement to Jean-Michel Benoit, Ned Duval, Marie Madeleine Fontaine, Nevenka and the late Norman Gritz, Brian Merrilees, François Roudaut, David Smith, Serge Vaucelle, Georges Vigarello and many others. To all I here express my thanks, which I must also extend to Routledge editors Samantha Grant and Kate Manson, for their patience and assistance.

Finally, I must recognize a debt of gratitude to three colleagues and friends who are the book's prime movers: Paul Bouissac, who first introduced me to the work of Arcangelo Tuccaro and whose intellectual vitality continues to set an example; Bruce Kidd, whose decanal generosity made it possible for me to teach sports history in the University of Toronto's Faculty of Physical Education; and Arnd Krüger, whose offer of a visiting professorship at Göttingen opened up my research into Roman sport, and who, beyond that, has been a hospitable and energetic model of sports scholarship.

Above all, of course, my gratitude goes to my wife and colleague Laura Willett. She has supported this project in word and deed, taken time from her own research to help me with mine, and kept me focused in the face of other distractions. It has been – and will continue to be – an unalloyed pleasure to work and think and talk with her in the sun-filled room that is our study.

Acknowledgements

Paul Bouissac and the Oxford University Press have given permission to reprint my article 'Sport' from the *Encyclopedia of Semiotics* (1998).

Illustrations 1–3 and 5–7 illustrating items in the collections of the Royal Ontario Museum, Toronto, are reproduced with the permission of the Museum. Permission to reproduce Illustrations 4 and 8 has been granted by the Biblioteca de San Lorenzo el Real de El Escorial (Spain) and the Château d'Oiron (France) respectively.

Financial support for my research was received from the Social Sciences and Humanities Research Council of Canada and from Victoria College in the University of Toronto, for which I am very grateful.

Chapter 1

Timelines, historiography, definitions

Between the years 28 and 2 BC Augustus, the first emperor, and the Roman senate in his honour, created three ostensibly permanent, quadrennial Greek-style athletic festivals, the *ludi pro valetudine Caesaris* (games to foster the emperor's long life and good health), the *Actia*, and the *Sebasta*, and elevated them to the same status as the Olympic and other 'crown' games that had been in existence for centuries (Caldelli 1993). These moves marked a new departure in the history of Roman sport. The Romans had previously considered Greek games to be oddities associated with the triumphs of victorious generals returning from the east. These new games, however, were part of a series of initiatives that would radically alter both quantitatively and qualitatively the sports that the Romans watched and practiced. Despite the fact that only the first festival of the three was held in Rome[1] – the other two took place in Nicopolis, Greece, and in Greek-speaking Naples respectively – they were perceived in retrospect as establishing a model for future emperors to follow and as achieving an assimilation of Greek and Roman culture.[2]

In June 1559, the French king Henri II similarly modified the course of sports history, though he did so inadvertently. Forty years old, politically defeated, and physically vulnerable, he hoped to recoup his prestige by jousting against a younger man he believed he could unhorse. As the two riders' weapons struck their mark, Henri's visor flew open and a large splinter of his opponent's lance pierced his eye and entered his brain. The best doctors were brought in and six criminals were beheaded to see if the wound could be replicated and a treatment devised, but to no avail. Henri's death 10 days later – perhaps the first time in history that a king had died from a sports-related injury – effectively brought to an end a sport the European nobility had practiced for six centuries and turned all its future manifestations into mere pomp and pageantry. The elimination of tourneying and jousting from the range of physical activities the upper classes might legitimately practice started an evolution that culminated in golf and lawn tennis.

Thus articulated, the dates chosen as terminals for this partial history of Western sport appear to derive from an outmoded historiography based on the notion of the 'great man'. They are more, however, than mere narrative conveniences. History is the sum of what humans did or failed to do, and some individuals have, historically, committed or omitted more – and more significant – acts than others. Historians, I think, all agree that Augustus's accession to imperial power in Rome introduced political and cultural innovations that radically altered the ancient world. Greek civilisation spread west and Roman civilisation spread east. Small towns throughout the Empire burgeoned into cities, and Roman architecture and literature dominated the Mediterranean world. Henri's death some 16 centuries later certainly had a destructive affect within France – religiously based civil war would shortly break out and last 35 years – but it also led to a realignment of Western European power structures that would ultimately produce the first new empires since the decline and fall of Rome. More importantly for our purposes, it coincided chronologically with a number of decisive developments in both science and art that in retrospect have been seen to have created the set of paradigms that we call modernity.

The modifications that were introduced in the last decades of the pre-common era and again in the middle of the sixteenth century are just as visible in sport as in other phenomena. By 30 BC Roman spectator sports had a history going back as much as several hundred years, but under Augustus and his successors sports spectacles increased in number and variety, became the monopoly of the state, and were housed in the monumental venues that we associate with them today. At the same time, personal athletic activities lost some of the proto-military character that had originally justified their pursuit. Under the guise of the *collegia*, associations of young nobles created by Augustus, they took on more of the character of the Greek gymnasium, acquiring a medical, hygienic dimension and moving from the parade ground to exercise rooms (*palaestrae*) built as annexes to the public baths or into the country villas of private individuals. In republican times, physical exercise was a sign of performing one's civic and national duty; under the Empire it became a sign of one's wealth, nobility, and social prestige. Most interesting, however, is the fact that Latin writers, beginning with those that lived into Augustus's reign and that were at least on the fringes of his court, started to deal with matters athletic in some detail. This reflects not only the increasing importance of sport as a social phenomenon under the Empire, but also a willingness on the part of Roman authors to put sport into language, to intellectualize what had seemed to be purely physical activities and to recreate them in sentences that conveyed the reality of physical contests to their readers. This subjection of gestures to words bespeaks the increasing dominance of the mind over the body in imperial Latin culture, the submission of the organic – and therefore innately chaotic – to the artificial rational order of grammar.

The changes in athletics attendant on the demise of Henri II correspond to criteria that are partially of a different order. Physical exercise, focused almost entirely on the training of future knights in the handling of weapons and horses, had certainly existed in the early Middle Ages but the transmission of its techniques was almost entirely oral. Tournaments were not quite ad hoc affairs, but they had little internal structure beyond the attempts by knights to capture the horses and persons of their adversaries and hold them for ransom. In the fourteenth century, however, spectacle, entertainment, and the display of chivalric prowess came to take precedence over the acquisition of booty as the determining factors in the tournament.

In the following decades, Renaissance humanists, usually employed as pedagogues, gave physical exercise a new articulation as part of general education and expanded its repertoire beyond the handling of weapons. They drew the authority for their pronouncements in this domain not from existing practice – though as Körbs (1938) pointed out, that is exactly what their programs perpetuated – but from what they knew of the sports of Greco-Roman antiquity. Almost simultaneously, various kinds of ball games – previously confined to ecclesiastics and rustics – began to interest the upper classes and, alongside dancing, joined with tourneying and fencing to create a new paradigm of knightly sports. There was also a change in ethic. Although competitiveness was still present, Castiglione's *Book of the Courtier*, published in 1528, stipulated that the most important thing for a noble was to ride, joust, swim, and play ball games with *sprezzatura*, a nonchalance that demonstrated to spectators his superior physical and athletic skills (Castiglione 1972). Three years later, Thomas Elyot's *Book of the Governor* also valorised sport and exercise as 'apt to the furniture of a gentleman's personage' and as both physically healthy and psychologically 'a laudable solace' (Elyot 1962/1531: 60). But in athletics as in other pursuits the Renaissance carried within it the seeds of its own undoing.

The social promotion of sport among the upper classes from the fourteenth through the sixteenth centuries certainly dribbled down into the bourgeoisie, probably through the schools, where recess became a time for competitive games, *cf.* Erasmus's 1522 colloquy on sport, 'De lusu' (Erasmus 1965: 22–30). It also attracted the attention of doctors, who debated with each other on the value of exercise, and came under the scrutiny of the bureaucratic mind. In the early fifteenth century tournament leagues were formed in Germany, with their attendant insistence on rules and regulations. There and elsewhere lances had to be stamped with official seals of approval, saddles and shields had to be uniform, and complex number-based scoring systems were adopted and applied. All these moves gradually robbed the chivalric sports of their spontaneity. Renaissance sport, as Semenza has said (2003: 13) 'bridges the chasm between the unrestrained disorderliness of Carnival and the orderliness of all rule-bound phenomena'. This shift towards rationalizing sport – in much the same way as Alberti rationalized artistic perspective in the early fifteenth century – was not to everyone's liking. Shakespeare certainly decried it (see Chapter 8) and Henri II had actually insisted that his fatal tournament be conducted 'à l'imitation des anciens tournois' (Tavannes 1838/1573: 225) rather than in the new style of scoring points cumulatively according to where your lance struck your opponent's body or shield.

This shift was concomitant with a new sense of decorum that in the course of the Renaissance permeated the nobility and the upwardly mobile bourgeoisie and cast opprobrium on physical movements that might require them to sweat or perform gestures that, if not graceful, would make the doer look ridiculous.[3] Up to about 1600 French and other European rulers and their courts were fairly avid tennis players, both indoor and outdoor, but by the 1660s the courtiers of Louis XIV (1643–1715) and Charles II (1660–85) were less concerned with playing strenuous games and more with fencing, hunting, dancing well, and appearing fashionable, although Charles himself liked to play tennis vigorously enough to provoke copious perspiration.[4]

Parallel to sport's transformation into a regulated, rationalized activity and to the distancing between the self and the body that is implicit in the notion of decorum, sports also became over the course of the Renaissance something you could write about and talk about among persons of culture. As in ancient Latin there began to exist in the modern languages a vocabulary and a syntax capable of clearly describing a succession of physical gestures. After 1530 numerous books started to appear giving instruction in swordplay, swimming, archery, tennis, etc., and many of these – swordplay is an exception – were written not by professional athletes but by learned outsiders who relied much more heavily on text than on illustration.[5] Paradoxically, as I shall argue in Chapter 8, the progressive intellectualization of sport both fostered an interest in the nature of athletic activity and led fairly quickly to its abandonment as an actual practice among upper and middle-class Europeans.

Sport and bodily activities in general can be experienced by both participants and spectators as purely physical events, a set of rapidly executed gestures that lie somewhere outside the domain of language and reason. By creating a literature that taught its readers how to play tennis, ride a horse, shoot an arrow, or wield a rapier – both bio-mechanically and strategically – the late Renaissance objectified these forms of play and robbed them of their mystery. It thereby gradually removed sport from the domain of the intuitive and spontaneous and made it into a rational object analogous to those studied by physics and anatomy. The rise of scientific method that began with Copernicus and Vesalius before 1550 and flourished with Galileo, Harvey, and Descartes in the early seventeenth century placed a premium on intellectual activities and downgraded leisurely physical pursuits to the level of children's games or mere popular amusements. Despite isolated British examples – the upper-class pursuits of golf, cricket, and horseracing were all institutionalized between 1750 and 1787 – and despite an interest shown by educators in physical education for children in the eighteenth century (Ulmann 1977), the decline of serious athletics among adults, of the kind envisioned by Bardi (1580) and James I (1996/1599), would last for another two centuries. It was really only after 1850 that sports – almost all (re)invented – began again to occupy the prestigious cultural position that had been theirs in ancient Rome and early modern Europe.

Between these two high points of sport – Rome in the first two centuries of the Empire and Western Europe in the later Middle Ages and the Renaissance – there was a long fallow period that has been attributed to a number of factors. The various Roman games – 177 days of them per year in the third and fourth centuries – continued to be held at their stipulated dates, but attention seems to have been diverted from them to more urgent issues. Under the pressure of barbarian incursions, the Empire that Augustus had united was split into two halves by Diocletian in 285, along a line roughly coincidental with the present boundary separating Croatia from Serbia. And by 395 these two halves had become four quarters. Similarly, Rome itself, though it retained its historical symbolic prestige, had long been abandoned as an imperial residence in favour of cities closer to the places where the threat to the Empire's northern boundaries seemed most real: Milan or Trier or Ravenna or Sirmium.[6] The Colosseum, the Circus Maximus, and Domitian's stadium, all built or enlarged between 80 and 114, still stood and athletic contests were still held there, but the people's real attention was focused elsewhere and on other things.

It was also becoming increasingly expensive and complicated to stage spectator sports. Augustus had concentrated the monopoly of the games in the hands of the emperor, but in later centuries they were left again to private initiative. When the Roman official Symmachus was obliged to organize games to celebrate his son's elevation to high administrative offices in the late fourth century, his correspondence reveals that he had to write desperately to various friends all over the Empire to get enough gladiators, horses for the chariot races, and wild animals for the *venationes* or wild beast hunts (*Letters*, Budé, books 2, 5, and 9). For these same reasons, provincial officials who bore the responsibility of staging games in the outlying administrative centres had gradually abdicated this responsibility, preferring to devote such funds as they had to more useful purposes (Hen 1995). In other words, sports were not worth the money and effort that was spent on them.

Another contributing factor in the decline of the Roman games was certainly the negative attitude towards them expressed first by pagan moralists – Seneca – and then by the Christian moralists who took up the theme – Tertullian, St Cyprian, Salvian. Throughout the Middle Ages, Christianity in fact remained opposed to games in general, as it did to any indulgence that brought pleasure to the body, and this opposition increased in direct proportion to the material and human violence that the games might occasion, whether they were popular or aristocratic. Equally significant is the fact that the essentially nomadic peoples who flooded into the Empire from the east and who by the year 500 ruled Western Europe in the place of the Romans had no athletic culture. Although the first generation of barbarian rulers tried to mount public games in the way the emperors had, they really did not know how to go about it (Cassiodorus 1973; Gregory of Tours 1927). As Sidonius (*Letters*, Loeb 1.2) reports in the fifth century and Eginhard (1967/828) again in the ninth, Frankish and Gothic kings lacked the aristocratic Roman's sense of personal dignity and liked to show off their athletic talents, but as they equated personal strength with authority, they did not want to enter into any sporting contests with their power-hungry vassals. Europe between 600 and 1000 was, in any case, 'profondément sauvage', as Georges Duby described it (1973b: 11), and not fertile ground for Huizinga's play element to take root.

When 'civilization' began to emerge after the first millennium in the form of princely courts and recognizable municipalities, such sports as did begin to appear were little more than violent encounters between rival groups of townsfolk or rival bands of knights. From late antiquity through the Middle Ages, and again through much of the eighteenth and nineteenth centuries, sport was an object of opprobrium among intellectuals and moralists. And though the Renaissance and the twentieth century did much to re-establish its prestige, the less than favourable opinions of sport that were prevalent among social critics are certainly reflected in the long unwillingness of modern scholarship to engage the history of athletics in the period I am covering here. They may also explain why the primary sources simply do not exist in the way they exist for Greek sports. Either no one wanted to write on a subject that was thought not serious, or perhaps even morally and physically dangerous, or if they did, these texts were not preserved. Before the late 1300s we know of almost no books in Latin, German, or the Romance languages that provide the same kind of detailed information we can get from Greek texts such as Lucian's *Anacharsis* or Philostratos' *Gymnastikos*.

However, the greatest obstacle to the study of Roman, Medieval, and Renaissance athletics was the wave of Hellenophilia that swept Western Europe in the nineteenth century. The origins of this movement lay in the Enlightenment and the Neo-classical aesthetic developed in the eighteenth century, but was given impetus by the Greek war of independence (1814–29) from the Muslim Turks, who had been for centuries a military menace to Western Europe.[7] One of the outcomes of this philhellenic movement was the revival of what purported to be the ancient Olympics in 1896 – the first archaeological excavations at Olympia had begun in 1829 – and the exaltation of what people wanted to believe was the pure, disinterested athleticism that had characterized ancient Greek sport (Young 1985).

Nineteenth-century Hellenophilia was accompanied by a certain anti-Roman prejudice that emphasized the decadence of the late Roman Empire and that, in the field of sport history, was most forcibly enunciated by E. Norman Gardiner (1910).[8] Echoing earlier English writers, Gardiner based his admiration for Greek games on the racial principle that the 'tall, fair-haired, athletic race' that had invaded Greece in prehistoric times had also 'spread...westwards as far as our own islands', and that it was 'no mere accident' that 'the physical vigour and restless energy' that would explain the Greeks' 'colonial activity and love of sport' were also characteristic of the British (Gardiner 1910: 8).

Gardiner's adulation of Greek athletes – he even went so far as to distort the motivations of the heroes competing at athletics in *Iliad* 23 (1910: 11) – was more deeply rooted, however, than a fanciful shared ethnicity with the ancient Greeks. It has been suggested that he was genuinely alienated by 'the stigma of Rome and its gladiatorial events', to the point of dropping the chapter on the hippodrome from the 1930 reissue of the book.[9] When he does speak of the Romans, Gardiner has little good to say about them: in the first century AD, 'the influence of Rome was degrading and brutalizing the public taste of Greece ... At Rome, scientific boxing

was of … little account' (1910: 172); Romans were 'not fond of competitions …
and their festivals … soon became mere spectacles, in which the performers …
were professionals belonging to subject races and the lower classes' (1910: 163);
the Romans had been 'brutalized by incessant war' and 'took more pleasure in
the gladiatorial shows … than in musical or gymnastic competitions' (1910: 164).
Twenty years later he would write that the Romans 'rode, hunted, swam, boxed
sometimes, or wrestled, but without any science … For competitions they had no
liking' (1930: 117; also Marrou 1981: 2.23).

Sports historiography in the twentieth century was so influenced by Gardiner
and by the Olympic movement in general that, as Martin Reis has written, for
many years the dominant opinion among classical scholars and sports historians
held that studying Roman sport was irrelevant.[10] Eight years later Bernard
Merdrignac found that people still believed that 'modern sport derived from the
Greeks' and that 'for the public at large (and perhaps also for most athletes?)
between the disappearance of competitive athletics in Antiquity and their revival
at the dawn of the twentieth century, there is no history of physical education'
(Merdrignac 2002: 9–10).[11]

Gardiner's motivation in excluding Roman athletics from the domain of sport,
however, may be owing to nobler feelings than mere snobbishness. Of the chief
forms of Roman spectator sports – gladiatorial fights, wild beast hunts, chariot
races, and Greek-style athletics – the first three produced, either purposefully or
accidentally, the killing or maiming of humans and animals.[12] Beyond his own
misguided belief in the refined moral and intellectual superiority of the Greeks,
Gardiner was articulating the same perplexity that had faced the admirers of ancient
Rome from the Renaissance onwards. The philosopher Michel de Montaigne, in
his essay 'On Cruelty' (1588), expressed revulsion at the Romans' willingness to
slaughter humans and animals in the name of sport and entertainment, dreading
that it was the mark of a fundamental human flaw:

> Once the Romans had become accustomed to spectacles in which animals
> were murdered, they moved on to men and gladiators. I fear that Nature
> herself attaches some instinct for inhumanity to humankind. No one takes
> pleasure in watching animals caressing each other and playing together, and
> no one fails to enjoy seeing them dismember and tear each other apart.
>
> (Montaigne 1965: 433)[13]

This revulsion in the face of physical suffering imposed on the weak by the
powerful had grown more acute from the late eighteenth century onwards,
particularly among the British (Thomas 1983). The attitudes towards Roman
games expressed by Gardiner and others were perhaps formed as much by their
hatred of cruelty and inhumanity as they were by unbridled Hellenophilia.

For all Rome's historical, geographic, and linguistic proximity to the early
modern states of Western Europe, there was something deeply disturbing about
ancient Roman culture. The paradox is explicit in the title of Roland Auguet's

pioneering study of the Roman games: *Cruauté et civilisation*, the normalized existence of extreme cruelty within civilized society (Auguet 1970). Another modern historian, R. H. Barrow (1949: 106–7), was so disgusted by the 'vulgarity and beastliness, the revolting horror of these shows', that he could not grasp the willingness of 'educated men, whose whole sympathies were on the side of humanity and decency … to provide entertainments whose barbarity shocked them as individuals'. In a book of over 200 pages that purported to give a full, if popular, account of Roman history and culture, he devoted only one paragraph to gladiatorial fights, wild-beast shows, chariot racing, and the theatre, though during the late Empire events of this sort occupied almost 180 days of the Roman year. As Keith Hopkins (1983: 26) has put it, 'The cultural divide between us and the Romans is difficult to cross'. Judging Roman culture from the vantage point of the twentieth century, the resultant mindset was that there was no such thing as Roman sport and that it was a waste of time to even look for it.

To some extent, the athletic pursuits of the Middle Ages and the Renaissance suffered from the same scholarly prejudice. Preoccupied with finding manifestations of more intellectual or spiritual human aspirations, historians of these periods and others have neglected until recently the activities of the body. Looked at from the vantage point of the twentieth century or the twenty-first century the games and other physical activities of the early modern era look to be amiably picturesque or unspeakably brutal, but definitely not sporting. Even contemporaries at times recoiled from them. Jousting and tournaments, at least before 1300, were barely different from actual warfare in their methods and their purpose (Duby 1973a). Scarcely less violent than gladiatorial fights had been, they very often caused severe injuries and even deaths (Anglo 2000). On those grounds, from at least 1130 onward, tournaments and jousting were frequently sanctioned by both royal and ecclesiastical authorities. The knights who participated in these events were a brutal lot (Goetz 1993; Kaeuper 1999), despite Medieval attempts to instil an ethic and make them seem noble and generous (Flori 1998), and they were certainly far removed from the supposedly disinterested athletes of idealized ancient Greece.[14]

In the cities, whose growing economic power obtained for them a certain measure of autonomy, the 'sports', as William Heywood designates them, were often rough-and-tumble vendetta fights between rival neighbourhoods that passed themselves off as games (Davis 1994). Much of the history of late Medieval local government is the history of efforts to restrict and control these contests and so limit the damage to people and buildings that they caused (Heywood 1969/1904; Rizzi 1995).[15] Even the ball games were risky to life and health. Field games like football, *soule*, and *calcio* were often occasions to settle grudges (Carter 1988; Mehl 1990), or at the least, as Richard Mulcaster wrote in 1581, characterized by 'bursting of shinnes, and breaking of legges' (Mulcaster 1994: 111). The more refined *jeu de paume* was played with a hard ball that could do real hurt if a player was struck in the head – there are reports of tennis players losing eyes or being killed. In the minds of many scholars, then, the manifestations of these kinds of at least semi-athletic popular culture were best forgotten (Davis 1994).[16] Even where no physical suffering was involved, Medieval and Renaissance sports are still thought by some writers as having been imagined in a manner quite different from that of more modern sports, and consequently as not being amenable to the same forms and premises of analysis, and perhaps not even being worthy of the name 'sport'. At best, they were mere pastimes or variants of children's play or enactments of folkloric ritual or expressions of social and class solidarity; at worst, forms of inter-personal brutality that passed themselves off as sports contests (Ulmann 1977; Guttmann 1978; Kidd 1996; Vigarello 2000, 2002).[17]

Despite this ongoing prejudice against even the idea of considering Roman, Medieval, and Renaissance athletic pursuits to be actually sport, there were isolated studies, often by antiquarians, that did approach the subject – although, to be honest, when they used the word 'sport', the authors did not necessarily mean what later writers intended by the term. The first books to be devoted at least in part to Roman athletics and spectator sports appeared in the mid-sixteenth century. They were often the work of medical doctors researching the prophylactic value of ancient gymnastics, which they had learned from reading Galen, and trying to understand – from archaeological remains – the functioning of the Roman baths. Thus Du Choul on Roman military practices, baths, and exercises (1555), Panvinio on the circus games (1600, but written before 1568), Mercurialis's influential *Ars gymnastica* (1569), Bacci on the baths (1571), Joubert on gymnasiums and exercises (1582), and Du Faur de Saint Jorry on Greek games and Roman chariot races (1592) all tried to create some understanding of physical pursuits in the ancient Roman empire, although sport itself is often incidental to their main subject. As humanists their concern was to both understand the past and draw from it lessons that were useful in the present.

Two further points need to be made concerning these early books. The first is that when ancient Roman sport and physical activity became subjects of study in Renaissance Europe, it was either as an appendage to Greek gymnastics, military and, especially, medical gymnastics, or as subsidiary to a larger field of historical or scientific research. Second, once these books were published, they were not superseded by subsequent, more informed studies, but simply reprinted or republished. Du Choul's book had reappeared five times by 1581, was translated into Italian in 1558, into Spanish in 1579, and into Latin in 1686. Mercurialis went through seven editions, the last in 1672, and Bacci was republished in 1588, 1622, and 1711. Du Faur de Saint Jorry was reissued in an expanded version in 1595 and thereafter there was really nothing new written on Roman sport until the twentieth century (Piganiol 1923; Robert 1940).

Early modern sports historiography might be said to have its start with Menestrier (1669) but it found its real *raison d'être* in the search for national identities that characterized the Romantic movement of the late eighteenth and early nineteenth centuries. Strutt's book on early English sport (1801) paved the way for similar research in other languages[18] and eventually led to the chronologically over-arching accounts of athletics by D'Allemagne (1880) and Bogeng (1926). More focused studies of early modern sport – they did not always call it by that name – were produced by Castle (1969/1885), Jusserand (1901), Heywood (1969/1904), Cripps-Day (1918), Coltman Clephan (1919), E. Mehl (1928, 1930a, 1930b, 1937), Körbs (1938) and Magoun (1938). In many cases, the work of these early historians has not been invalidated or replaced, though it does not always adhere to the scholarly standards and forms of discursive analysis now considered normal.

After the Second World War, the antiquarian strain appeared to die out (except for Henderson 1947 and Hole 1949), and by the 1960s occasional professional scholars came to be interested in the subject without being deterred by the conventional wisdom that held Roman and early modern sports history to be a trivial pursuit. Lily Stone (1960) produced a small scholarly volume on sports and recreations in Tudor and Stuart England and Michael Grant (1967) wrote perhaps the first book on gladiators since the encyclopaedia articles in Pauly (1893–1972) and Daremberg and Saglio (1877–1919) that was less concerned with inscriptions and more with the actual phenomenon. He thereby launched what has become the most explored sub-field within the overall area covered here.[19] Other books followed in the next two decades that dealt with Roman sports phenomena in various ways and that were addressed to a variety of publics (Balsdon 1969; Auguet 1970; Harris 1972; Cameron 1973, 1976; Isidori Frasca 1980; Savi 1980; Weiler 1981; Lukas 1982; Clavel-Lévêque 1984; Briceño Jáuregui 1986; Humphrey 1986; Golvin 1988; Nardone 1989). After 1990, the subject became even more popular, as will become clear in the following chapters, though reference should be made here to the collections of primary Latin sports sources published by Shelton (1988), Wistrand (1992), and Mahoney (2001).[20]

Early modern sports have not fared so well from a scholarly point of view. Brailsford (1969) did root his landmark study of seventeenth-century sport in the Elizabethan period, but his focus was forward to the eighteenth century rather than back to the Renaissance. Rühl (1975) also deals with the end of the period under study here, but the most valuable publication for research into early modern sport was Carlo Bascetta's two-volume compilation of primary Italian materials from the fifteenth to the eighteenth centuries ranging across the entire field of athletics (1978). Six collections of essays that originated as conference papers appeared from the early 1980s to the early 1990s (Ariès and Margolin 1982; Krüger and McClelland 1984; Fleckenstein 1985; Anglo 1990; Mehl 1993; Malato 1993),[21] and in the same years J. M. Carter published two slender, but very useful, studies of Medieval sport (1988, 1992) as well as co-editing a volume of papers that touched on the subject (Carter and Krüger 1990). Barber and Barker's generously illustrated study of the Medieval tournament (1989) usefully digested and completed – and considerably enlivened – the stern scholarship of earlier books in that field, while J.-M. Mehl's massive study of French Medieval games and sports (1990) established the legitimacy of early modern sport within the groves of academe. Still and all, the history of athletics in the Middle Ages and the Renaissance has attracted only sporadic scholarly interest, though it ultimately does generate publications of a very high quality: Clare (1983) on the sports used for training jousters (but practiced as sports in their own right), Morgan (1995) and Gillmeister (1997) on the history of tennis, Anglo (2000) on the Renaissance martial arts, Fontaine (1999), Semenza (2003) on the place of the body and sport within the political and literary debates of Renaissance France and England, Flannery and Leech (2004) on golf, and Vaucelle (2005) on equitation and fencing. Merdrignac (2002) gives a comprehensive account of Medieval sport, especially in France, and the appendix to his book provides excerpts from a number of primary sources translated or transliterated into modern French.

None of the foregoing books, however, covers both Roman athletics and those of the Middle Ages and Renaissance, with the exception of the encyclopaedic histories that strive to cover sport from the beginning to the present: D'Allemagne (1880) and Bogeng (1926) mentioned above, and more recently Diem (1960), Ueberhorst (1972–89), Ulmann (1977), Baker (1982), Mandell (1984), and Guttmann's impressive series of both general and more specialized studies (1978, 1986, 1996, 2004). Further, only a few of those who have written on the athletics of these centuries (e.g. Weiler 1981; Thuillier 1996b) actually challenge the prejudicial notion that the physical competitions of the Roman empire and/or Medieval and Renaissance Europe cannot be called sports in the same way that we apply that name to the athletic activities of the ancient Greeks or to those of the nineteenth to the twenty-first centuries. Some scholars do not bother to use the word 'sport' at all, and so the question does not even arise. Others choose to use 'sport' in its widest possible denotation, in the way the term is defined in the first edition of the *Oxford English Dictionary*: 'participation in games or exercises, esp. of an athletic character or pursued in the open air'. The result is that their books usefully demonstrate the persistence of all manner of physical activities throughout the periods in which these pursuits have been neglected by historians, but they do not really make the case that we ought to consider these pursuits to be sport.[22]

The remainder of this chapter will be devoted, then, to examining the notion of sport and seeing if a definition can be developed that will fall between the all-inclusive and the all-exclusive and at the same time fit, without distortion, all of the forms of organized athletic contests that his book will cover. It is obvious that such a definition risks appearing to be purely *a posteriori*, i.e. its terms will be framed in such a way as to allow me to label as 'sport' the forms of competitive play that I want to be so labelled. At the same time, it is equally obvious that if 'sport' is to have any meaning, that meaning has to be restrictive in some way and distinguish between activities to which the term can be legitimately applied and those to which it cannot.

The crux of the argument lies, then, in the grounds on which the distinction is established, and up to now these have been most often derived *a priori* from a particular ideology or at least a specific ideological position, e.g. the concept of sport as defined by the International Olympic Committee (IOC). It is frequently the case as well that those who argue in favour of the specificity of modern sport take as their starting point the kinds of popular games that are recorded as flourishing during the seventeenth and eighteenth centuries, without understanding the athletic practices of the Middle Ages and the Renaissance (e.g. During 1984).[23] Of course, Guttmann (1978) founds his characterization of modern sport more objectively on the appearance of seven phenomena – secularism, equality, specialization, rationalization, bureaucracy, quantification, records – which he believes were either not found in earlier versions of sport or were there only in an embryonic form or were unevenly applied. This assertion has been debated (Krüger and McClelland 1984, Carter and Krüger 1990), but ultimately it does not really help to examine existing definitions and to try to either refute them or extend their denotation to include the forms of athletics that are the subject of this book.

Sport – or modern sport – it is said, arises either because of a catastrophic change in the nature of play (Huizinga 1962); or incrementally through the progressive addition of new distinctive features to competitive play (Guttmann 1978); or by introducing morality and competition into proto-military gymnastic (Ulmann 1977); or through the desire to preserve and institutionalize in a symbolic way an activity once thought essential, i.e. some form of work, but now obsolete (Sansone 1988). Semiotically speaking, these explanations depend on there being a sign-system that is at least partially shared by both sport and its antecedent(s).

It is, of course, easy to demonstrate that this is the case. Like play, sport is a functionally gratuitous activity whose performance produces no immediately measurable material benefit, except monetary, whose content seems culturally determined, and which appears to convey meanings, but meanings that turn out to be drastically different from those of play. To the untrained eye, there may be little fundamental distinction between school children kicking a ball around a field and professional soccer teams playing a league match, but in fact, the former is almost completely unstructured and the latter tightly controlled by a bureaucracy that has gradually monopolized all aspects of the sport. Like physical training, sport consists of series of rhythmically executed, graceful, goal-oriented gestures that demand muscular discipline and coordination, but they do not share the same teleology. Like hunting – now mostly irrelevant as a means of obtaining food – sport can be both a solitary and a collective effort, both competitive and communal, both sensitive to the terrain and, with some exceptions, deliberately indifferent to the weather; both the hunter and the athlete wear special costumes that signify the nature of their activity and both display the trophies that index their success. In other words, sport emerges from previous practices with the same set of signifiers, but with new signifieds.

Most of these efforts to explain the origin of sport and to define it, as well as others previously mentioned, have used the insights of anthropology, educational science, and sociology. In their place, I propose to try to understand sport by borrowing models from the disciplines of linguistics and semiotics. The first move will be to situate sport within the nexus of activities with which it has been most frequently contrasted or otherwise linked: play, work, and war, rather than seeing it as one pole of a binary opposition or as the end-product of a set of ever-expanding, disjunctive dichotomies (Guttmann 1978: 9). The second will be to perform a kind of Cartesian analysis, breaking sport down into its smallest conceivable elements, and then reconstituting it as the sum of its parts. The aim will be to formulate an intellectually rigorous set of parameters that maintain the principle of distinction between what is sport and what is not.

Before going further, it should of course be kept in mind that though we may want to think of sport as an abstraction, as some kind of Platonic ideal, like any other human creation it exists only as the sum of all the sporting events that have ever taken place and ever will. Since no one of those events is exactly like any other, sport as a conception is in a constant state of evolution. In addition, as more forms of competition are added to the list of internationally recognized sports, the conception is necessarily being enlarged and re-imagined. Secondly, all sporting events, whether professional or amateur, simultaneously exist as a reality in the minds of at least three different groups: the promoters or organizers, the athletes, and the spectators. The first group may be concerned mostly with making money and avoiding expense, the second may be thinking of the contest as means of employment or self-promotion, while the third may have bet on the outcome or be concentrating on the communal advantages – inter-city, intercollegiate – that can result from a victory. Concomitantly, all three groups, being human, may be caught up at different points in the excitement of the match and the displays of athletic skill, so that at any given time the same sports event may be sport in the eyes of some who are involved and something else in the eyes of others.[24]

The first model to be applied here, commonly called the semiotic square, derived originally from Aristotle's logic (*De interpretatione* 17[b]17–20[a]15; *Prior Analytics* 51[b]5–52[b]34) but has been most clearly enunciated and explored as a semiotic concept by A. J. Greimas (1987). Creating the square is a cognitive procedure whose purpose is to transcend the synonym-antonym pattern and understand semantic relationships, and the substance behind them, as more complex than a simple antagonistic juxtaposition of opposites. It consists of placing two positive but seeming antithetical terms at the upper corners of a square and two negative terms diagonally opposite to them. Logically speaking, the two positives are normally recognized as contrary to each other, but not mutually contradictory, whereas the two negative terms are just that, though the nature of this contrariness and contradiction is not immediately clear. Further, the contradictory term is usually revealed to be the hinge that allows the semantic passage from one positive to the other.[25]

Definitions of sport usually derive out of the seeming opposition of work vs play that dictates the alternating rhythms of most people's lives. Virtually all cultures and societies connote both these terms positively – albeit in different ways, and at times grudgingly – but since they appear mutually antithetical, we may use them as our basic pair (Figure 1.1).[26]

Work ⟵⟶ Play

Work and play are not, however, contradictories. In early childhood education, children are taught to make certain forms of play into work by using the game to produce some kind of artefact. And adults, bored with their tasks, use various strategies to make them into games without sacrificing productivity. But beyond the possibility of transmogrifying play into work and vice-versa, the one characteristic they share, and that is essential for most forms of play and work to become successful, is cooperation among the players or workers. Play and work are thus linked by a complementarity, and may now be restated as in Figure 1.2.

Cooperative

Work ⟵――――――――⟶ Play

There is, however, a third form of human activity that is considered to override both work and play and that is the waging of war. Since war undoes what work has accomplished, it is not simply unproductive in the way that play is, it is destructive and therefore the contradictory of work. Because war is purposefully deadly, it is obviously the contrary to play. On the other hand, the two are complementary in the sense that both are wasteful of time, resources, and energy – although war is wasteful to an immeasurably greater degree. Paradoxically, war is also an intermediate term between work and play, because it shares with work the characteristic of being serious – deadly serious, one might way – but it then turns that seriousness to futility (Figure 1.3).

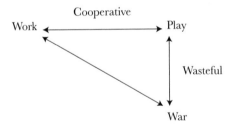

Filling the fourth corner of the square is, as Fredric Jameson (1987) pointed out, the most challenging task in completing the cognitive structure, and it is also the most contentious and the most illuminating. Obviously, here, it will be filled by sport. Given that sport is often considered a sub-set of play or simply a more intense variant with greater emphasis on victory (Michael Salter, quoted in Chick and Loy 1996), it is difficult to consider it as the contradictory of play. Yet, as will become clear later in this chapter and in the rest of the book, in many ways sport controverts play, though it does not do so in the negative fashion imagined by Huizinga (1962).

Because sport occurs in the time of leisure, it is the contrary of work, and because it is not supposed to generate either destruction or death, it is the contrary of war. At the same time it is complementary to work because at the highest level athletes are paid and sport generates various forms of economic activity – at one or two degrees of separation, of course, because the physical actions executed during a sporting event are themselves unproductive. Sport is also complementary to war in that both are competitive – though war more intensely so – and strategic and that many of the basic sports were, in fact, skills useful in warfare and in personal combat. In the first representation of sport in Western literature – book 23 of Homer's *Iliad* – the athletes are all soldiers and the contests are all warlike. Many centuries later, during the First World War, British officers thought that war could be conducted as if it were a sport, and soldiers attacking the German trenches at the battle of the Somme in 1916 kicked a soccer ball ahead of them (Ferguson 1999; Keegan 1998).

The final form of the square looks then like Figure 1.4.

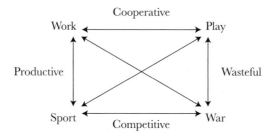

Examined and situated in this way, sport is no longer relegated to being the irreconcilable opposite of work, but is understood as part – and not the end part – of a continuum that stretches from the innocent and the innocuous to the deadly serious. Moreover, this continuum is not a finite line but actually a square within a circle whose arcs – the set of complementarities – diameters, and chords – the set of cognitive axes – reveal that any defined point on the circumference is linked to the other three in a semantically complex relation. Sport cannot be defined simply as an 'autotelic, ludic, physical contest' (Guttmann 1986:4) because it has many more dimensions than that.

The realization that sport might be conceived in this manner derived from an earlier attempt to understand its specificity using another semio-linguistic model first proposed by Morris Halle (Jakobson and Halle 1956).[27] It is referred to as distinctive feature analysis and its underlying principle is that meaning is generated by a set of often minute differences between two phenomena. Its methodology is thus empirical and pragmatic rather than theoretical and conceptual and relies on close, detailed examination and finely drawn distinctions. As a result, its problematic is centred on the determination of which differences are significant, i.e. are signs, and which are simply non-signifying variants. In English ball games, for example, the question as to whether players could touch the ball with their hands or use only their feet was merely a matter of local convention and ad hoc decision until the 1860s when it became the basis for deciding that there were in fact two different sports, rugby and soccer-football (Magoun 1938).

First, then, sport is a physical activity that, like play, is ostensibly pleasurable but functionally gratuitous. However, it differs from play by being also disciplined and necessarily competitive. The competition may be immediate and the sport therefore involve defensive as well as offensive manoeuvres; or the athletes may simply be striving to achieve their personal best and have no opportunity or wish to hinder other competitors; or they may – simultaneously or not – be attempting to establish a record and be competing against a previous performance more or less removed in time. Sport is therefore serious and teleological and these features have been increasingly articulated in the form of a quantification that has extended beyond what is needed to establish records.

In consequence of this general mindset, sport normally sets out to determine which athlete or team is the best in a given league or at a given tournament or set of games. In some cases this determination is reached by a process of elimination: the winners of the first heat or round or set of playoffs compete against each other at a second level, and so on up until a champion is proclaimed. There are exceptions to this process – sometimes the champion is just the person or team with the best overall score, sometimes the evaluation is more qualitative and subjective – but the end result remains the same.

Because sport is agonistic and oriented towards victory, it requires physical training and psychological preparation, and more than that, strategies to achieve that purpose. For that reason, many forms of sport specifically include warm-up or practice sessions to which spectators are admitted, prior to the match itself. At the same time, it is also ritualistic, being performed according to rules, regulations, and conventions and at set days or times of the year or at specified yearly intervals. Some of the rules and regulations may be practical, but most are arbitrary and consequently ceremonial and a-realistic. Within the rules, however, sport, being a human creation, is innovative. It encourages the imaginative exploitation of the rituals and regulations and feats of individual prowess not originally conceived as being possible. Because of these features, sports are evolutionary, either in terms of their general practice or of the degree to which the rituals are observed. Ultimately, the rules may be changed in order to institutionalise desirable innovation.

Sporting contests represent 'possible worlds' in which the rules and rituals are enforced by bureaucracies and applied equally to all. These possible worlds are thus also perfectly moral worlds and this morality is usually indexed by as precise forms of measurement as are available. The measurements – and hence the moral autonomy of the world that sport expresses – are customarily visible as real or symbolic barriers around the place of sport and often subdivide the interior of that space into areas that are hierarchically related to each other.

As the icons of possible worlds, sports had in ancient times and have had again since the nineteenth century their own permanent, reserved spaces, which they may share with other ludic activities but not, generally, with any practical pursuit; sports are thus physically isolated from, and even counter to, the places of the ordinary train of life. This isolation is also marked by the resort to special costumes and equipment that are peculiar to each sport and that are generally unused or even unusable outside the sport to which they belong.

Concomitantly, but with a very few notable exceptions, sports are temporally autonomous: their time stops and starts according to the motivated decision of the judge or referee; or they may be conceived as a contest between the athlete and time; or, on the other hand, they may have no time at all, any given contest lasting until a winner can be declared according to the system of rules. In addition, the time of sport may be understood as seasonal, in some cases for obvious practical reasons, but in others, perhaps, to perpetuate in a ludic mode rhythms of life that have been superseded by technology.

Just as sport resides outside normal human time, it also, for the most part, either ignores the weather or makes it part of the competition. It is thus as heedless of meteorological contingencies as it is of physical or, at times, mortal injury, even when contact with other athletes or a hazardous terrain are not officially involved. Sport, since ancient times, has implied pushing the body to or beyond the limits of normal physical capabilities, often using means deleterious to health. Sport is thus excessive and ostentatious in the expenditure of the athlete's energy. These two features are obviously linked to what has been called the 'quest for records' but they are also compensated by the requirement that prowess be graceful, controlled, almost nonchalant.

Correlatively, sport does not shy away from the acceptance and infliction of injury. By the same token, participation in sport is necessarily willing, at least in the long run. This is most obvious in combat sports and, to a lesser – but no less real – extent, in the heavy contact sports. A boxer or wrestler whose opponent dies or is seriously maimed is not held responsible, provided that the blows struck or the holds used were legitimate. In ice hockey, rugby, and North American football, serious injury may also result accidentally and within the rules, but surreptitious, intentional harm is an unspoken but accepted part of the game. This is equally true of those non-contact sports where the athletes are required to perform at very close quarters.

Nevertheless, it is also through physical excess and ostentatious indifference to danger that sport displays another essential feature, passion. An athlete's intense emotional individual desire to win may in turn become collective, as it is transmitted to teammates, and finally communal, as it affects spectators and instigates action on their part. An athlete's or a team's victory is interpreted as a victory for the communities that wish to claim the athlete or the team for their own. On the other hand, sports, being ideal worlds, are also conciliatory. Passionate competition ceases with the end of the event, and equilibrium, iconicized by the initial disposition of the athletes and the terrain, re-established. A sporting event is thus digressive and not permanent, because it does not fundamentally alter the relations of force among the competitors.

Finally, sport, in sharp contradistinction to play, is primarily economic. From earliest times athletes have competed for real monetary rewards and their competition has generated such transactions as purchasing equipment, erecting facilities, paying groundskeepers, charging admission, attracting tourists, and, more recently, selling goods and services whose price is arbitrarily linked to specific athletes and specific sports events. Given that the most spectacular athlete generates the most money, sport has become increasingly democratic. Previously operative social and ethnic barriers to participation have yielded to sheer talent. The meaning of sport, anthropologically speaking, is a function of the kinds of financial dealings that are its end product and its justification.

The 35 or so features that have been identified here as the connotative signs of sport can be observed to varying degrees in the practice of almost all the forms of high-level athletics at the present, and less intensively in amateur sports as well. Taken together, they constitute a determinative paradigm of what we may call sport. However, any attempt to define 'sport' as an activity displaying some minimal number of these features is fraught with perplexity: the long-distance swimmer is as much of an athlete as the professional hockey player, even though their respective sports are not commensurable according to the paradigm. The absence of certain signs may thus be deemed inconsequential. What is consequential is not that in some ludic activity any of the foregoing features be reduced to the degree zero, but rather that they be negated; that the participant(s) insists on not recognizing their obligatory character as a sign of sport and try to substitute some contradictory features in their place. The remaining chapters in this book have been conceived in the light of these two semiotic models and on the principle that we can label as sport the competitions and contests to which they seem to apply. This approach, however, will not constrain the argument or preclude the introduction of many other kinds of considerations.

It cannot be determined with any degree of certainty just what Augustus personally and wilfully contributed to the marked change in Roman sports that can be observed during his reign and after. Nor can the impact of the jousting death of Henri II be really measured, at least in so far as it affected sport. The following essays are nonetheless predicated on the assumption that what appears from our vantage point to have been true at those remote times was in fact the case. Augustus brought together and institutionalized a disparate set of competitions requiring athletic skills, thereby expanding and formalizing what the Romans thought of as games (*ludi*). He did the same for the physical education of the youth and encouraged personal sport among adults. Henri II was fond of all manner of 'rough sports and exercises' and he practiced them with unbridled enthusiasm (Baumgartner 1988). But the gusto with which he played these games and that made him prefer old-style tourneys to the new ones was already at odds with the emerging standards of controlled refinement that would characterize the gentleman, the *honnête homme* of the next century. Strenuous sports were on their way out, at least among the nobility that set the norms of social behaviour. Henri's unexpected death merely made it happen faster.

Chapter 2

Sport in the forgotten centuries (1)

The primary sources to 600 AD

The historiography of the evolution of sport since the later nineteenth century is very much predicated on sources that are considered factual and that concentrate on sport itself. The bureaucracies that govern the various games and competitions that constitute current sports have been, some of them, in existence for a very long time. The Society of St Andrews Golfers began in 1754, the Marylebone Cricket Club in 1787, and others proliferated – and have continued to function – throughout the nineteenth and twentieth centuries. The archives that these bureaucracies have created and preserved afford the historian with matchless sources of material. They can be supplemented if necessary with the documentation that became technologically possible and socially approved after 1800: individual team and club records, newspaper reports, eye-witness accounts, photographs, film documentaries, and the like. In the presence of so many 'scientific' sources of knowledge – and of the resultant mindset that privileges facts over insight – no one thinks now of turning to fictional and artistic representations of athletics for reliable information on a particular sport. It is not so much that they are untrustworthy as it is that they have been rendered irrelevant.

But it is precisely these 'irrelevant' sources that of necessity constitute a good percentage of the raw data for the historiography of sport in earlier times. Much of the written material discussed in this chapter and used in this book will thus be problematical from an historiographical point of view and fall into categories that the historian of modern sport will normally eschew. As Allen Guttmann recognized (2000: 152), those who write on ancient sports must often 'draw conclusions based on the shaky basis of a single literary text…or a single visual image'. For the sports of the ancient world, the problem lies in the fact that the passage of time has erased many of what would have become the primary sources, and so the history of sport has to be reconstituted from the bits and pieces that have survived.

After the advent of Christianity, it was rather the case that sport was not taken seriously and so was left unrecorded. Yitzhak Hen (1995: 207) points out that the 'sources which refer to the secular culture of early Medieval Gaul are pitifully meagre', because they are mostly religious and ecclesiastical. For the later Middle Ages,

Historians...often ignored tournaments altogether, or noted only the briefest details, so we have to hunt the smallest scraps of evidence and piece together what we can, from account books, letters, the odd note in a chronicle and (with great caution and as a last resort) the chivalric romances.

(Barber and Barker 1989: 2)[1]

In other words, the primary sources were lost or never even existed, so scholars of Roman and early modern sport have to eke knowledge out of metaphors or mere passing mentions found in texts whose central subject is far removed from the domains of sport and athletics.

To deal first with the sources that are now considered purely literary, writers from Virgil to Shakespeare have included in their work long or short accounts of athletic feats and contests. These frequently contain narrative exaggeration whose purpose is to excite the reader. But since these works are not science fiction, they are necessarily marked by the presence of details that Roland Barthes (1982) baptised 'effets de réel', elements that provide the artistic message with a stability that is anchored in the experience of the reader or viewer and that thereby guarantees the veracity of the work's principal subject. Latin authors surely operated under this aesthetic constraint, for they, like other writers of fiction up to the time of Cervantes, functioned in a world where there was very little distinction between literature and history or social commentary.[2] During the Middle Ages and on through the Renaissance, realism in what we now call 'imaginative fiction' was a virtually doctrinal obligation (Auerbach 1957). Whether in Chrétien de Troyes' twelfth-century description of knights donning their armour for a joust (Chrétien 1955/1160–70: 22–23, ll. 707–26) or in Shakespeare's 1613 description of a young man swimming to shore from a shipwreck (*The Tempest* 2.1.108–13), we have a sense of palpable observed reality, of 'this is the way it was actually done', of an effort on the part of the writer to extract the same accuracy from words that an artist might achieve by painting. Ancient and early modern representations of sport were, to be sure, decorative and entertaining in their intention. At the same time they were also a mirror of life around them, in ways that modern art and literature are not necessarily intended to be, or may even be discouraged from trying.

This is not to say that the historian has to rely solely on fictional literature and that factual information is absolutely not available for the sports of the late ancient and early modern periods. Philosophical, biographical, and epistolary texts do include references to Roman sport that would seem objectively true. As well, the Romans felt the same need as we do to preserve and publish data, and they did so in the rather cumbersome form of carved stone or cast bronze inscriptions – cumbersome, but also virtually imperishable, though now often broken or blurred. These exist in very large numbers and, given the ancient world's interest in sport, a reasonable proportion of them deal precisely with athletic exploits.[3]

For the early modern period, on the other hand, inscriptions concerning sport are virtually non-existent. In their place we do have, as the Middle Ages become the Renaissance, an increasing number of chronicles and histories that make at least passing references to sport. Beginning in the thirteenth century there are biographies and later memoirs of participants in athletic events, especially tournaments. These are not without their fictional elements, as the authors try to present themselves or their subjects in the best possible light, but it is nevertheless possible to weed out the glorification and reach a reasonable sense of what really happened. Still and all, trying to write satisfactory history of sport from the creation of the Roman Empire to the rise of scientific method in the mid-sixteenth century obliges the scholar to rely on texts whose absolute veracity is not always guaranteed.

Some of the ambiguities of the verbal texts on matters of sport can, of course, be palliated by turning to pictorial, architectural, and sculpted sources. The Romans erected many panegyric monuments to athletes and they liked to decorate the interiors of their homes and public places with murals, mosaics, and sculptures that often featured representations of athletic pursuits. Nor did a Roman's interest in sport end with death. The funerary sarcophagi of the wealthy were usually ornamented with stone carvings in high or low relief, and although these were often mythological or pastoral in nature, some at least depicted chariot races or other athletic contests.

In the Middle Ages and Renaissance the visual sources are richer, better preserved, and less constrained in their execution by the nature of the materials and the surfaces. Manuscripts were illuminated and tapestries woven with pictures of sport, and depictions of games and athletes might be painted onto utilitarian objects. Artists were apparently attracted to the representation of men in the act of sport. Leonardo da Vinci cites pall-mall and tennis as games that painters liked as subjects, because the physical exertion required of the players' bodies made them interesting to draw (da Vinci 1952/1500: 42). Before the invention of printing and especially after, entire books were filled with woodcuts and engravings demonstrating the best way to practice one sport or another, usually fencing and wrestling. Apart from the books, however, most early modern images of sport can be found only on objects or in places that are unique, and hence not widely accessible.

Whatever their subject, painters were, however, as much concerned to produce a beautiful picture as they were to record the reality of actual events.[4] The issue is thus naturally raised as to the reliability of the information the painting conveys. When examining the pictorial images executed in ancient and early modern times, we are nonetheless obliged – following the same principle of the 'effets de réel' that was operative in literature – to believe that many of the incidentals are an accurate version of what really did pertain at that time, and that a valid history of sport can be written using such data as sources. Roman mosaic images of chariot races certainly emphasized the violence of crashes, but they did not misrepresent the way chariots were constructed or the Circus Maximus was laid out or the fact that crashes took place. In more modern times, from at least the beginning of the fourteenth century, painters and sculptors were required to 'ape nature', to be realistic in their depictions of the human body, its costumes, and its implements, even if constraints of space and viewpoint imposed some distortion (Baxandall 1985/1972; Arasse 1996/1992). In the many late Medieval-early Renaissance pictorial representations of ball and club games, for example, gestures such as the swing, actions such as the face-off, the shapes of the clubs, the configurations of the playing surfaces, and the targets – planted sticks, holes in the ground, gates in walls – are all accurate, precisely because they are non-contentious, non-signifying elements of the picture. The painter therefore had no reason to alter them. If, as the proverb says, the devil is in the detail, so too is the truth, at least as far as the sports historian is concerned.

Another source of information about Roman sport in particular resides in the remains of the often huge arenas, circuses, amphitheatres, stadiums, and public baths that were constructed to house gladiatorial combats, wild-beast shows, Greek-style games, chariot races, and spaces for exercises, ball games, athletic training, and swimming in heated pools.[5] Structures of this sort were common not only in Italy but also throughout the northern parts of the Empire (King 1990). Private homes and country villas also possessed facilities for bathing, exercise, and sport (Balsdon 1969). Reading these buildings archaeologically is difficult, however, because in later centuries the urban populations converted the larger ones to other uses, e.g. defense against the marauding barbarians (Ward-Perkins 1984), or appropriated their stones to make churches and palaces, or simply destroyed them. Private houses, whether as palatial as the great Villa del Casale near Piazza Armerina in Sicily or the simpler villas of land-owning aristocrats, fell into disrepair, were abandoned, and gradually buried with dirt and vegetation.[6]

For the Middle Ages and the Renaissance archaeology is of practically no use, since no permanent sports structures were built during those centuries, with the exception of enclosed tennis courts, and enough of these have survived untouched to permit a thorough understanding of how *jeu de paume* was played during its heyday between 1300 and 1750. On the other hand, wooden barriers and stands were erected for jousting and ball games in palace grounds or open fields near towns or around public squares. Although these wooden structures left no permanent trace, contemporaries did make drawings of them, and these drawings stand in for archaeology and permit an imaginative reconstruction of the events.

The pictorial, sculptural, and archaeological sources that are essential to the understanding of Roman and early modern sport have been frequently reproduced in the last 30 years, often quite lavishly (e.g. Jacobelli 2003; Flannery and Leech 2004). They will not be discussed in the remainder of the chapter, which will confine itself to analyzing the verbal sources and, for the Middle Ages and the Renaissance, books that contain illustrations.

Allusions to sport – even detailed accounts of sports events and achievements – are frequent in Greek literature from its very beginnings in the Homeric epics. In Latin literature too, mentions of sport can be found in the earliest texts, but at best they are sporadic, anecdotal, and very brief until the last years of the pre-Christian era. Nonetheless, these scattered references in the writings of republican

Latin authors attest to the awareness and the importance of contemporary sport in the minds and lives of their readers. The founder of Latin literature, Quintus Ennius (239–169 BC) invokes the spectators' emotions at the start of a chariot race to illuminate a moment of tense expectancy in a political contest (*Annals*, Loeb, 86–91).[7] In one of the comedies of Plautus (254–184 BC), a poor fisherman ironically compares his hard physical work to the wrestling and exercising the upper classes do in the gymnasium (*Rudens* [*The Rope*], Loeb, 2.1). And on a more popular level, the prologues to the third performance of a play by Terence (190–158 BC) tell the spectators that two earlier productions failed because nearby displays of athletic skill caused the audiences to desert the theatre or be distracted (*Hecyra* [*The Mother-in-law*], Loeb, prol. 1.4–5 and prol. 2.33–34 and 39–40).[8]

A century or so later, in three books composed toward the end of his life, the philosopher Cicero (106–43 BC) uses allusions to sport for various ends. He complains – resorting to an age-old commonplace of academic discourse – that students desert lectures on serious topics in order to practice athletics. In other contexts, he uses boxers, gladiators, and track and field athletes as standards of positive and negative comparison when discussing behaviour that is appropriately Stoic, when praising the strength, courage, and endurance of veteran soldiers, and when contrasting attitudes to pain, suffering, and death – gladiators are the dregs of society, but they offer a model of comportment that others could imitate. In a more technical vein, he compares public speakers to athletes in combat sports. The former can learn from the latter when it comes to being both graceful and effective in marshalling and delivering their arguments.[9]

The same kinds of allusions to sport crop up in poets either contemporary with Cicero or of the two generations immediately following. Catullus (84–54 BC) makes fleeting references to racing boats (*Poems*, Loeb, 4.1–5), to chariot races (55.3–4), and to Greek-style games (63.59–60). Tibullus (55–19 BC) speaks briefly of hunting boar and deer (*Elegies*, Loeb, 3.14) and Propertius (50–16 BC) displays an isolated but technically knowledgeable interest in Spartan athletic practices, which he finds praiseworthy when compared to Roman usage (*Elegies*, Loeb, 3.14.1–13).[10]

Horace (65–8 BC) frequently alludes to sports in one way or another, in a manner that reveals just how important athletic pursuits, both personal and professional, were to the Roman upper classes.[11] He is the first, I think, to give a reasonably complete list of the proto-military exercises the Romans practiced on the Campus Martius (*Odes*, Loeb, 1.8) and in several places indicates they were practiced competitively and attracted an audience (e.g. *Epistles*, Loeb, 1.18; *Odes* 3.7). He contrasts Roman athletic vigour with the idle games the Greeks now practice – their fondness for 'athletas' is a sign of their decadence, *Epistles* 2.1 – and gives us several names of apparently famous gladiators (*Satires*, Loeb, 1.7, 2.7). In retirement, he compares himself to another well-known gladiator who refused to return to the arena despite pressure to do so (*Epistles* 1.1). His book of advice to aspiring writers, the *Art of Poetry*, contains parallels between playing sport and writing in a couple of places (ll. 379–81, 412–14) and in another epistle

(1.19) Horace tells his readers that a debate between a writer and a critic may be a game ('ludus') to start with, but it quickly leads to a more antagonistic encounter ('certamen').

The last of the Golden Age poets, the controversial Ovid (43 BC–18 AD) also invokes sporting events in a number of places, most of them brief but some of them quite telling. One poem in particular (*Amores*, Budé, 3.2) might be titled a 'Day at the Races', for it provides a vivid picture of the atmosphere of the Circus Maximus, both on and off the track. In the *Art of Love* (Loeb, 1.135–76) he details the ways in which to make seductive approaches to a lady at the Circus or when betting on gladiatorial fights, and elsewhere in the poem often compares the would-be lover to a charioteer, a hunter, a fowler, or a fisherman. Later, when exiled to Tomi on the Black Sea, Ovid nostalgically recalls Romans exercising on the Campus Martius (*Tristia* 3.12.17–22) and compares the taxing effects of exile on the soul to the way in which wrestlers and gladiators tire in the course of a fight.

What is important to note in all the foregoing is that in republican Roman writers, allusions to athletic pursuits, however informative, remain as very intermittent references within a body of writings that are mostly concerned with other things. In authors whose lives spanned the beginning of the Empire in 31–27 BC, sports come to play a more significant role. As in the earlier writers, they continue to possess metaphorical value or serve to characterize individuals, but what were formerly rapid allusions are more frequent and more complete, fleshed out with concrete detail to the point of occupying an entire poem, as in Ovid. In other words, by the end of the first century BC there had come to be in Latin literature a recognized discourse of sport where there had been none before; a discourse that fitted in alongside the already existing discourses of love and loss, of country vs city life, of praise and vituperation. It is a discourse that exists in its own right and also as a reference, a mode of comparison, for other discourses. For all that, the point of view of this discourse is almost always that of the spectator – to be sure, a spectator who understands to a certain degree what the athlete is doing – hence it remains external to the sport itself. There is little to suggest that the poets who describe sports actually participated in them.[12]

Virgil's *Aeneid* takes allusions to sport much farther than any of the contemporary texts that have just been mentioned.[13] This nationalistic epic recounts in 12 books the travels and struggles of the Trojan hero Aeneas, who, having escaped the destruction of his city by the Greeks, was mandated by his mother, the goddess Venus, to found the new Troy – Rome – in Italy. Although no athlete himself, and though just as likely as his colleagues to use sport as a passing metaphor,[14] Virgil composed in book 5 of his poem the first account in Latin of a fully-fledged sporting competition. Curiously enough, this account – at least superficially – retails in 500 lines a version of the kind of Greek athletic festival that the Romans supposedly did not like.[15] Literarily speaking, the athletic competitions in *Aeneid* 5 are very much a replica of two Homeric models: Patroclus's funeral games in *Iliad* 23 and Odysseus's competition with the Phaeacians (*Odyssey* 8).[16] They are organized to commemorate a death – in this case the death of Aeneas's father the year before – and feature many of the same contests as the *Iliad*, but with two significant changes. The competitions that Aeneas announces are, in order, a boat race, a footrace, a javelin or archery contest, and a boxing match, though in fact the javelin throw does not take place. The games end with an elaborately convoluted equestrian display called the *lusus Troiae* or Troy game that was not originally specified as part of the competition.

The first of these events is in itself surprising. The *Iliad*, Virgil's model here, had used a chariot race as the premier event, and chariot racing is generally thought to have been the *ur*-sport of ancient Rome; among the spectator sports of imperial times, it alone could be practiced by the nobility without any loss of social status, although they did not compete against professional drivers. In fact, though the Greeks raced boats occasionally, Virgil seems to have been the only writer in Antiquity to describe such a race (Harris 1972). Whatever his motivation (see Chapter 4), the boat race in the *Aeneid* occupies over 170 lines of the poem and is, together with the *lusus Troiae*, the competition that is described in greatest detail.

After the boat race, the crowd of spectators moves away from the seashore to a different site, which is described as a 'grassy *campus*', a label that recalls the *Campus Martius*, Mars' field, where the Romans traditionally practiced their proto-military training and exercises (5.287–89). In addition, the space for the field events is bounded by a ring of curving hills (*collibus curvis*) that replicate the location of the Circus Maximus in Rome, between the Aventine and Capitoline hills. From earliest times, this was the venue of the traditional games, the *ludi* (Livy, *History*, Loeb, 1.35.7–10) and other 'spectacle entertainments'. In Virgil's day, on the other hand, Greek-style games were held in temporary structures in the Campus Martius (Suetonius, *Julius Caesar*, Loeb, 39). By having 'Greek' games held in a quasi-Roman setting, Virgil is promoting the fusion of Greek and Roman culture that was an explicit element of Augustus's political goals.[17] This identification of the Sicilian site with the Circus Maximus is made even more explicit by the metaphor 'theatri circus', by an allusion to its elongated shape ('longo circo') and by the fact that Aeneas sits to direct the games on a raised structure, just as Augustus himself presided over the Roman chariot races and other sports spectacles from the elevated imperial box at the Circus.[18]

Three of the events held in this natural amphitheatre are largely rewritings in Latin of the same events in *Iliad* 23 (footrace, boxing, archery), although Virgil's boxers do evoke gladiatorial fights (Lovatt 2004). The descriptions have rightly been described by Gardiner (1930: 124–7) as athletically uninteresting, but the Troy game at the end stands out from the rest. The participants are not the Trojans heroes but their sons, Aeneas's son in the lead (5.545–603). Like the description of the boat race, the account of this labyrinthine exercise involving three teams – which owed nothing to any Greek model – demonstrates a remarkable ability on the part of Virgil to put very technical matters into precise, clear language, to the point where the game can actually be reproduced.

Although there are other descriptions of athletics in the *Aeneid* (see Chapter 4 below), it is only at the very end of the epic that there is a genuinely Roman form of contest that parallels the nationalistic dimension of the *lusus Troiae*. The final lines of the poem (12.887–952) describe a combat between Aeneas and Turnus, whose army is the last obstacle the Trojans have to face before achieving their purpose. Turnus is so badly wounded he is forced to surrender and begs to be spared. He does so both verbally and by stretching out his hand, a gesture found in many depictions of gladiatorial fights (*cf.* Augenti 2001). Aeneas wavers for a moment, but then furiously plunges a sword into his chest ('ferrum adverso sub pectore condit fervidus'). Every detail of the encounter, and particularly its finish, evokes the emotional and physical reality of two gladiators facing each other (Hardie 1986).

Creating the history of Roman sport from the work of Virgil's contemporaries and predecessors is essentially an inductive process, arguing from isolated examples to general propositions. On the other hand, the *Aeneid*, for all its concreteness of detail, remains abstract. It tells the historian neither what Roman sport had been nor what it was, but rather what, in Virgil's mind and Augustus's, it might have been and might become.

For a sense of what really went on in this area at the turn of the Christian era, nothing reveals more the emphasis that Augustus placed on spectator sport than does his list of his own achievements, the so-called *Monumentum Ancyranum* (Augustus 1923/14).[19] In it (Chapters 22 and 23) the emperor records that he gave eight gladiatorial shows involving 10,000 fighters in all, 26 wild animal shows (*venationes*) in which 3,500 animals were slaughtered, and a mock naval battle (*naumachia*) on an artificial lake, with 30 ships and 3,000 fighting men. He also staged traditional *ludi* 27 times; revived one set of annual games (the *Ludi Saeculares*); and inaugurated another (the *Ludi Martiales*). In the midst of these extravagant numbers, he mentions only three sets of Greek competitive games – these are presumably in addition to the three ongoing festivals that he and the Senate had founded. Although the Greek games are comparatively few in number, it is worth noting that in this record Augustus lists them as stand-alone events, on an equal footing with other kinds of games, and not just as eastern curiosities brought in to illustrate his triumphs.

Other sports historical sources contemporary with Augustus include the historians Livy and Dionysius of Halicarnassus. They, however, make only scattered allusions to athletic pursuits and sports spectacles. They will be cited as the occasion arises, but beyond the *Monumentum Ancyranum* and the retrospective accounts given by second-century historians (Plutarch, Tacitus, Suetonius, Appian), the major source of our information concerning Roman sport in the first century is the Stoic moralist and playwright Seneca (4 BC–65 AD). More than anyone else Cicero's intellectual heir, Seneca discusses physical fitness, athletics, and sport in several of his *Letters* and other writings.[20] In letter 15 he condemns those who are overly fond of developing their physique and advocates short and simple exercises that save valuable time for nobler pursuits: running, weight-lifting, and various kinds of jumping: the long jump, the high jump – this is one of only two mentions of the high jump in all of ancient literature – and something he calls the *saliaris* or the *fullonius* and that probably designates running or repeated jumping on the spot.[21]

Variants on this theme return in letters 56 and 80. In the former he complains that he lives above a bathhouse and details all the noises to which he is subjected: the grunts and groans of the weight-lifters; the slapping sounds made by the masseurs; the shouts of the score-keepers in the ball games; the sounds of those who like to sing in the bath; the reverberations caused by the swimmers who do cannonballs into the pool; the yells of those who are having their armpits plucked; and all the other cries and noises produced when the police arrest rowdies and pickpockets and the cosmetologists and food-sellers vocally advertise their goods and services.

In a typically Stoic vein, letter 80 contrasts the training and life of the mind and the soul with people's enthusiasm for spectacle sports – Seneca implies that the results are rigged – and professional athletes' obsession with their own muscular bodies. Athletes are a drain on society, whereas the virtuous man does not require any resources that lie outside himself. Beyond this criticism, Seneca does provide incidentally an impressive tableau of the pancratiast fighting a succession of opponents all day long in the burning sun and dust, covered in his own blood.

Spectacles are also the subject of the often-quoted letter 7. He reports that he went into a 'spectaculum' at noon one day, expecting to find amusement and relaxation. Instead, he discovered he was attending one of the varieties of execution that the Romans were adept at devising (Kyle 1998): convicted criminals, armed but wearing no protection, were forced to fight each other to the death. Seneca's main concern is the deleterious effect these shows have on the spectators, who are aroused to paroxysms of cruelty and who prefer these 'homicidia' to the fights of true gladiators. These, we are led to understand, were displays of fighting skills and might feature 'postulaticiis', request matches that pitted two specific fighters against each other.

Beyond the written sources, the externals of Roman sports practices from the first century AD onwards can be deduced from mosaics, wall paintings, sculptures, and architectural remains. Archaeological excavations of the sports edifices constructed in Rome and in the provinces – the Roman Empire, from northern England to the Syrian desert was dotted with such structures – have allowed sports historians to understand much of the mechanics of putting on spectacular athletic shows, as well as their social and political dimensions: how the spectators, wild animals, chariots, horses, and athletes got into the arenas and circuses, how they moved about once they were there, and how the seating reflected the social hierarchies.[22] On the other hand, the actual athletic practices are harder to grasp from archaeology alone. Fortunately, the cognitive shortfall is compensated from other sources. The very popularity of these large-scale sports spectacles led to their being depicted in decorative floor and wall panels, bas-relief sculptures, ceramics (particularly oil lamps), and occasional statues and statuettes.

It is consequently possible to reconstruct some elements of the gladiatorial combats, *venationes*, Greek-style games, and chariot races from the mosaics at Zliten in Libya (Aurigemma 1926; Auguet 1970; Kyle 1998), the Villa del Casale in Sicily (Lee 1984; Catonze 1999), the baths at Ostia end elsewhere (Newby 2005), and the Torrenova mosaics in the Galleria Borghese in Rome (Nardone 1989; Augenti 2001), to name only the most complete sets. In particular, Pompeii, almost instantly buried in volcanic ash by the eruption of Vesuvius in 79, preserved some specimens of gladiatorial armour, numerous inscriptions (both official and amateur), decorated household objects, wall paintings of wild animal shows, statues of gladiators, and a detailed bas-relief depicting the stages of a gladiatorial show and a *venatio* (Jacobelli 2003). In the nineteenth century, Friedländer (1908–13/1862–71: 2 and 4) was able to create a typology of the different types of fighters that up until very recently was still considered reliable. Others (e.g. Wiedemann 1992) have refined this picture, tracing an evolution of fighting styles over several centuries as new gladiatorial types emerged to replace others.[23] However, written material on gladiators is particularly hard to come by and no manual detailing the best principles of gladiatorial fighting has come down to us (Nardone 1989; but see Junckelman 2000b). The same can be said for the *venationes*.

We may extrapolate, however, from the rare literary descriptions that describe such competitions or that narrate analogous encounters. There are long and technically precise descriptions of chariot races in Statius and Sidonius Apollinaris (see below) but for gladiators we have to resort to the approximate. Virgil's account of the hand-to-hand combat between Aeneas and Turnus referred to before (*Aeneid* 12) is short on the concrete details of Roman sword fighting, but he does capture the emotions of the winner and the loser. Although defeated, the latter does not want to die. The former can only dispatch his adversary by summoning up enough strong feeling to overcome his natural pity and to furnish the energy needed commit a physically demanding act that required speed, accuracy, strength, and a certain savagery. Wiedemann (1992: 118–24) points out that gladiators who lived in the same *ludus* or training school and knew each other well might have to fight each other. The visored helmets they wore had the effect of depersonalizing them, making it 'less nerve wracking' for their opponent 'to destroy an anonymous target'.

A century after Virgil, Valerius Flaccus described in his *Argonautica* (Budé, 4.206–314) a boxing match between Pollux and Amycus that also ends fatally and that too may borrow something from gladiatorial fights.[24] Flaccus deals first with the mental states of the two boxers, showing how Pollux, the ultimate winner, nervous at the beginning, takes advantage of Amycus's rashness and headstrong over-confidence. More importantly – and unlike his Greek models – he also shows Pollux developing a definite strategy, holding back, using footwork to his advantage, moving his head out of the way of blows before passing to the attack, feinting with his right, then striking with his left, and finally stepping deftly aside – his move is reminiscent of a bull-fighter subtly avoiding a charging bull – so that his enemy loses his balance and is easily killed with a blow to the back of the neck. Flaccus may have based his description of the Pollux–Amycus bout on his observation of traditional Roman boxing (Hershkowitz 1998). It might be more revealing, however, to read his account as a transposition of what he had seen as a spectator of gladiatorial combats.

A more extensive description of athletics (558 lines) was provided by a better-known contemporary of Flaccus, the court poet Statius (40–96). In his Virgilian-inspired epic poem, *Thebaid*, he devoted book 6 to an account of the first celebration of the Nemean Games, an event founded in mythology but that historically took place in the early sixth century BC.[25] These are funeral games, and in his choice of sports the poet follows, with some variation, the models of the *Iliad*, the *Odyssey*, and the *Aeneid*: a chariot race, a foot race, discus, boxing, wrestling, an armed single combat which – like the corresponding event in *Iliad* 23 – is stopped before it gets started, and an astounding feat of archery.[26] Although Statius imitates his models in places very closely, and although his narration is larded with similes and extended comparisons drawn from mythology and the natural world, *Thebaid* 6 is often more picturesque, more precise, more technical when it comes to describing what the athletes actually do to increase their chances of winning. The chariot racers lean forward over their team urging them on or bend backwards almost double at the knees when reining the horses in (*Thebaid*, Budé, 6.416–19). To limber up, the runners stretch their lower legs, exercise their arms and chest, and practice making fast starts (587–92). The discus throwers rub sand on the disk to improve their grip, search out the best place to hold the lower edge with their hand, and involve their whole body in the throw – the judges use an arrow to mark the point where the discus touched the ground (668–715). The boxers, wary at first, measure each other with their eyes until the more impetuous of the two launches an attack (750–69). The wrestlers tuck their heads in, but one gets the advantage over the other by lowering his centre of gravity (850–53). Despite the epic's often flowery mythological similes and the fact that it is ostensibly describing events that occurred in remote Greek antiquity, the *Thebaid* succeeds better than the *Iliad* or the *Aeneid* in actually capturing in language the physical and psychological reality of competitive sport within the framework of an international meet.[27] At the same time, this description has become a purely literary exercise, undoubtedly capitalizing on the growing popularity of Greek games, but lacking the political motivation that inspired Virgil.

The keen interest in sport that Statius and Valerius Flaccus demonstrated, and the skill they displayed in writing about its mechanics, coincided – not surprisingly – with the construction of two of the most impressive monuments to Roman spectacle and imperial power, the Colosseum (80 AD) and Domitian's stadium (86). But the fact that these two buildings were constructed on such a monumental scale, and that just a few years later Trajan (98–117) rebuilt and enlarged the Circus Maximus on a similar scale to hold at least 150,000 spectators suggests that the qualitative changes that Augustus introduced into the sponsorship of spectator sports (Kyle 2003) produced significant quantitative results in the sensibilities of the Romans as well as in the shape of their cities.

This change can be measured in the increased frequency with which sports of all kinds become a topic, not only of comparison but as a subject in their own right, in Roman and Hellenistic thought, literature, and historiography. The libertine poet Martial (40–104) wrote a series of 37 epigrams, grouped under the title *De spectaculis*, that recount the 100 days of *ludi* and other shows that marked the opening of the Colosseum celebrations and that sporadically give an insight into the sports that were involved. In the remaining 12 books of his *Epigrams* he provides a devastating account of late first-century AD Roman society and, along the way, more references to athletes, whether gladiators, hunters, or charioteers, and to the athletic pursuits of the Roman upper classes than can be found in any other poet. His contemporary, the satirist Juvenal (c. 50–130) is famous for his criticism of the Roman populace, who have abandoned their political power and are now content with bread and circuses, i.e. chariot-racing (*Satires*, Loeb, 10). Others of his poems are equally informative of the Roman taste for athletes and sporting shows, such as his anecdote of the Roman matron who left her husband and ran off with a gladiator to Egypt – ancient Rome's California (*Satire* 6). The historian Tacitus (55–120) confirms what Juvenal has been saying, when he complains that his students' minds are engrossed with stage actors, gladiators, and chariot races, to the point where they talk of nothing else in the lecture halls (*Dialogue on Oratory*, Loeb, 29).[28] His complaint is not surprising, given that the great educational theorist of the late first century, Quintilian (35–95), larded his treatise on the education of the public orator, the *Institutions*, with about 40 extended passages drawn from sport and athletics. Like Cicero, but to a greater degree, Quintilian saw many parallels between the training and work of the orator and those of the gladiator and athlete. One can easily imagine that his lectures similarly relied on material of this sort.[29]

Other Romans writing at this time devote some space to sport, whether by choice or by obligations. Pliny the Younger (61–114) was one of the Emperor Trajan's chief administrators. In his official correspondence from his postings in Gaul and the Near East, Pliny advises his master on the deleterious moral effect of Greek games (*Letters*, Loeb, 4.22) and how to deal with towns that want a new gymnasium (10.39 and 40) and the complaints of Greek athletes who were not, by their standards, being paid in a timely fashion (10.18). In a long text praising Trajan's accomplishments, he speaks of the inspiration to courage that comes from watching gladiators and describes the rebuilt and refurbished Circus Maximus (*Panegyricus*, Loeb, 33 and 51). In other letters (2.17, 5.6) he describes his country houses with their swimming pools, exercise rooms, ball courts, and riding tracks. The biographer Suetonius (70–128), in his *Lives of the Twelve Caesars*, enters into considerable detail with respect to the games, gladiatorial shows, wild beast hunts, and Greek athletic festivals that the emperors mounted and that were so important to the Romans. In particular he wanted to pique the interest of his readers and so he recounted with some relish the actions of the more depraved emperors who put on pseudo-athletic shows that would not be out of place in a present-day World Wrestling Entertainment spectacle.[30] As a source for sports history, however, Suetonius is not limited to retailing accounts of imperial cruelty and extravagance. He also describes his subjects' interest in more private forms of athletics (see, e.g. *Augustus*, Loeb, 83) and in addition, he wrote in Greek an account of recreational games in which he gives the earliest version of the rules – or, more accurately, conventions – governing various ball games (Suetonius 1967).

Ball games are also reported briefly but no less significantly in a panegyric of Calpurnius Piso, a member of the Roman ruling class at the time of Nero. The anonymous poet lavishes extravagant praises on Piso for all his considerable talents, not the least of which his ability to play ball games so spectacularly that others stop their own game to watch him (*Laus Pisonis*, Loeb, ll. 185–89). On a more amusing note, two satirical novels, Petronius's *Satyricon* (before 66) and Apuleius's *Metamorphoses* (before 170) both give humorous glimpses of provincial Roman life and sport from the underside. In the former, a *nouveau-riche* ex-slave plays three-cornered catch at the baths but disdains to pick up any ball that has touched the ground. His drinking goblets are decorated with the fights of two famous gladiators and he wants all the fights of one of them depicted on his tomb (*Satyricon*, Budé, 15.27, 52, and 71). In the latter, the narrator – a man who has been transformed into a donkey – describes a newly elected local official who has to scramble to find some gladiators for the show he is putting on to celebrate his success (*Metamorphoses*, Budé, 10.18).[31]

Roman writings in this period often reveal crucial information about private games and large-scale spectacle sports, but the authors 'seldom express their views about *spectacula* or *ludi* directly…My overall impression is that they were *neutral*; the existence of various shows are mostly reported or referred to as simple facts without any value judgement at all' (Wistrand 1992: 11). In quantity and importance too the Latin contribution to the history of imperial Roman sport remains insignificant, compared to what was being written in Greek. It is further the case that the Romans – after Statius and Valerius Flaccus and perhaps Quintilian – view the subject of sport from the outside. They tell us much about the material conditions and *desiderata* surrounding sporting events, but nothing of what actually transpired in a physical sense between two gladiators or the competitors in a foot or chariot race. They are also non-committal with respect to the games and shows they describe,

Among the Greeks, the biographer Plutarch (c. 46–125), like Suetonius, also sees sport from the outside, in his *Lives* of famous Greeks and Romans and in his *Moralia* – especially his *Quaestiones Romanae*. The other Greek writers, however, although they mostly limit their focus to ball games and track and field events, deal with their subject from the inside, often in a much more intense and personal way. The first among these, curiously enough, is the Stoic philosopher, Epictetus (55–135) who, like Seneca, treats athletic training almost existentially.

Of course, like any good moralist, he criticizes the ungifted man who spends too much time exercising, copulating, and generally devoting himself to the concerns of the body instead of the mind (*Enchiridion*, Loeb, 41). In his longer *Discourses* he disparages both people who are overly interested in gladiators, horses, and athletes (Loeb, 3.16.4) and those students who, after his lectures, go to work out or attend chariot races or gladiator fights without connecting what they have learned from him to what they see or do (3.16.14). On the other hand, he resorts even more than Seneca to favourable comparisons between athletic endeavours and the attempt to reach Stoic perfection. The energy and discipline one needs to expend on the soul is equivalent to participating in the Olympic Games (3.22.50–52), and he then goes on to say that this effort is the greatest athletic contest of all (3.35.2–7: *ton agōna ton megiston*).[32] For that reason the would-be Stoic has to train with the same assiduity as athletes and gladiators (1.24.1–2, 2.17.29–31, 3.15.1–7) and has to know his strengths and limits in the same way they do (3.23.1–2, 4.4.30–32). Human bodies are not all suited for the same type of competition (3.1.5–6) and – presumably by extension – not all human personalities are fit to face the same challenges (4.4.30–2).[33]

The prevalence of athletic comparisons in Epictetus's work is not surprising, given that after his exile from Rome in 95 he created a school in Nicopolis, which was the site of a long-standing sports festival that Augustus had appropriated to create his own Actian games (Harris 1972). More unexpected is a lengthy passage full of technical vocabulary in which he compares Socrates' behaviour at his trial to the ball game *harpastum* (*Discourses* 2.5.15–21).[34] The qualities that are required for playing ball are good form (*eurythmia*), skill (*technē*), speed (*tachos*), and gracefulness (*eugnōmosynē*) and Socrates displayed all of these at that critical moment. More importantly, like any good ball player *vis-à-vis* the ball, he refused to have any emotional involvement in the outcome of the trial, and thus his comportment is a model for Stoics, who are expected to keep their emotions at bay. Despite his condemnation, Socrates won a great victory, akin to an Olympic victory, except that he was defeating 'something more than these cheap boxers and pancratiasts and the gladiators who resemble them' (2.18.22–23). Like Seneca then, Epictetus informs us both of the contradictory status of athletes and gladiators within Roman society – their pursuits are trivial but the determination with which they pursue them is exemplary – and of the ways and means and language of ancient sport.

In a more technical vein, Galen (131–201), the chief physician of his time and a surgeon to gladiators (Scarborough 1971), frequently wrote on matters athletic. His *Hygiene* is a particularly informative source on ancient thought concerning the role and effects of massage, exercise, and personal trainers in maintaining good health (Galen 1951/200). It was translated into Latin in 1517, under the title *De sanitate tuenda*, on the protection of good health, and was thereafter the single most influential book on the value of sport. In addition Galen wrote an *Exhortation for Medicine* that condemned professional athletes and their training methods, and a pamphlet (*Exercise with the Small Ball*) that advocates ball play as a means to good physical and intellectual health; it also gives some indication as to how the game *harpastum* was played.[35] Among Galen's Greek contemporaries, the rhetorician Pollux expanded Suetonius's treatise on ball games, thereby providing us with a reasonably clear understanding of how they were played, and in particular a team game called *episkyros* (Pollux 1967/190; also Miller 2004).[36] A more relaxed writer, the encyclopaedist Athenaeus (c. 200), delves sporadically into the subject of sport and gives, in particular, a spirited account of men playing a ball game he calls *phaininda*, although he says that the new name for it is *harpastum* (*Deipnosophistae*, Loeb, 1.14–15).

Genuinely full-scale treatments of Greek sports in the imperial period, however, are to be found in the satirist Lucian (125–180) and the more sober-sided, and somewhat mysterious, Philostratos (late second–mid-third c.). The latter's *On Gymnastics* is a virtually complete account of Greek athletics, including the seamy side of bribes and cheating,[37] while the former's *Anacharis* ostensibly describes Greek sports as they were in early sixth century BC to a naïve though learned outsider. But since Lucian could have possessed little information as to what Greek sports were like in the remote past and to the ways they might have differed from the athletic practices of his own time, Newby (2005) argues that the purpose of his dialogue is to set out the pro and contra positions concerning the value of these sports in the second century.

Although writing in Greek, these authors – like Epictetus and Plutarch before them – were addressing themselves to a cultivated audience who were perfectly fluent in Greek, even if Latin was their native tongue or *lingua franca*, and for whom the athletic practices encouraged by Rome were the standard. In his encomium of the blessed state of the world under Rome's domination, the Greek orator Aristides (1983/155) twice mentions the abundance of organized competitive athletic festivals – in Greek, *agōnes* – as a sign of the benefits and progress that the Roman emperors had conferred on Greece.

Latin writers at the end of the Empire and the beginning of the Dark Ages are more forthcoming than some of their predecessors about the concrete details involved in mounting shows and playing games. The correspondence of Symmachus (345–405), prefect of Rome under three emperors, reveals how complicated it was to organize the lavish games that were expected of high officials on certain occasions – in this case his son's accession to high office in 393 and again in 398 (*Letters*, Budé, books 2, 4, 5, and 9). As mentioned in Apuleius, gladiators were *de rigueur*, and so too were horses for the chariot races, wild animals and hunters to hunt them, and bears to be baited and unusual dogs to bait them.[38] To assemble all these participants required many letters and favours from friends and even the emperor himself. Symmachus's correspondence is often quoted as evidence that the great Roman spectacular entertainments eventually petered out because of the considerable expense and extraordinary effort they demanded.

Two of Symmachus's contemporaries, St Augustine (354–430) and Vegetius (fl. 385–400) are similarly informative, in an incidental sort of way. In his autobiographical *Confessions*, the former makes a number of allusions to Roman athletic practices, whether private or public, and to his own involvement with sport, but a particular passage is often quoted. In it he describes the psychological reactions of a friend, Alypius, who had scorned the brutality and cruelty of gladiator games and refused to attend. However, once lured to a show, he found his attention riveted on the combat and thereafter became an avid fan (*Confessions*, Budé, 6.8). Vegetius's *De re militari* [soldiering] includes an important section on the training of soldiers that allows the reader to glimpse the use of athletic contests as a way of encouraging recruits to acquire – and veterans to maintain – the skills necessary for warfare (Vegetius 1995/fourth c.: 1.9 and 2.23)

These are very late sources, and hence their validity for earlier periods may deserve some scrutiny, but in a sense they are harbingers of some still later writers who are even more precise and informative. The first, chronologically, is the fifth-century Gallo-roman aristocrat and later bishop (and saint), Sidonius Apollinaris (430–486). He mentions sport in passing several places in his works (Carter 1992) but the texts richest in detail are a lengthy narration of a chariot race and a similarly precise account of a spontaneous ball game. The former text is part of a panegyric of the accomplishments of Consentius, one of Sidonius's friends, who won a race organized in Ravenna by the emperor Valentinian III (425–55). Like his model Statius, Sidonius supplies both concrete details – the drivers drawing lots to see who gets which chariot and which horses, already installed in the starting pen, the trumpet sounding to start the race, the colours worn by the drivers – and dramatic, but realistic, descriptions of the drivers leaning over their horses as they urge them on, the tactics used by Consentius and his team-mate to secure a victory, and the accident that befalls an overly rash opponent (*Poems*, Loeb, 23.307–427).

In the latter text (*Letters*, Loeb, 5.17), Sidonius gives a reasonably precise account of a presumably real *harpastum* match that took place on 2 September 469.[39] It is presented as a strenuous – perhaps even a contact – upper class sport played by young students. An older man tries to join in, but is quickly so tired out he has to quit. Like the world he evokes in other letters, Sidonius's description is to say the least idyllic and not quite in keeping with contemporary realities (see Chapter 7). He may be trying to keep alive the image of a disappearing Roman world, but whatever his real preoccupations, his letter presents the sports historian with an accurate picture of a Roman game neither physically or socially unlike North American touch football.

A later writer with a similar aim was the sixth-century civil servant Magnus Aurelius Cassiodorus (480–575). Cassiodorus was principal secretary to the Ostrogothic king Theoderic (455–526), the second Germanic ruler of Rome after the collapse of the Western half of the Empire was consummated in 476. Since Theoderic wanted to conserve Roman imperial culture, the letters that Cassiodorus penned on his behalf contain many details outlining Roman practices. Two in particular (Cassiodorus 1973: 3.51 and 5.42) are the most complete accounts we possess on the history, symbolism, and actual practice of chariot races and wild beast hunts. The first of these letters mentions a specific charioteer whose success has assured him of receiving the same monthly pay, but Cassiodorus then goes on to describe the Circus Maximus in some detail, explaining the meaning of each of its parts, of the team colours, and of the seven laps and their markers. In the second letter he seems to be describing simultaneously wild-beast hunting shows, public executions in which the condemned – rendered immobile – were killed by animals, and intermediate displays in which criminals, poorly armed or encased in elaborate contraptions, were pitted against animals who almost always won.

Finally, Isidore of Seville (560–636) made the most systematic attempt to preserve classical and Christian Greco-Roman civilization by creating an encyclopaedic dictionary of all current knowledge as it was embodied in the Latin language (Isidore 1991/600). Entitled *Etymologies*, Isidore's book devoted the eighteenth chapter to Roman warfare and Roman games (*de bello et ludis*), the latter occupying sections 16–69.[40] Under the general heading of *spectacula*, games are defined as 'gymnic' (the term covers both physical exercise and Greek competitions), chariot racing – this is the game to which he devotes the most space – theatrical plays, amphitheatre shows (both gladiators and *venationes*), table games (mostly involving variants of dice), and finally ball games. Isidore's knowledge of the specifics of these sports is sketchy, incomplete, and definitely bookish rather than first hand.

In Sidonius, the discourse of sport still speaks of real events and attests to the continued importance of both personal and spectator sports, at least among Romanophile provincial elites feeling threatened by the Frankish incursions. By the time of Cassiodorus's letters, this discourse has become largely archaeological in focus, telling less of what Roman sport is and more of what it used to be. When we come to Isidore the discourse has been voided of any meaningful reference to lived experience and has been reduced to little more than dictionary entries. Greco-Roman antiquity and all of its athletic culture has come to an end and can now be experienced only as a memory. By the year 600 the discourse of sport no longer has a real object; its content has become a mere remembrance of things past.

Chapter 3

Sport in the forgotten centuries (2)

The primary sources 600–1700

It is in the work of Isidore's contemporary, Gregory of Tours (538–94), who was writing in the northwest corner of the former Roman Empire about the same time as Isidore was writing in the southwest, that the Dark Ages of sport become a reality. Gregory apologizes for his poor Latin grammar by likening himself to an ox doing exercises in a private gymnasium ('palaestrae ludum exerceat') or a donkey trying to play ball among organized players ('inter spheristarum ordinem', Gregory 1922/594: 5). The references are brief to the extreme and may owe more to literary convention than to any real acquaintance with wrestling rooms or team games. They are, in any case, the last recognizable allusions to Roman athletic practices and to the game *harpastum*, or indeed to any definable ball game, for the next 800 years. Other sports fare no better. In his major work, the *History of the Franks*, Gregory mentions that the Franks were avid hunters and liked animal baiting (Gregory 1884/594: 8.36) and that in 577 King Chilperic I (561–84) built circuses and put on *ludi* in both Soissons and Paris (1884/594: 5.11[17]). It seems unlikely that these shows included chariot racing, but may have involved beast-baitings and – in emulation of the Byzantine court – displays of juggling and gymnastics (Gregory 1927/594: 1.441–2).

After Gregory and Isidore, references to there being any kind of sport in Western Europe become so sporadic as to pass unnoticed. From the seventh through the eleventh centuries, we can discover little evidence of there being a sporting culture at all, despite our unwillingness to imagine a world in which strenuous, relatively non-violent, physical competition did not exist. Both written texts and the pictorial record are similarly silent on anything to do with physical activity.[1] The huge circuses, arenas, and private villas the Romans had built throughout the Western Empire were a continued, albeit dilapidated, presence, but nobody could remember what to do with them. The *Versus de Verona* written around 800 describes the local amphitheatre as a labyrinth, i.e. a puzzle, a clear sign that the building was no longer understood (Ward-Perkins 1984).

Brief glimpses of sport are afforded us from the ninth century onwards, but they omit more than they tell. Biographers and historians start to make short references to apparently spontaneous athletic activities, a hint that such references were emerging as a common-place and that physical games were not necessarily to be decried. It is worth noting in this connection that these details crop up in texts whose authors could have, for the most part, only legendary proof of the sporting activities they mention. In turn this may suggest a desire on the part of these writers to perpetuate some part of the ancient athletic tradition in order to maintain a link between the prestige of Rome and their own sense of living in lesser times.

For example, a ninth-century life of the sixth-century St Malo claims that, as a schoolboy, the future saint and his fellow pupils habitually took time away from their studies to run footraces on the beach (Bili 1979). More significantly, the *Historia Brittonum* (written c. 829–30) states that fifth-century wise men searching to discover a boy who, it had been foretold, would threaten the Celtic King Vortigern's rule, found him playing ball ('pilae ludum') with some other boys and getting into a fight about it (Nennius 1985/830: 92–5).[2] When questioned, he replies that his father was 'unus de consulibus Romanorum', a member of the Roman consular class, i.e. a person at the very top of the socio-political scale. This story thus links three themes: ball games, upper-class behaviour, and the faintly recalled prestige of Roman culture.

In almost the same year, a member of Charlemagne's court who had become secretary and adviser to his son Louis the Pious, wrote a biography of the Frankish emperor. Among other things he reports that Charlemagne was a big man and was fond of physical exertion:

> His body was large and robust, his height above average.…He vigorously and purposefully practiced both riding and hunting,…for there scarcely can be found any people in the world who can equal the Franks in these skills. He enjoyed the steam from the naturally hot thermal baths [in his capital at Aachen] and swam frequently to exercise his body. He was an extremely good swimmer, to the point that no one could beat him at it.…[When he swam] he invited a crowd, so that there might be a hundred or more men swimming with him.
>
> (Eginhard 1967: 66–8)[3]

We note that in the space of a few lines Eginhard has managed to characterize Charlemagne's physical person and sporting pursuits with three superlatives plus a number intended to impress: the Franks are better than other people, Charlemagne is the biggest and best of the Franks, and he is not afraid to demonstrate this in front of others. Competition is intimated, but is of no account.

Eginhard recorded Charlemagne's skills at riding, hunting, and swimming as a grown man. Later biographers and novelists will tend to shift the display of athletic accomplishments forward in the lives of their heroic subjects. Sports achievements will be no longer parallel to triumphs in politics and war but precursors to them. Before coming to this, however, there is another sports reference that emerges from the Carolingian era, embodied in an event reported by another ninth-century chronicler – and illegitimate grandson of Charlemagne – Nithard. When his kingly cousins Charles the Bald and Louis the German met in 842 to sign a mutual non-aggression pact, their two polyglot armies – composed of racially diverse units that had atavistic reasons to hate each other – often engaged in ritualized mock combats. These are described as 'ludos causa exercitii', which may be rendered as games whose purpose was to keep the soldiers in training. The sport consisted of equal numbers of foot soldiers from the two armies attacking each other at high speed. Abruptly, one army would pretend to turn and flee ('terga versa'), hiding behind their shields ('protecti umbonibus'); then the roles were reversed and the opposing army did the same. At this point the two kings would ride in brandishing their lances and accompanied by all their young nobles. They pursued those who were fleeing and brought the game to an end. Despite the warlike nature of the contest, it remained playful throughout and no attempt was made to inflict injury (Nithard 1926/843: 110–13 [3.6]).

Beyond the undoubted symbolic value of this show and hence its importance for onlookers – Nithard refers to a 'multitudo' of spectators and twice calls the game a 'spectaculum' – the description implies that it required some preliminary rehearsal if accidents were to be avoided. The game certainly demanded of the participants the same expenditure of physical energy as a real battle. More significantly, Nithard underlines the differences between this and other instances of mock combat – by implication these seem to have been fairly frequent – where genuine violence might result even though the combatants were few in number and knew each other. In short, in his report of this playful encounter between two armies, Nithard is arguably relating the birth of what would become the chief aristocratic sport of the Middle Ages, the simulacrum of battle known as the tournament.

Parallel to the re-emergence of sport as a legitimate topic of serious discourse in written texts, sports and games similarly became the subject of pictorial discourse, appearing in mural paintings and decorative illuminations in manuscript books. Most often these books had no connection to sport, indeed were even books of religious devotion expressly lettered and decorated for the high nobility.[4] It is curious that these detailed images of sport are not only present in prayer books and the like, but often constitute the border surrounding a liturgical or devotional text. Perhaps the intent was to juxtapose the life of the flesh and the life of piety.[5]

One such source, more monumental than the others, is the 70-metre long Bayeux Tapestry (c. 1080) that depicts the Battle of Hastings (1066) and the events leading up to it (see Wilson 1985 for a reproduction). Along its upper and lower borders it reveals incidentally some Medieval leisure activities (Carter 1992) but for knightly sports the main body of the tapestry is particularly informative. Segments 50–56 show massed cavalry attacks with some riders using couched lances, a tactic that required a good deal of equestrian skill and skill at handling weapons while on the unsteady seat of a rapidly moving animal. The images of the tapestry imply that the victorious Norman cavalry had undergone many hours of training to learn to control notoriously skittish horses and to charge in close formation. If not exactly sport – we cannot know if competition was involved – such training was at the very least athletic.

A more detailed written version of knightly sports is found in Geoffrey of Monmouth's versified *History of the Kings of Britain* (1985–91/1136), where the author recounts the athletic activities that were supposedly undertaken at the legendary King Arthur's coronation. After the ceremony and the banquets the knights began to compete in various sports and games, mostly of a military nature. The list varies from edition to edition – Geoffrey's book was very popular and later copyists did not hesitate to make changes and additions – but it almost always includes wrestling and dice (see Chapter 5 for a detailed account) and it is almost always mentioned that a crowd of appreciative ladies watched the knights from the battlements. At the end of the games, Arthur distributes rich prizes to the winners or, in some versions, to all the knights, and these included cities, castles, archbishoprics, bishoprics, and abbeys (Geoffrey 1985–91/1136).

From a sports historical point of view there are elements of Geoffrey's account that are both old and new. As in *Iliad* 23 and *Aeneid* 5, the games appear to be organized quite spontaneously, as an interlude between the battles already fought and those yet to come – the knights, of course, had participated in the campaigns that brought Arthur to the kingship. Second, although the prizes are rich, Geoffrey finds it necessary to state that the competitions are carried off in a friendly manner, even if they sometimes do involve brutal physical contact. In other words, the knights have learned not to confuse sport with war or mock fighting with personal animosity, and they are more inspired by the contest than by the rewards. Finally, Geoffrey's *History* establishes – or at least is symptomatic of – a paradigm that will determine the narrative warp of Medieval historiography and historical romances. Henceforward texts that recount heroic deeds will make some reference to sporting events, usually tournaments, held in connection with a celebration such as a wedding or a coronation.

Contemporary with the *History of the Kings of Britain* is the Spanish epic, the *Poema de mio Cid* (1140). It recounts in a somewhat fictionalized form the exploits of the eleventh-century Castilian knight, Rodrigo Díaz, who fought against the Moors and who rose from relatively humble beginnings to become virtual king of Valencia. During celebrations there feting his military victories, he wants show off by jousting in front of his wife and daughters ('delante de su mugier e de ses fijas querié tener las armas'). He then does a solo *corrida* on his new horse, with mock weapons, in front of the crowd. And to conclude, his vassals joust and play at a kind of quintain ('armas teníen e tablados crebantavan'; *Poema* 1963/1140: 193–94, ll. 1577–1602). The difference between this poem and Geoffrey's *History* is that here and elsewhere in the Spanish text the sports really only occupy a line or two of verse and are thus mere details of the larger picture, whereas Geoffrey promotes them to the status of independent events worthy of an itemized report. But also, as in Geoffrey, there is no indication of the quality of the athletic performance, it simply being taken for granted that everything is executed at a superlative level.

Although Geoffrey based his work on earlier histories, and consequently used their vocabulary, he could only have understood the sporting terminology as it was used in his own day. In this respect, at least, the *History of the Kings of Britain* is less an account of the past as it is a tableau of the noble sports of the early twelfth century.

Another text from the same century as Geoffrey's *History*, William Fitzstephen's description of London of 1175, reveals the medieval bourgeois counterpart to the recreations of the aristocrats. His encomium of the English capital praises all aspects of the city's life, but closes with what is certainly the most extensive written account from that period of popular competitive sports. Significantly, Fitzstephen stresses that his portrait of London has to mention the leisure pursuits (*ludi*) of the bourgeoisie, because a city has to be 'pleasant and cheerful' as well as 'useful and serious-minded'. These recreations included Saturday horse-racing with professional jockeys – conducted as part of the weekly animal market – and, on various feast-days, for students and male youths in general, cock-fights, ball-games of an indeterminate nature, more horse races, mock equestrian combats,[6] water-jousting, archery, running, jumping, wrestling, shot-putting (using heavy stones), javelin-throwing, and fencing. In the winter the young practice boar, bull, and bear-baiting and various ice-sports such as sliding and skating – this latter also including a kind of jousting. Adult males go into the countryside to hunt with both hawks and hounds but otherwise are just spectators at the games that their sons play. Fitzstephen resorts for his description to words connected with ancient Roman spectacles (*ludi, agmen*) and with Greek athletics (*certamen, agonisticus*) but is at pains to point out that these English games are merely analogous to the practices of the Roman world; in essence they are of a totally different nature (Fitzstephen 1908: 224–28; 1961: 959–61).

Other twelfth and thirteenth-century writers, almost too many to mention, also make references to sports events, but like most of their Roman and early Medieval predecessors, they do so in passing or as part of a total picture. They are not so much interested in the sports themselves as they are in what the participation in sport reveals about their subject, or about the characters and plot of their fiction. In some cases, however, the descriptions are sufficiently expanded to be of some sports-historical value. Fitzstephen's French contemporary, Chrétien de Troyes (1130–90), the literary creator of the legends of King Arthur's Round Table, is one such writer. In his first long poem of knightly adventures, *Erec et Enide* (1955/1160–70), the hero – son of a minor Breton king and now a member of Arthur's court – jousts and fences with another knight, Ydier, in front of a large group of spectators, just to determine whose girlfriend deserves to have a hunting falcon that has been offered as a prize at a local *fête*. Although this is intended as a sporting encounter, Erec's motivation runs deeper – Ydier had inadvertently shown him and Arthur's queen Guinevere disrespect – and things turn violent. Coats of mail are shredded, helmets split open, both men are wounded, and finally Erec has his opponent at his mercy. In a scene reminiscent of the fight between Aeneas and Turnus that closes the *Aeneid* – but with a Christian twist to it – the defeated knight pleads for his life, and Erec takes the high moral ground, spares him, leaves him his sword, and imposes only a symbolic punishment (Chrétien 1955/1160–70: 27–32, ll. 863–1040).[7]

Erec then marries Enide and a two-day tournament takes place as part of the festivities surrounding the marriage; of course, it is Erec who is adjudged the winner (Chrétien 1955/1160–70: 64–68, ll. 2072–2206). As in the description of the earlier fight, Chrétien's account of this mock battle is full of concrete, although still spectacular, detail. He conveys simultaneously an impression of both considerable splendour and enormous disorder and violence, itemizing all the colours of the flags, shields, armour, and weapons, but more so the incessant rain of clashing lances and sword blows and of knights knocked from the saddle. In other places his narrative is very technically precise, e.g. when relating the way Erec dons his various pieces of armour, leaps into the saddle, and is equipped with his sword, shield, and lance before fighting Ydier (Chrétien 1955/1160–70: 22–23, ll. 707–26). For all their daring-do, there would seem to be a prima facie case for thinking that the descriptions of the fight and the tournament in *Erec et Enide* are valid sports-historical documents.

Tournaments and jousting play a similarly important role in Chrétien's later romances of knightly adventure, but most often from the point of view of the spectator, as might be expected of a court poet. There are two tournaments in *Cligès* (Chrétien 1957/1176: ll. 2838–2917 and 4543–4929) and one each in *Lancelot* (Chrétien 1958/1177–81: ll. 5339–6056) and *Perceval* (Chrétien 1959/1180: ll. 4816–5655). In *Yvain* (Chrétien 1942/1173: ll. 2500–2684) Gawain and Yvain obtain leave from their king to go tourneying for a year, but stay away longer; no account of their victories is provided. Generally, the purpose of these tournaments is to fulfil some function in the plot, usually in connection with the knight's *vie sentimentale*, and Chrétien does not hesitate to include sensational elements to titillate his readers.[8] The descriptions of knightly sport in Chrétien's later novels are thus short on the kind of technical details found in *Erec*, but what they do speak to is the assumption on the part of a Medieval audience that a chivalric romance will have to include a tournament in order to be complete.

The non-fiction equivalent of Chrétien's idealized stories of knights errant, and by the same token a text that confirms Chrétien's veracity, is found in the early thirteenth-century biography of William Marshal (1144–1219), known in his own time as the greatest knight that ever lived.[9] Marshall's career in a sense followed that of the Cid: he started out life near the bottom of the feudal nobility, but through his own deeds rose to the top, becoming Regent of England during the first three years of the reign of King Henry III (1216–72). What is of particular interest in William's life, though, is that for some years he earned his living as a professional athlete, as a freelance tourneying knight. William's biography – 19,215 lines of verse (William 1891–1901/1220) – was commissioned by his son shortly after his death in 1219 and was written by someone who was apparently an eye-witness to at least some of the 20 or so tournaments in which William participated. Of particular interest is the first of these, because the poet narrates in great technical detail how the tourneyers stayed up late the night before, making sure that each piece of their armour and equipment fit and was in good shape (William 1891–1901/1220: ll. 1231–50).

The biography then goes on to describe the unfolding of that tournament – the initial massed charge of 40 or so knights to a side, after which each knight goes after what he thinks is the richest prize – and of a second tournament that took place immediately after. William's team decided not to take part, but William galloped day and night, arrived at the last minute, and in the fray five knights ganged up on him. He fought them off, but his helmet got twisted back to front. He withdrew for a moment, removed his helmet with great difficulty, hurting his hand badly in the process, threw some water on his face, and went back into the battle, where he fought so vigorously that he was awarded the prize. The sports historical value of a source like the Marshall biography lies in the fact that, even if the author wants to add excitement through the use of superlative expressions, he is nonetheless psychologically constrained to report what he actually saw. The modern reader is able to see beyond the exaggeration, and beyond the popular image of knightly chivalry, to understand the reality of the first professional sport of modern times.

Of these essentially twelfth-century writers, William Fitzstephen remains an exceptional case – nobody else wrote of bourgeois sports and that is why he is quoted so often – but Geoffrey, Chrétien, and the anonymous biographer of William Marshall established a paradigm. In later chivalric romances and, more significantly, in the biographies of the knights who were the heroes of the Hundred Years War between France and England (1337–1453), it became *de rigueur*, in France at least, to include passages on their athletic achievements.[10] In his life of Bertrand du Guesclin (1320–80), Cuvelier (1990/1400) recounts how, as a young man, the future hero and Grand Constable of France – unappreciated by his father – jousted incognito in tourney in Rennes and dazzled everyone with his skill; when his identity was revealed, the father regretted his mistake and promised appropriate recognition (ll. 562–787). As in other texts, the description of the jousting is marked by an abundance of realistic detail as to technique – Bertrand lowering and aiming his lance during the charge, and striking his opponent right in the visor of his helmet – and to the concomitant dangers – the other knight's horse is killed, while he is knocked unconscious to the point of being thought dead.[11]

The biography of the next generation's military hero, Jean Le Meingre, called Boucicaut (1366–1421), lays even greater stress on his athletic capacities (Boucicaut 1985/1400). In Chrétien de Troyes and Cuvelier, proficiency in the sport of the tournament was semiotically prophetic, the sign that a young man will achieve great things as a soldier. Perhaps for the first time in the historiography of early modern sport, Boucicaut's biographer begins this process in his subject's adolescence, relating that he invented a regime of exercises that made him physically superior to every other man of his class.[12] Even after he had become famous for his military deeds, he continued an active amateur career as a jouster, meeting challenges from other knights and finally, with two friends, offering to take on all comers during a 30-day period in the spring of 1390. The place chosen was St Inglevert, near Calais, because the English were the intended opponents, but the challenge was advertised all over Western Europe.

As to the actual unfolding of the event, Boucicaut's biographer is most likely unreliable, since his hero far outclasses all the other jousters. However, the St Inglevert jousts promised to be such a spectacular – and, one would guess, politically important – occasion that the historian Jean Froissart accompanied the English team in order to record what happened. His chronicle of the Hundred Years' War devotes 35 pages in the modern edition to the encounter (Froissart 1963: 676–710), and gives a more sober view of such games than is common in the other sources we normally have to turn to. Most notably absent from Froissart's version are the superlative adjectives and the extraordinary feats, and in their place are mundane details much closer to the truth: Boucicaut getting a bloody nose when his helmet was knocked off, or the jousters frequently missing each other because their horses veered away.[13]

Equally informative as to the organization of a jousting tournament and the sequence of events are the fifteenth-century *Mémoires* of Olivier de La Marche (1422–1502), who was master of the household and captain of the guard to the duke of Burgundy. Astounded by the spectacle of a joust organized by the duke in 1443 – the first set of jousts he ever attended as a young man – he gives a day-by-day, blow-by-blow account of the event. We learn that there were special dressing tents for the knights and that three nearby castles had been appropriated as hospitality suites. The jousters were an international crew, some of them talked a better joust than they actually performed, and – though La Marche was not surprised at this – as a lot they missed their targets at least as often as they hit them (La Marche 1883/1500: 282–335).[14]

Middle-class memorialists and amateur chroniclers – who did not have the direct access to aristocratic events that was afforded Froissart and La Marche – also make a point of mentioning tournaments, jousting, horse races, and other sporting events (e.g. Sardo 1845/1400, Del Corraza 1894/1438; *Récits* 1887; *Journal* 1854), sometimes adding details the official historians leave out. The fifteenth-century 'bourgeois de Paris', for example, reports that the winter of 1423 was so cold and snowy that the Seine froze over for 18 straight days. In order to keep warm, the Parisians chose to play rough ball games: 'souller, crocer, jouer à la pelote ou autres jeux' (*Journal* 1975: 182).[15] He is also the only one to record the appearance in Paris in 1427 of an expert woman tennis player from southern Belgium named Margot. She played both forehand and backhand shots with such strength, cunning, and skill that she beat all but the most powerful men (*Journal* 1975: 222).

The inclusion of sporting achievements, particularly jousting, in the biographies of famous knights continued well into the sixteenth century with the life of Bayard (1473–1524), the famous 'chevalier sans peur et sans reproche', by the Loyal Serviteur (2001/1525). Like other chivalric heroes, Bayard demonstrated his prowess by participating in tournaments, and winning them, while still a very young man, and the biographer supplies vivid accounts of knights jousting and then fighting with axes and swords.[16] Although a cavalry charge with lances had long since been an obsolete military tactic, it remained an aristocratic ideal and jousting persisted as a sign of a noble's courage and soldierly skills. It continued thus to be practiced as a spectator sport destined to impress others, and biographers and historians (e.g. Brantôme and his gossipy lives of France's great military leaders [1864/1614]) recorded these events in some detail as elements important to their narrative. Shakespeare even includes an, off-stage, tournament in *Pericles, Prince of Tyre* (2.1–3); its purpose is to enable a princess to select a suitable husband on the basis of his knightly prowess.

More extensively, the Medici family in mid-fifteenth century Florence commissioned two pseudo-epics to celebrate the jousting tournaments of 1469 and 1475 in which Lorenzo the Magnificent and his younger brother Giuliano displayed their military prowess and confirmed the family's right to rule Florence (see Chapter 6). The latter poem (Poliziano 1976/1475), composed of 171 eight-line stanzas, was left unfinished when Giuliano was assassinated in 1478 and contains no direct account of any athletic activity. The former, 1280 lines long (Pulci 1986/1471), describes in precise but often flowery terms a kind of tournament *en masse*, like the tournaments in Chrétien's *Erec* and the William Marshall biography, but in which there are no teams. Individual tourneyers simply single each other out and charge like jousters without lists or a laid-out course. Unlike the jousts at St Inglevert, none of the encounters are arranged in advance and there are neither challengers nor defenders. Although Pulci does provide a clear sense of what was a very complex athletic competition, his narrative reaches that point only after 800 lines of mythological imagery and descriptions of the tourneyers' splendid costumes. There were already hints in La Marche (1883/1500) that in the fifteenth century tournaments had become as much occasions for elaborate display and spectacle as they were for knightly sport. In the sixteenth century sources it becomes increasingly clear that actually striking and unhorsing your opponent has taken second place to the pomp and circumstance that precedes and follows (e.g. Cimilotti 1587; Gaiani 1619; Messeri 1894).[17]

Early modern sports other than the tournament had a difficult time making their appearance in fictional, biographical, and historical literature, with the exception of real (or royal) tennis. The poet Charles d'Orléans (1394–1465) saw the game as an allegory for the way his life was unfolding: a triples match with Age, Worry, and Fickle Fortune on one side and the poet, Hope, and Good Luck on the other (Charles 1966/1465: 1.144–45). In a somewhat parodic fashion, the Burgundian court historiographer Jean Molinet (1435–1507) used the tennis metaphor to describe the capture of Ghent in 1492 and the ongoing struggles between the French king and the duke of Burgundy (Molinet 1936–9: 1.254–7).[18] In this vein, Molinet had English precursors, some anonymous writers and versifiers who imagined Henry V's capture of Harfleur in 1415 as a tennis match in which the English artillery served cannon balls (Gillmeister 1997: 111–17). Shakespeare much later used some of this material in Henry's often-quoted tirade rejecting the gift of tennis balls the French have sent him (*Henry V* 1.2: 'When we have match'd our rackets to these balls, / We will in France, by God's grace, play a set…').

Allusions of this sort are, like similar allusions in the Roman poets, simply passing mentions that only inform us that the poet is ingenious and that his readership understood what he was saying. Other, more extensive, examples of athletic games making their way into literature are found in fifteenth-century Italy as well. Gentile Sermini's *Giuoco della pugna*, the game of the fists, i.e. a collective fist fight, of 1425 (Sermini 1968) and Giovanni Frescobaldi's *Giuoco del calcio*, the 'rugby' game, of about 1460 (Frescobaldi 1973–5) are respectively prose and versified descriptions of semi-folkloric games.[19] Sermini writes from the viewpoint of the participants, Frescobaldi from that of a spectator who knows – and names – all of the players and all the moves they make. These descriptions, unlike the contemporary appropriation of tennis as a metaphor, possess a definite interest for the sports historian. They attest not only to the popularity of certain games and to the poet's ability to manipulate the lexicon of sport, but actually bring the modern reader into contact with the reality of the game.

Popular games like *calcio* and *la pugna*, like the games mentioned by the 'bourgeois de Paris' (*Journal* 1975), inadvertently generated another primary source of sports historical information, of the kind that seems indisputably authentic. They both wasted the players' time – at least in the eyes of the authorities – and produced injuries and even deaths. Thus they provoked the intervention of church, the state, and the city governments in ways that left their trace in the bureaucratic archives: royal, ecclesiastical, and municipal decrees that attempted to control these games and redirect the participants toward more useful exercises – usually archery – transcripts of trials, and requests for pardon from those condemned for committing violent acts on the field of play or shortly thereafter. Although these documents are short on the specifics of the games actually being played, they do represent a corpus of texts from which an understanding of these sports can be derived at a couple of removes.[20] They are not, however, a very readily accessible source of information and will not be dwelt on here.

Much more significant in determining the development of sport and the ways in which it was conceived and practiced in the early modern period is the Germanic emperor Frederick II's book on hunting with falcons, *De arte venandi cum avibus*, written before 1250 (Frederick 1955). This is an encyclopaedic work, as much a treatise on ornithology and veterinary medicine as it is on actual hunting. It draws its information from Arabic and ancient Greek sources, and hence reconnects with antiquity and Aristotelian method after the rupture of the Dark Ages. But it is also based on close empirical observation of avian and human behaviour and so combines the theoretical with the pragmatic. However, its real significance lies in the fact that it is both descriptive and prescriptive. Frederick extracts general rules and abstract criteria from the materials he has assembled and formulates a set of rational principles for future practice. In one sense, the *De arte venandi* is part of the tradition of Greek treatises that raised practical matters almost to the level of an applied science, as exemplified by Xenophon's books on hunting with dogs (*Kynēgetikos*) and horsemanship (*Peri hippikēs*), but with one important difference: the *De arte venandi* demonstrates that a physical activity conducted purely for pleasure, can be analysed, i.e. in the literal sense of the term, deconstructed into its component parts, in the same way as scientific phenomena and purely mental pursuits; and that these parts can then be classified and organized into a pedagogy. In short, that hunting with falcons – and by extension all forms of physical sport – can be apprehended intellectually and executed by applying sound *a priori* concepts grounded in reason and personal experience.[21]

Other books on hunting would follow, not all so scientifically minded as Frederick's, but all usually trying to present hunting as a science, or at least as a methodical endeavour, and not merely as a pragmatics. Almost all of them are by aristocrats or even kings and are addressed to an aristocratic audience for whom hunting was a sport. They limit their subject matter to deer – the noblest game animal – or wild boar – the most dangerous and exciting – or to falconry – the most complex form of the chase – as well as to the training of dogs and the stocking of otherwise empty forests with suitable prey (e.g. Charles IX 1857/1573: 1–3).[22] That said, the content of the most widely read hunting book of the Middle Ages (Crescenzi 1965/1305: 127–93) had, as its modern editor puts it, 'nulla di "sportivo"', nor anything aristocratic either, for that matter. Pietro de' Crescenzi was a thirteenth-century Bolognese lawyer who owned extensive country estates. Late in his life he wrote a large book on estate-management, distilling his experience but also bringing into it the intellectual fruits of his training and education. His book, the *Liber ruralium commodorum*, or book of country pleasures, consists of 12 chapters, each concerned with a different aspect of systematically and scientifically making the best use of the land. The tenth chapter is devoted to hunting, which for Crescenzi was part of agriculture, a useful exercise that provided food for the table and eliminated animals that might otherwise destroy crops. His prey thus ranged widely to include rabbits and other small game that were normally the only animals that peasants were allowed to hunt. The methods and techniques he advocated undoubtedly worked, for his book survived in 130 manuscripts and 60 printed editions.

A similarly successful hunting book, but one more specifically addressed to an aristocratic, sporting audience, was written by Gaston Phoebus, comte de Foix, around 1387–9 (Gaston 1998). It displays the same kind of system, method, and scientific approach that characterized the work of Frederick II and Crescenzi and became thus a model for conceptualising hunting, especially in those countries where suitable game abounded. Gaston did not limit himself to noble prey, but included animals such as otters, hares, wildcats, badgers, and even reindeer – he had travelled to Scandinavia. The book quickly became very influential and many manuscript and printed editions in French and other European languages followed in the next 200 years.[23]

The systematic analysis, and hence the theorisation, of hunting, i.e. of an activity heretofore considered to be purely pragmatic and empirical, spread quickly to another aristocratic pursuit, swordsmanship. Now published as *The Medieval Art of Swordsmanship* (Forgeng 2003), the earliest surviving manual of sword fighting happens to be almost contemporary with the *De arte venandi*. It depicts 38 combat sequences opposing a teacher – the Priest – and a pupil – Scholar. Each one of the images is accompanied by a brief explanatory text, in Latin, with occasional German technical terms inserted. Other pedagogies of swordsmanship followed in the fourteenth and fifteenth centuries: Liechtenauer's *Kunst des langen Schwertes*, the art of the long sword, dated 1389, but perhaps written earlier (Liechtenauer 1965, 1985), Fiore dei Liberi's *Flos duellatorum*, the flower of combatants, of 1410 (Fiore 1902), Hans Talhoffer's *Fechtbuch*, or book of fighting, that exists in three very different manuscripts dated 1443, 1459, and 1467 respectively (Talhoffer 1887, 1890, 1893, 2000), Filippo Vadi's *L'arte cavalleresa*, the chivalric art of 1482–7 (Vadi 2001), and the first book of weapons handling to be printed, in 1516, Andreas Pauernfeindt's *Ergrundung ritterlicher Kunst der Fechterey*, a fathoming of the knightly art of fighting (Pauernfeindt 1538).

What is characteristic of these books, and there were others of the same sort, is that they remained essentially pictorial:[24] a series of images – sometimes very many images – depicted two combatants in various postures of attack and defence, often including straight unarmed wrestling. Each image was usually accompanied by a brief written text intended to clarify what was happening between the two men, and the fighting positions were customarily arranged into sets or sequences. Unfortunately, as Sydney Anglo has pointed out (2000: 46, 182), when these manuals are read at a distance of 500 years, they are pedagogically lacking.

There are still vast gaps between what is depicted and what would have to be done in order to move from one posture to another. The fighting system was an effective one but the techniques for recording it were seriously deficient. Talhoffer and the majority of his fifteenth-century German colleagues generally failed to describe adequately how a fighter was to achieve any particular manoeuvre. They also experienced the utmost difficulty in matching words and pictures.

In the one book where that relationship between word and image is clear, Albrecht Dürer's *Fechtbuch* of 1512 (Dürer 1910), I am inclined to think that the artist was not really intending to write a commercial manual of hand-to-hand combat. The book consists of 120 drawings of wrestlers demonstrating various holds and throws; and 80 of men fighting with a variety of weapons, but though the wrestling section is copiously annotated, the part devoted to weapons is not. Of course, the quality of the illustrations is vastly superior to those of any contemporary combat manual – and of any later one, for that matter, with only a couple of possible exceptions – but in fact they were not even done from life. Dürer was really just re-drawing in a much more satisfying manner the holds and fighting postures of an earlier manuscript, the so-called Codex Wallerstein.[25]

What is curious in these manuals of single combat, both in the fifteenth century and later, is the complete absence of boxing and the ambiguous role accorded to wrestling. Although they enjoyed ancient Olympic prestige as independent sports, the latter was at best an appendix to other forms of fighting and the former is not mentioned, except to make fun of peasants (see Terry 2003). In some circles, particularly Germanic ones, wrestling was a highly esteemed chivalric skill; in others, it was decried as a purely lower-class form of fighting, since it involved none of the ostentatious panoply of other knightly sports: horses, fancy armour, elaborate weapons. That said, there were independent wrestling masters who taught their skills and techniques outside the tradition of weapons fighting, and who encapsulated them in written treatises. For example, the wrestling master to the dukes of Austria, Meister Ott, wrote an unillustrated wrestling book, *Ringbuch*, in the fourteenth-century. It was alluded to by Liechtenauer and actually appended to the 1443 version of Talhoffer, along with some illustrations that supposedly pertained to it but that did not (Anglo 2000). Another teacher, Fabian von Auerswald, published his *Ringerkunst*, art of the wrestler, in the mid-sixteenth century (Auerswald 1539). This was the first wrestling manual ever to be printed and was graced with 85 woodcuts by Lucas Cranach the Younger.[26]

The question arises, of course, as to whether these manuals were teaching their readers a sport or simply a series of moves that would maim or even kill your opponent. And if the latter, why bother discussing them in book that is devoted to the former? The first answer is that in the combat sports, the difference between a hold or thrust aimed at producing injury and a harmless version of the same move lies not in the gesture's geometry and biomechanics, but rather in its physical intensity: killing someone with your hands or a sword and pretending to do it differ from each other only in the final step. It follows that, if you are going to train someone to be a soldier or a duellist, that person has to rehearse his skills first by *not* killing his practice adversary – who is either his teacher or another pupil like himself – before going on to the real thing.

Second, fencing masters customarily conducted their classes in public. Montaigne (1983/1580) went as a spectator to fencing schools in both Augsburg and Bologna, complaining in the former case that he had to pay twice, once to get in and a second time to get a cushion to sit on. In London, the Company of the Masters of Defence organized public demonstrations in which students of fencing qualified to move up from one level to the next: free scholar, provost, and master in turn. These shows were widely advertised, attracting as many as 4,000 spectators, and were played in enclosed, usually rectangular spaces: markets such as Leadenhall, inn courtyards, and, after 1570, public playhouses (Berry 1991: 1–14). The fact that spectators were not only admitted but actually sought out undoubtedly encouraged competition among the students, though I suspect that the pedagogy itself had a similar focus.

Indeed, martial arts teachers were often explicit about the fact that wrestling and swordplay were both training for more deadly purposes and sports, even if in training sessions and prize contests the results went beyond what is now permissible. Henri II put out a servant's eye in a practice match (Brantôme 1864) and the wrestler in Shakespeare's *As You Like It* has broken his opponents' ribs and promises to break their limbs (1.1–2). Antonio Manciolino (1531: 3rᵒ) speaks of the 'diletto di giocare con variie & diversi giocatori', literally, the pleasure of [sword]playing with various and diverse [sword]players, while almost in the same breath mentioning that getting wounded by a friendly adversary is part of the game. But in any case, the proliferation of instructional books on the art of weapons handling means that from the fifteenth century onwards, they become the major source for our knowledge of early modern sport and athletics, reducing to lesser importance the literary, (auto)biographical, and historical sources of the earlier Middle Ages.

Other areas of sport and physical activity that became the object of concentrated intellectual attention in the fourteenth and fifteenth centuries included tourneying and jousting – on their way to obsolescence, although no one knew it – and physical education, which would become an increasingly important component of general pedagogical theory. About 1350 Geoffroy de Charny, a knight himself, formulated a set of *Demandes pour la joute, les tournois et la guerre*, questions about jousts, tournaments, and war (Muhlberger 2002) that demonstrated the legalistic complexities of these activities. Not just a matter of two men in armour charging or hacking at each other, chivalric sports in this period still involved the acquisition of booty – usually the loser's horse – and even holding defeated knights for ransom. However, once some kind of ambiguity or imprecision crept in, then could the winner still take the horse? Charny's questions are many and complex, but what they essentially speak to is the desire for certainty in practical matters that was becoming more and more insistent during the 'calamitous fourteenth century', as Barbara Tuchman aptly called it (1978). The mindset implicit in Charny's reflections can be traced back to the *Statuta armorum*, statute on [the use of] weapons, an English document regulating the tournament that was first circulated in 1267 and ultimately promulgated as a decree in 1292 (Denholm-Young 1948). It can also be traced forward to a more precise articulation a century or so later in the various published sets of rules for the conduct of jousting tournaments, in the formation of tournament leagues, and in the devising of objective scoring systems that awarded a different number of points according to the nature of the hit.[27]

The most celebrated attempt to analyze the tournament and prescribe rules for its practices was René d'Anjou's *Livre de la forme et devis d'un tournoi*, the book of the form and devising of a tournament, of about 1460 (René 1986). Lavishly illustrated, between its text and its pictures it remains still today the best source of our information as to how a tournament actually unfolded from beginning to end, what the armour looked like, what the weapons were, how the prizes were awarded, and so on. Ultimately of much greater retroactive significance to the history of sport, however, was the c. 1434 book by king Duarte of Portugal (1433–38), *Livro da ensinança de bem cavalgar toda sela*, the book of instruction on how to ride well in a full saddle (Duarte 1944). Probably because it was written in Portuguese, although the manuscript is conserved in Paris, Duarte's work has been largely neglected, with only a very brief section ever being translated into English (Barber and Barker 1989 – but now see Anglo 2000). Duarte is the first writer on jousting actually to give instructions on how to hold the lance, both as the knight starts his course and as he approaches his opponent, and also to delve into the psychology of the jouster who, as he sees a lance approaching him, is very much inclined to close his eyes and thus miss his target altogether.

By the end of the fourteenth century Italian humanist writers, especially those charged with the education of the children of their noble or royal patrons, began to formulate analytical systems for upper-class pedagogy. These almost always included a multi-purpose section on physical education that mentioned first the kind of training in weapons that was already the most important component of the heretofore unwritten training of young nobles. But since the humanists' goal was to make their future masters into replicas of ancient Greek and Roman statesmen, their advocacy of physical education and the practice of sport was much influenced by their understanding of the role exercise and strenuous games played in the moral life of the ancients. With the passage of time, Galen's thinking on the medical value of exercise began to infiltrate humanist thought as well, and the prophylactic argument was added to the moral and military aims of physical education.

By far the most influential of the advocates of exercising the body was the Italian doctor Girolamo Mercurialis (1530–1606) whose *De arte gymnastica* (Mercurialis 1672/1569) was still being republished in the early eighteenth century. The beginnings of the movement, however, go back to Pier Paolo Vergerio's *De ingenuis moribus et studiis* (c. 1400), the studies and character of a free-born youth (Vergerio 2002) and to Leon Battista Alberti's *Libro della famiglia* (c. 1434–44) (Alberti 1913, 1969). Other educational theorists who prescribed the addition of physical exercise to the standard pedagogical curriculum – or whose view of the necessary role of sport implied such an inclusion – included Maffeo Vegio, *De educatione liberorum* (1444), the education of children – significantly, both boys and girls (Vegio 1933–6); Juan Luis Vives, *De tradendis disciplinis*, on the transmission of the [scholarly] disciplines (1913/1531); Thomas Elyot, *The Book Named the Governor* (1962/1531); François Rabelais, *Pantagruel* (1994/1532) and *Gargantua* (1994/1534), Roger Ascham, *The Scholemaster* (1904/1570); Michel de Montaigne, 'De l'institution des enfants', the education of boys (1965/1580–92); and Richard Mulcaster, *Positions for the Training up of Children* (1994/1581).

But the most influential book by far is not really a treatise on education *per se*: Baldassare Castiglione's *Libro del cortegiano*, the book of the courtier (1972/1528) is a dialogue-debate that defined the manners and *mores* and abilities required of the modern upper-class male. Among these requirements, physical dexterity in a variety of sports plays a prominent role, and that in turn implies that the future courtier will have begun to play these sports during his school years. And, of course, chief among these sports in all the theorists – with the exception of Mulcaster – are riding well and handling the weapons of war; the young Renaissance man they are intending to educate will still, like his Medieval predecessor, spend at least part of his life in the military.[28]

After 1530, by which time the 'printing revolution' that had begun in the mid-fifteenth century had fully taken over the means of communication (Febvre and Martin 1971; Eisenstein 1983), books that instructed their readers on the techniques and niceties of swordplay were published with increasing frequency. Marozzo (1536) was the most popular of these, at least to judge by its numerous reprintings and re-editions up to 1615, but it remains mired in the Medieval pragmatism that characterized the manuals of Fiore dei Liberi and Talhoffer. Egerton Castle considered him to be 'the greatest teacher of the old school, the rough and undisciplined swordsmanship of which depended as much on dash and violence as on carefully cultivated skill' (Castle 1969: 35).[29] Although Marozzo's book is heavily illustrated with 82 woodcuts, these remain secondary to the verbal text.

Marozzo represents the end of a certain pragmatic tradition in athletics that, nonetheless, continued to live on despite other developments. A new theoretical approach was first enunciated by Antonio Manciolino, whose *Opera nova*, new book (1531) established several original principles. First, weapons manuals should be concise and should bring enjoyment to their readers.[30] Second, fencing/duelling is an activity in which the whole body is implicated and not just the sword arm. Co-ordination of the movements of the hands and feet is a prerequisite to success.[31] Second, fighting always involves an adversary. Hence the swordsman cannot act as an isolated individual, but must move in dialectical concert with his opponent, whose personality and style will be different from those of his other opponents. Third, Manciolino brought to the pedagogy of swordplay a new vocabulary that signalled a different way of conceiving the actions of the fencer: 'bellezza', beauty, 'leggiadria', lightness, and 'grazia', gracefulness, terms which could not be used when speaking of heavy weapons like the two-handed sword, and which reflect the language Castiglione used in the *Book of the Courtier* of 1528 to characterize the general deportment of a noble; 'scienza' and 'ragione', science and reason, that imply an intellectualised approach to what had been theretofore a strictly physical endeavour; and most importantly, 'tempo' and 'misura', that denote rhythm, precision, and control in the fencer's movements.

Another important step forward was achieved by Francesco Altoni, whose *Monomachia*, or single combat (c. 1538) enunciated the need to impose a prior conceptual model onto the skills of fencing. He dissected the various thrusts and parries that constituted the repertory of swordsmanship and regrouped them into sets and subsets of the nine major postures, or guards, the fencing body can adopt. The body in Altoni's thought – and this includes the sword – is understood as an organic whole; hence the need for the fencer constantly to keep his balance and to relate all movements in one direction to simultaneous compensatory movements in the opposite direction. More than Manciolino, Altoni articulates his argument through a vocabulary that is derived from architectural geometry as applied to human movement: harmony, proportion, fixed measurements, composition, tempo. He founds this geometry on the notion of the module or basic unit, which is the normal pace of a well-proportioned man and is equal to one-third of his height, although this will necessarily vary in the course of fighting.[32]

Like other fencing masters, Altoni invokes as a reason for writing his book the claim that his predecessors had got it wrong. Here he seems to have had both

Manciolino and Marozzo in his sights, decrying other teachers' use of the word 'gioco', a game or form of play – it is Manciolino's favourite word – to designate fencing itself as well as its various components. For Altoni, fencing is not a 'gioco' but an 'arte', a rationalized technique. He also condemns the illustrations in previous books – it sounds as if he is speaking about Marozzo – claiming they drove him crazy ('mi impacciavano') rather than helping him to understand.[33] Altoni's book was never published but appears to have been known to Camillo Agrippa, whose *Trattato di scientia d'arme* (1553) takes the process of the geometrification of swordplay much farther. Unlike almost all other authors of weapons manuals, Agrippa was a mechanical engineer and thus 'interested in the engineering principles underlying the movements of the human body when engaged in fencing' (Anglo 2000: 48). He rationalizes these, reducing Altoni's nine guards to four, and replacing the three-dimensional body with two-dimensional geometrical analyses; in sum, making fencing into a branch of abstract mathematics free of material contingencies.

The next generation of fencing masters tended to back down from Agrippa's more extreme position, remembering perhaps what he himself had said: after you have learned the 'theorica' of any science or technique, you have to 'vivificarla con la prattica', make it come alive in a practical way (Agrippa 1553: f. A1^v–A2^r). The writer to do so most successfully, in my opinion was Giacomo di Grassi (1570), who retained some of Agrippa's geometry but put everything back onto a human scale. Perhaps disingenuously, he claims to have had no experience in teaching 'la ragione dell'armi', the rationality of weapons practice, but being ill and down on his luck ('assai debole & bassa fortuna') he is now going to do so, in order to thank some noble lords who helped him out of a bad situation. Grassi's opening stance is to assert that since all the best masters teach different styles of fencing, the result is a 'confuso & infinito numero de' colpi', an unclear, almost infinite number of cuts and thrusts. He will make sense of these by starting with the basics ('le cose piu semplici') and going up from there to the more complex ('poi alle composite ascendendo'), basing his whole system on the 'linea retta e circolare', straight lines and circles (1570: f. *3^{r-v}). Grassi's more down-to-earth approach led to his having more international influence than most of the other masters. Henri de Sainct Didier (1573) based his fighting manual, the first to be written in French, on Grassi, and in 1594 an English translation of Grassi was the first to appear in that language; it was followed fairly quickly by two original English texts, Saviolo (1595) and Silver (1599), the latter being a jingoistic refutation of the advantages of the Italian rapier and style of fighting.[34]

From Marozzo on, these manuals have this in common that marks them as modern, both in their presentation and in their way of thinking. By eschewing the exclusive reliance on images that was characteristic of the Germanic tradition, these books transformed swordplay into an endeavour that could be made the object of verbal discourse. A picture might be worth a thousand words, but the 200 or so words that filled up the space in the book that would have formerly been occupied by a drawing or woodcut had to be arranged according to the contemporary conventions for writing expository prose. Prose that was, moreover, of a very utilitarian nature. If the book was to sell, potential duellists had to understand clearly what was meant. In other words, the new language of the fencing manuals represented a triumph of the intellectual over the visual, the ability to communicate physical gesture in language. The illustrations, still very numerous and important in some texts, are both reduced to an adjunct role and endowed with a different semiotic function. Up to and including Marozzo, the images are essentially anecdotal; beginning with Altoni, they are almost exclusively analytical.[35]

Concomitant with the reduced role accorded images in printed fencing manuals is the decreased frequency of sports iconographical sources generally (Francioni 1993). The disappearance of the manuscript book entailed, of course, the disappearance of the illuminated miniatures that often showed legendary or real heroes performing athletic feats. The rise of humanism and the taste for ancient mythology altered decorating styles, so that chests and other pieces of furniture that might in the past have shown tournament scenes (Barber and Barker 1989) were either simply stained and shellacked or painted with pastoral scenes from Greek literature.[36] Murals and tapestries also shied away from sport, with a few notable exceptions: the Sala dei Giochi, or games room, in the ducal palace of Ferrara, the Palazzo del Te in Mantua (men swimming c. 1530), the Château d'Oiron in west-central France (men playing ball, see Ill. 8), or the *Histoire de Gombaut et Macé* (c. 1580), a set of tapestries in the Musée de Saint-Lô in Normandy, one of which depicts a version of pall mall (reproduced in Flannery and Leech 2004: 118–19). In fact, until the mid-seventeenth century, pictures of one sort or another are virtually our only source of information concerning ball and club sports such as billiards, the varieties of golf, and a kind of mini-baseball played by both men and women.

The vogue for text-based instructional books teaching the principles and practice of single combat spread quickly, although less numerously, to other fields of athletics. The Swiss humanist Nicolas Wynman's wrote the first instructional book on swimming in 1538, *Colymbetes, sive de arte natandi,* and in 1545 Roger Ascham, tutor and secretary to three successive English monarchs, outlined the principles of archery in his *Toxophilus, or the Schole of Shoting* (Ascham 1904), defending it as a sport not unworthy of intellectuals. Following an argument with his patron, the duke of Ferrara, over a call he made while refereeing a tennis match, Antonio Scaino undertook the first typologically based categorization of ball games, the *Trattato del giuoco della palla,* a treatise on ball games (1555). A priest and Aristotelian scholar, Scaino laid down the rules and tactics of the varieties of tennis and other ball games, according to the implement used to strike the ball – hand, racquet, paddle, etc. – the size of the court, and whether or not a 'net' was used – actually just a slackly strung fringed rope. Scaino's book was supplemented by an anonymous and unfinished *Discorso del giuoco della pallacorda,* an essay on the game of net tennis (c. 1560) that deals largely with tactics and with determining the angles and speeds at which the ball will ricochet off the various parts of the court.[37] Tennis's unusual scoring system continued to puzzle people. Guillaume Gosselin tried to solve the conundrum in a pamphlet of 1579, and his solution was reprinted by Forbet L'Aisné (1599) as an appendix to his translation of Galen's *Exercise with the Small Ball*. Forbet also was the first to codify the rules of tennis, supposedly in 1592, though he seems not to have published them until the appearance of his book.[38]

Scaino included in his book a brief account of *calcio*, a rambunctious sort of rugby football that the Florentines adopted as their peculiarly native game, and in 1580, Giovanni Bardi, a humanist, mathematician, and musicologist – he is credited with inventing opera – subjected the game to a full-fledged treatment in his *Discorso del calcio fiorentino*, an essay on Florentine *calcio*. Bardi sets out the game with arithmetical precision (size of the field, number of players, distances between them (see Ill. 10), methods of determining the score), but though he celebrates *calcio* – and though it continued apparently to be a fixture of Florentine social life into the late seventeenth century (Lassels 1670) – there are hints in his essay that the game is dying out and that the city's Medicean rulers are unwilling to support it.[39] *Calcio* is also described in a curious encyclopaedia of Florentine games and sports that was undertaken anonymously in the mid-sixteenth century, but left incomplete and never published (*Ammaestramenti* c. 1550). The table of contents lists 97 physical activities, but many of these are not actually described. Some are just children's, or childish, forms of play, others require some athletic ability, e.g. walking on stilts, while still others are actual sports – *calcio* and *pome*, this latter described in Chapter 7.

Francisco de Alcocer (1559) actually published a similar encyclopaedia in Spain, the *Tratado del juego*, or treatise on games, but his work was much more focused than the *Ammaestramenti*. Alcocer was concerned to classify games, and particularly games that might possess some moral overtones, according to whether or not it would be licit to practice them. The purpose of tournaments, for example, is 'para exercitar las fuerças en las armas y tomar algun regozijo y recreacion', to exercise one's strength in wielding arms and at the same time take some enjoyment and recreation (1559: 286). However, since there is a probable danger of death in tournaments on horseback, it is a mortal sin to participate in them. Dancing, on the other hand, is not a mortal sin but just a waste of time (1559: 301).

The *Ammaestramenti* and Alcocer are a prefigurement of a later and almost equally neglected attempt at an encyclopaedia of sports and games, Francis Willughby's *Book of Games*, left unfinished at his death in 1672 (Willughby 2003). Like the *Ammaestramenti*, Willughby covers table games as well as more strenuous activities – tennis, footraces, football, jumping – games now thought more suitable for children but played by adults in the seventeenth century, e.g. 'prison barres', and games that have since disappeared or left only faint traces – stowball, 'stoole ball'. Willughby's book presents, however, the considerable advantage of supplementing the verbal descriptions with simple diagrams showing, e.g. a geometrical analysis of a tennis ball ricocheting off the walls and floor.

Between the *Ammaestramenti* and Willughby, several other landmark athletic manuals were published. The Cambridge physicist Everard Digby studied the means to propel the body through water and to keep it afloat in his *De arte natandi* (1587, 1595). His concerns lead him into such arcana as how to cut your toenails while keeping you head above water, but he does describe a number of different swimming strokes, e.g. 'to swim like a dog'. The stroke he prefers, however, is 'to swim upon his side'. It is 'more laborious' than the other strokes but it is also 'swifter'. Digby's book remained the authoritative manual on swimming into the nineteenth century. A contemporary manual of gymnastic feats, both with and without apparatus, had a similarly long-lived influence. An entertainer at the imperial and royal courts in Vienna and Paris, Arcangelo Tuccaro created a rational pedagogy for the training of a young acrobat in the *Trois dialogues de l'exercice de sauter et voltiger en l'air*, three dialogues on the practice of leaping and somersaulting in the air (1599). His book is both an illustration of what he himself could do – he had a European-wide reputation (Garzoni 1585, Schindler 2001) – and a system that a trainer could adopt to take a young boy from the first physical exercises right through to the point absolute mastery of all the varieties of elaborate front, back, and side somersaults (Bouissac 1973, Schmidt 2006, 2007). Many of the illustrations show a geometrical analysis of what the acrobat is attempting to do (see Ill. 9). More or less contemporary with Tuccaro, another Italian entertainer, Giocondo Baluda, wrote a very complex and sophisticated *Trattato del modo di volteggiare & saltare il cavallo di legno*, a treatise on vaulting and leaping over the wooden horse (c. 1630). Like Tuccaro, his method is rational, and like Agrippa's book on fencing (1553) he reduces three-dimensional shapes to two-dimensional geometrical schemata.[40] Digby, Tuccaro, and Baluda are all copiously illustrated, but the verbal text remains the primary means of communication. More significantly, with the exception of Forbet, Tuccaro and Baluda, the authors of these instructional manuals were not professionals in the sport they analyze, but learned outsiders bringing to athletic activity the insights and methodologies of other disciplines.

Of course, non-technical sources continued to speak of sport and to tell us something about how it was actually practiced, as opposed to the version we might derive from the ideal world of the instructional manuals. What changes between the fifteenth and sixteenth centuries, particularly in northern Europe, however, is that the references to sport are no longer confined to the private world of the personal diary or journal, but are expressed in texts that are potentially intended for publication. Perhaps in emulation of imperial Roman writers, Renaissance humanists found it appropriate to speak of sport in a variety of contexts. Sixteenth-century dialogues by Vives ('Leges Ludi', the laws of playing; Vives 1970/1540), Erasmus ('De Lusu', sport; Erasmus 1965/1522), and Mathurin Cordier ('Lusus pueriles', young men's games; Cordier 1585) covered a range of sports played by students. The purpose of the dialogues was to show young men that they can play sports and talk of everyday subjects just as well in Latin as in their own language – the same exercise was repeated in the early seventeenth century by Bretonneau

(1628) – but to the modern historian they present secondary advantages: it is from Vives, for example, that we can date the introduction of the stringed racquet into tennis.

Court poets like Pierre de Ronsard (1524–85) and Sir Philip Sidney (1554–85) boast of their athletic prowess. Scattered throughout the former's works between 1552 and 1560 are numerous references to his fondness for fencing, tennis, hunting, shooting the harquebus, swimming, wrestling, horse vaulting, foot racing, and 'ballon', i.e. a field game involving an inflated ball (Ronsard 1914–75: see Ill. 8). In one of the sonnets of the *Astrophil and Stella* sequence (no. 41) Sidney describes his skill with the lance that won him the prize in a tournament, perhaps in 1581 (Sidney 1962: 185). In other texts he praises good horsemanship and advises his brother on what manuals – all Italian – he should read in order to acquire expertise as a rider (Sidney 1965: 95 and 144; Duncan-Jones 1991: 170–1).[41] Other, less likely, sources for early modern sports history include a university professor who provides the first description of Florentine *calcio* since Frescobaldi in 1460 (Filopono c. 1518);[42] a disgruntled bourgeois who recounts in his memoirs how a ceremonial *calcio* game was badly organized in 1558 and how he and his friends went the official organizers one better (Tenagli 1538–66); and a school teacher who explains to a noble patron just how pall mall is played (Ricci c. 1978/1553). Shakespeare – 'the happy hunting ground of all minds that have lost their balance', according to James Joyce – is also a mine of sporting references: wrestling and duelling in *As You Like It*, tournaments in *Pericles*, tennis in *Henry V*, swimming in *The Tempest*, fencing in both *Hamlet* and *Romeo and Juliet*.

Travel writers also report on local sports. Montaigne toured through Switzerland, southern Germany, Austria, and Italy in 1580–1 and recounted in his travel diary (*Journal de voyage*, Montaigne 1983) a number of different sports and displays of athleticism that he managed to see: a stadium for archery contests, displays of fencing skill, horse races, ball games, horse vaulting, etc. He was especially delighted to have been invited to spend an afternoon talking with some Florentine nobles about horses and swordsmanship, the kind of opportunity he could not yet have in France (McClelland 2003b). Robert Dallington's *View of Fraunce* (1604) reports that the French practice vigorous exercises even when the temperatures are hot, that pall-mall is a game worthy of a gentleman since it is not strenuous and the players can chat among themselves as they walk from one target to another, that there are two tennis courts in France for every church, and that more people pay tennis there than drink ale in England. Some decades later, the English recusant priest, Richard Lassels in his *Voyage of Italy* (1670) gave a very circumstantiated account of how a *calcio* game is organized and played when he came to describe the things a tourist should see in Florence.

Foreign ambassadors and fawning biographers also reported on the athletic proclivities of the royal courts on which they were spying or the noble personages whose lives they were detailing. The former sources are unfortunately tucked away in Calendars of State Papers and similar archival repositories whose perusal demands enormous patience and palaeographical skills. The latter are not always trustworthy, at least when it comes to the level of their subjects' athletic performance, but both kinds of sources allow us to measure the role that sport played in early modern lives. For example, the earl of Lincoln, on a special mission to France in June of 1572, was taken to watch King Charles IX play tennis, as a prelude to a private interview in which the French monarch confided his plans to Elizabeth I's representative (Nichols 1823).

The importance of the practice of sport as part of a monarch's public persona is further illustrated by the chroniclers' accounts of the jousting and other sports in which Henry VIII and François I participated during their historic meeting in 1520 at the Field of Cloth of Gold (Russell 1969). A Venetian ambassador's 1561 report on Cosimo I, archduke of Tuscany, reveals that he excelled at 'lifting weights, handling weapons, tournaments or ball games…fishing and swimming' (Hale 1977: 137), all activities that he must have performed in front of at least a limited public. At the end of the sixteenth century England's King James I (1603–25) underscored the role of monarchical sport in his advice to his son and heir presumptive on how to prepare himself for kingship. The young man should play at 'running, leaping, wrestling, fencing, dancing, and playing at the catch or tennis, archery, pall-mall', but should eschew 'the football, meeter for laming than making able the users thereof', and limit 'games on horseback… such as the tilt, the ring, and low-riding' to exercises in handling weapons; they are no longer displays of manly prowess. The real way for a prince to show his qualities lies in his horsemanship: 'for it becometh a prince best of any man to be a fair and good horseman. Use, therefore, to ride and daunton [subdue] great and courageous horses' (James I 1996: 166–7).

From England too come the primary sources for our knowledge of more popular forms of athletics. In an effort to resolve some religious disputes (see Chapter 5) the same James I set out in his so-called *King's Book of Sports* (1617) a list of athletic games that might be practiced on Sunday afternoon by English men and women who had attended Anglican church services in the morning (James I 1982/1617): 'daucing, either men or women, Archerie for men, leaping, vaulting, or any other such harmlesse Recreation,…and the setting up of May-poles and other sports therewith used' – *inter alia*, bowling was forbidden.[43] More or less simultaneously with the publication of the *Book of Sports*, a provincial notable, the English lawyer Robert Dover, undertook in 1612 to reinvigorate some annual country games in the Cotswold Hills by refashioning them into a kind of replica of the ancient Olympics. In their new guise the games persisted until just after the outbreak of the English Civil War in 1642, but along the way they generated a volume of laudatory poetry entitled the *Annalia Dubrensia* published in 1636. It is in fact this volume that is our only real source for knowing what sports were actually used: 'wrestling, leaping, dancing, pitching the bar, throwing the hammer, music, leap-frog, shin-kicking, running races, horse-racing, hunting the hare, coursing, singlestick fighting, handling the pike, tumbling, and card games and chess, held in tents' (Whitfield 1962: 19).[44] Obviously these games had very little about them that was actually 'Olympic', but Renaissance scholars had already done enough research into ancient Greek sports (see Chapter 1) for the term to have acquired a patina of prestige, even if the term's actual referent remained obscure. For example, in 1555 Pierre de Ronsard announced his intention to found a sacred festival in honour of his patron Odet de Chastillon (Ronsard 1914: 8.73). It will feature games 'à l'exemple des Romains & des Grecz', the competitions will include wrestling, foot races, javelin, and fighting with pikestaffs, the winners will be crowned with laurel, and their names published 'comme au lustre Olympique', as they were in the quadrennial Olympic games.

Two final texts will be invoked here as signs of where sport was headed. The pattern that had started in the mid-fifteenth century with itemized, but still very local, *ad hoc* rules for jousting tournaments, gradually worked its way into other competitive sports. The impetus for establishing an orderly set of regulations for fencing/duelling is clearly present in a number of books we have not mentioned but that attempt to set the grounds on which fighting is legitimate. The most accessible of these is Girolamo Muzio's *Il duello* of 1551, which was the basis for William Segar's *Booke of Honor and Armes* (1590) and which formed in English translation the second part of Saviolo's *Practise* (1595); there are allusions to this code in both *As You Like It* (5.4) and *Romeo and Juliet* (2.3). The move toward systematizing athletic practice can be observed in all the fencing manuals, in Ascham's *Toxophilus* (1904/1545), in Scaino's book on tennis (1555) and Bardi's on *calcio* (1580), but the rules of play adumbrated in these books – if 'rules' they can be called at this stage – remain embedded in what is after all humanistic discourse; not the prose of grammarians and accountants but cultivated conversation that imitates the dialogues of Cicero and the discursive style of Seneca.

The devising of itemized rules for non-military sports seems to have begun with Vives's six 'laws of playing' in 1540 (Vives 1970) but took a more decisive turn in 1592 with Forbet's formulation of the 24 components that collectively make up his *Ordonnance du royal et honourable jeu de paume* (Forbet 1599; De Luze 1933). Two further documents accentuated the move away from the (semi-)literary and pictorial sources that have been the subject of these two chapters and towards the kind of 'scientific' bases of sports historiography that are now the historian's stock in trade: the *Loix du paillemail*, rules for pall-mall, of 1655, and the *Capitoli del calcio fiorentino*, the 'headings' for Florentine *calcio*, of 1673. The former consisted of 83 separate rules printed on a single page and copiously corrected by hand (see Flannery and Leech 2004: 159, pl. 161); the latter of 33 regulations extracted from Bardi (1580) and published in the third edition of his *Discorso* and again in Bini (1688) and Bascetta (1978: 1.131–3). Although these attempts at rule-making leave much to be desired when read from the vantage point of the twenty-first century, they do succeed in two things.

First, they simplify our modern efforts to understand the historic basis of certain rules and practices still current in some sports today. With patience we can get beyond obscurities of language and what is left unsaid because it seemed obvious to contemporaries and reconstruct the games the way they used to be played. Second, they allow us to measure the shift in mentalities correlative to the rise of scientific method. The humane and very human discourse of sport that characterized La Marche and Frescobaldi in the fifteenth century, Ascham, Scaino, and Bardi in the sixteenth has yielded to a new mode of expression – and concomitantly to a new way of thinking about sport. Rules imply logic and hierarchies of thought, but also boundaries drawn around action. Spontaneity is replaced by sober second thoughts.[45]

The Latin discourse of sport that we identified as coming into being at the end of the last century of the pre-Christian era succeeded in fusing a technical language, i.e. perfect clarity, and the conventional forms of literary expression, i.e. a language of approximations. The modern reader could thus understand both the sports themselves and the manner in which they were integrated into the experience of the Roman bourgeois and upper-class collectivity. The degeneration of that discourse from a sociology of knowledge in Statius and Sidonius into an archaeology, a remembrance of things past, in Cassiodorus and Isidore marked the evacuation of a particular paradigm that had determined at least one dimension of Roman life. The history of sport from Eginhard through to the sixteenth century is partially the history of the efforts to restore that paradigm to prominence, to make sport a subject of civil conversation. But it is also the history of the rise of a conflicting paradigm that prized method over intuition and that ultimately oriented modern life away from the Roman model. Frederick II's *De arte venandi* (1955/1250) is not a scientific book in any current sense of that term, but it did initiate an alternative to purely humanistic thinking about sport. Like the other arts that depended on mathematics and precise measurement – but in the Middle Ages these were not arts but skills – sport could be reduced to a geometry and in the end communicated as an itemized set of disincarnate rules voided of any psycho-somatic content.

Chapter 4

The sports, the athletes, the material setting

Viewed retroactively – and with the historian's desire to separate the incidental from the essential – Roman sports divided neatly into amateur and professional. There was overlap in the area of chariot racing and equestrian events because young nobles could practice these sports. On the other hand, they never did so in competition with professional drivers and jockeys. And there are also examples of upper class Romans of both sexes – and even eight emperors – becoming enamoured of gladiators and Greek athletics to the point of being trained in these sports and practicing them in public – but again, only among themselves, never against the professionals (Juvenal, *Satires*, Loeb, 6.246–64; Barton 1993).

To deal first with the professional sports, because they are the more familiar, ancient Roman athletic spectacles were heterogeneous in nature and involved contests that differed radically from each other in a variety of ways and on many levels. More than that, they entered Roman culture at specific dates stretched out over many centuries, their origins were ethnically diverse, they became acclimatized in different ways, and – to the extent they were signifying, symbolic praxes – meant different things to the Roman(ized) populations of the capital and the provinces. Although in later centuries the word *ludus*, game, came to be applied to all of them, for a long time there was no specific label that referred to the entire set.

For the sake of clarity and brevity, historians have adopted a convenient stenography and categorized these sports into three different groups: the *ludi* (chariot races and other events), the *munera* (gladiatorial shows, to which were often linked the *venationes*, wild beast hunts), and the *certamina* (Greek-style games). Although the Romans themselves did not observe this terminological distinction, either diachronically or synchronically, with all the rigour we would like, the three labels retain their usefulness as a kind of historiographical shorthand. Since by the end of the first century AD each of the three branches of sport had its own permanent, imposing marble venue, the distinction appeared to become concretized, as it were, and so remains useful as a basis for discussion.

The *ludi* were the ceremonial Roman games, essential parts of the regularly scheduled religious festivals that punctuated the year; their earliest manifestation dated back to at least the sixth century BC. They consisted, so Cicero tells us, of physical contests in running, boxing, wrestling, and chariot racing, with a view to determining a winner.[1] To this list should be added the peculiarly Roman phenomenon of the *desultores*, jockeys who rode two horses at once, jumping from one to the other at full gallop (Livy, *History*, Loeb, 23.29). From the fourth century BC onwards, stage plays (*ludi scaenici*) became part of the program of these religious festivals, although they were held not in the Circus but in nearby theatres and on days other that those devoted to sport. Private individuals might sponsor unscheduled *ludi* for various reasons; for example, either to curry favour among the voters or, as victorious generals returning to Rome, to demonstrate their success. In the latter case, they might add Greek games and wild beast shows and hunts to the traditional events we have enumerated. We may cite as an extravagant example of these occasional games the grandiose set of *ludi* Julius Caesar organized in 46–5 BC to celebrate his own military triumphs and to commemorate his daughter, who had died seven years before. The biographer-historian Suetonius describes these games thus:

> He gave entertainments of various kinds: a combat of gladiators [*munus gladiatorium*],…as well as races in the circus [*circenses*], [Greek] athletic contests [*athletas*], and a mock sea-battle [*naumachiam*]….For the races the circus was lengthened at either end and a broad canal was dug all around the track; then young noblemen drove four-horse and two-horse chariots and rode horses for displays of vaulting [*equos desultorios*]. Two troops of older and younger boys performed the Troy game. *Venationes* were presented on five successive days….Athletes competed [*athletae certaverunt*] for three days in a temporary stadium built for the purpose near the Campus Martius.
>
> (Suetonius, *Divus Julius* [the deified Julius], Loeb, 10 and 39)[2]

After the accession of Augustus, however, the state and its agents monopolized the *ludi*, though in the later empire it was expected that officials elected or named to high office would put on some kind of a show at their own expense (Symmachus, *Letters*, Budé).

Of all the Roman spectator sports chariot racing, and the *ludi* in general, are the least problematical for the historian, even though they were marred by the Nika riots of 532, in which 30,000 people died in the Constantinople hippodrome. Chariot races may well, in fact, be history's longest-lived sport, having lasted almost uninterruptedly in Rome for 1,200 years or so, from the sixth century BC to the mid-sixth century AD.[3] In the eastern half of the Empire they continued to be run regularly at least into the ninth century and sporadically as late as the twelfth (Cameron 1973; Treadgold 1997).

In primitive times the races were staged in the largest open space in Rome, the flat valley between the Aventine and Palatine hills; later the Circus Maximus was built on that site and, after being partially destroyed in Nero's fire of 64, was rebuilt there by the emperor Trajan around the year 100. Generally speaking, the circuses in which chariot racing took place were oblong structures curved at one end, whose inner measurements ranged from 244 to 580 metres in length by 51 to 125 metres in width (Meijer 2004b: 218–19, following Humphrey 1986). There were more than 100 such structures dotting the length and breadth of the Empire, and most of them were monumental in nature, in the literal sense of the term. They stood, as Pliny the Younger said of the Circus Maximus, as 'a throne worthy of a people that had conquered the nations' (*Panegyricus*, Loeb, 51: 'digna populo victore gentium sedes') and could hold immense numbers of spectators. The Elder Pliny estimated that a quarter of a million people could fit into the Circus Maximus in the first century AD (Harris 1972), but it is now thought that 150,000 is closer to the real number (Thuillier 1996b).

The canonical form of the chariot race consisted of 12 four-horse chariots running seven laps around the circus for a total distance (in the Circus Maximus) of just over five kilometres. For variety's sake, however, some races might have only four or eight chariots. At speeds ranging between 30 km per hour at the turns and 70 on the straightaways, the race would last about 10 minutes, according to Meijer's calculations (2004b: 95–6).[4] Originally the centre of the racing surface was marked only by the two *metae* or turning posts, but over time, the up and down lanes came to be separated by a line of statues, fountains, and obelisks which, joined together, formed the *spina* (the word is first used, however, only by Cassiodorus in the sixth century, see Ill. 2). There were normally 24 races a day, but the number might be as high as 36, and they were interspersed with other events such as foot races, boxing, the two-horse jockeys (*desultores*), etc. In Augustus's time there were 17 days of races per year, but by the fourth century that number had risen to 64.[5]

In addition to the four-horse chariots (*quadrigae*), there were two-horse (*bigae*) and three-horse vehicles (*trigae*) but these were normally driven by apprentices, called *aurigae* (a charioteer who had earned the right to drive a *quadriga* was called an *agitator*; Thuillier 1987). The charioteers themselves were mostly slaves or at least of slave families, according to Horsmann (1998) and for that reason he wonders whether it is legitimate to call chariot-racing a sport – drivers who were slaves had no choice, after all.[6] Cameron (1973: 155–9) attenuates that view slightly: 'Actors, dancers, and charioteers were all members of the entertainment profession', i.e. social undesirables, and the fact that the mothers of some of them were well-known might indicate that the profession of charioteer was hereditary. It might also explain why drivers appear to have embarked on the career at a very early age, perhaps as young as 13 ('it was skill rather than physical strength and stamina that counted'). The drivers wore a distinctive costume that included a leather helmet with a projecting flap and a tunic – both helmet and tunic bore the team colours – over a skin-tight leotard. The tunic was tightly bound with a protective rope harness, and when driving, the charioteer would wrap the reins around his chest – he carried a small knife to cut himself free if necessary. The dangers of an accident (*naufragium*) were real and were depicted in the mosaics at Zliten and elsewhere, but still some charioteers had long and successful careers and a few actually won fabulous sums of money. A relatively small number became very famous – many of the horses were also very well known – and despite their marginalized social position, even had statues erected in their honour on the *spina* (Cameron 1973).[7]

The one characteristic of chariot racing that distinguished it from other Roman spectacles was the manner of its organization. Being an expensive sport to put on, the procuring of horses, chariots, and drivers was farmed out to associations of businessmen known as the factions. The team colours – red, white, green, and blue – identified the factions on the course and fan interest seems to have focussed on them rather than the individual drivers or horses (Younger Pliny, *Letters*, Loeb, 9.6). Eventually, only two factions – blues and greens – survived, but the increase in the frequency of race days meant that they grew very rich, and the unshakeable fidelity of their fans ultimately gave them considerable political power (Cameron 1976).

Chariot racing was a military exercise in ancient Greece (*cf. Iliad* 23), but chariots were not used by the Roman army and when the sport was introduced to Rome via Etruria in the sixth century BC (Livy, *History*, Loeb, 1.35.7–10), it was as part of other equestrian events associated with the agricultural festival called the Consualia. Religious and ritualistic in origin, Roman chariot racing was thus always a deeply-rooted symbolic praxis that was automatically included in every new set of *ludi* that over the centuries was proclaimed and added to the annual calendar. The only change was that its cultic associations shifted from the supernatural gods to worship of the emperor beginning with the reign of Augustus.[8] The first emperor's palace on the Palatine hill looked directly down onto the Circus Maximus and he could – and did – watch the races very attentively (Suetonius, *Augustus*, Loeb, 45; Collart 1978). As Cameron (1973: 180–2) points out, when in the late third century the capital of the Empire was moved around from Rome to one or another of the frontier cities, one of the first things built was a palace/circus complex 'in direct imitation of the *domus Augustana/Circus Maximus* complex at Rome'. Indeed, the idea of the circus and chariot racing were so closely linked to the emperor's self-image that Maxentius (306–12) actually constructed a second such complex in Rome itself, on the Appian Way (*La villa* 1999). The fact that Roman chariot racing should have died out so completely in Western Europe after the barbarian invasions, the conversion of the Empire to Christianity, and the elimination of the emperor demonstrates that, semiotically speaking, it had become disconnected from the popular imaginary and possessed no meaning beyond its own actualization.[9]

The chronological third in the triumvirate of Roman spectator sports was the *certamen*, the Greek-style athletic contest. Some elements of controversy surround it, both historically and historiographically speaking, but these do not relate to the events themselves. The first example of *certamina* taking place in Rome dates from 186 BC when a victorious general returning from the east, Fulvius Nobilior, staged Greek games and a wild beast hunt (*venatio*) as exotic symbols of Rome's conquest of foreign lands (Livy, *History*, Loeb 39.22.1–2). The latter eventually became a fixture on the same programs as the gladiatorial fights (*munera*), but the former took some time to catch on and were usually presented as isolated festivals. The most egregious example of this occurred in 80 BC, an Olympic year, when Sulla held some Greek games that may have been the Olympics themselves, or may simply have pre-empted the Olympics by drawing all the athletes to Rome for the rich prizes (Crowther 1983; Matthews 1990). After 60 BC Greek athletes became more common in Rome and a fixture in all privately mounted sets of games. Nonetheless, before Augustus's accession to power, Greek games at Rome were at best sporadic: Caldelli (1993) lists only nine known examples between 186 and 46 BC.

Traditional scholarship – always pro-Hellenic – has usually maintained that refined Greek-style games were never very popular among the bloodthirsty Romans or in the Latin west in general (Gardiner 1910; Harris 1972; Briggs 1975).[10] More recent, less prejudiced research has shown, on the basis of mosaics, other archaeological findings, and a closer reading of the texts, that Greek games were quite popular in Rome, at least by the second and third centuries AD, and that Greek festivals founded by the Romans had a relatively long life both in Rome itself and in the western provinces (Ghiron-Bistagne 1992; Caldelli 1993; Newby 2002, 2005). It is, of course, significant in this relation that the two fullest accounts of athletic competitions in Roman literature are of games that follow a Greek model (Virgil, *Aeneid 5*) or that purport to represent actual games that took place in Greece (Statius, *Thebaid* 6).

The first attempt to institutionalize the *certamina* in Rome itself were the *ludi pro valetudine Caesaris*, games held in Rome to foster the emperor's long life and good health. They started in 28 BC, became irregular after 16 BC, and ceased to be held after 9 AD (Newby 2005).[11] A second attempt, this time less thematically linked to the life of a particular individual, occurred at Nero's initiative in 60. It was intended that these games, the *Neronia*, be quadrennial, like the original four Greek crown games and like the *Actia* and the *Sebasta*, the festivals that Augustus had founded in Nicopolis and Naples respectively (see Chapter 1). The *Actia* lasted into the third century, the *Sebasta* (*sebastos* is the Greek equivalent of Augustus) into the fourth (Caldelli 1993). The *Neronia*, however, were only repeated once, in 63 or 65 – the sources are unclear – and perhaps this repetition included only one of the three components that came to characterize the Roman version of the Greek *agōnes* (i.e. the *agōn gymnicus*, the *agōn equestris* and the *agōn poeticus*).

It was only then in 86, when Domitian founded the *Agōn Capitolinus* and constructed both a permanent stadium for the field and combat events and a theatre – the *Odeon* – for the literary and musical competitions, that genuine Greek games became a permanent part of the athletic panorama of the Latin west. Sited on the Campus Martius, the space where Romans traditionally exercised, the buildings were erected on the same place as earlier wooden stadiums constructed by Julius Caesar and Augustus and perhaps on the very spot where Nero had built a narrower stone stadium for his own *Neronia*. Domitian's Stadium, 275 metres long by 106 wide and 18½ high, seated 30,000 spectators and was still one of the wonders of the city in 357. Its outlines can be observed in modern Rome's

Piazza Navona, whose access streets and surrounding buildings incorporate some elements of the original structure (Duret and Néraudau 1983).[12]

This festival continued to be organized into the middle of the fourth century and became a model for similar games in the Roman world, in the same way that the Olympics were the model for other sets of games in the Greek east. They are hence the games for which we possess the most information – at least as far as the competitors are concerned. Surviving inscriptions indicate that the winners of the *Agōn Capitolinus* came from all parts of the Empire, from Bordeaux on the Atlantic to cities in Syria and Egypt, and so it had a genuine ecumenical effect – with this proviso, however: athletes that competed in the track and field events as well as boxing, wrestling, and *pancratio* were all Greek or Hellenized Middle Easterners or North Africans. Competitors of Latin or Latinized origin seem to have won only in the artistic disciplines. Significantly, all the participants in the *certamina* were either free men or freed men and thus susceptible of accepting the grant of Roman citizenship that was often one of the apanages of winning an event. This social distinction separates the *certamina* from the other Roman spectator sports.

The athletic events in the *certamina* were the same as in the Greek crown games (*stephanitai*) and the games where money prizes were awarded (*thematitai*) – running, wrestling, boxing, pentathlon, etc. – with the addition of poetic and musical events as in the Panathenaic festival.[13] Where the games became controversial in Rome was first in the athletes' costumes. In Greece they competed in the nude, but the Roman sense of decorum would not tolerate public nudity and so they had to wear some kind of loincloth or shorts. Even then it was thought that festivals of this sort encouraged dissolute behaviour (Younger Pliny, *Letters*, Loeb, 4.22). More serious was the fact that the Greek athletes were public heroes in Greece, where they were entitled to a victory parade when they returned from a festival abroad and where they might be granted the municipal title of 'councillor' (Roueché 1993). As far as Rome was concerned, however, they were on the same social level as stage actors – they shared the same synod or union – and other entertainers, though unlike actors and gladiators they were not *infames*. The emperor Trajan and his officials held them and other *Graeculi* in such low esteem that they tried to delay paying them as long as possible (Younger Pliny, *Letters*, Loeb, 10.118–19). However popular, Greek games never enjoyed the same prestige as the traditional Roman sports.

Between the *ludi* and the *certamina*, chronologically speaking, came the gladiatorial fights, introduced into Rome in 264 BC. They were labelled *munera* (*munus* in the singular), dutiful benefactions, because they were originally staged as gifts to the citizens in honour of a recently dead relative, though later the connection between the dead person and the public show became tenuous. From being originally sporadic, nominally private, events, they gradually became an integral part of Roman festivities, and the most contentious part at that. As Georges Ville (1979: 656) perceptively puts it, speaking of gladiatorial shows but the same holds true of other spectacles, 'The Romans were horrified by gladiatorial shows, or at least some Romans were, or, to put it in stricter terms, all Romans were half horrified'.[14] The commonly held image of the *munera*, fostered by Christian apologists, nineteenth-century painting, and twentieth-century movies, is that of two men fighting until one of them is too wounded to continue. At that point, the screaming crowd turns its thumbs down, the emperor gives a sign, and the winner kills the loser.

This image partly derives as well from a tendency to conceive all gladiators and gladiatorial shows as being identical, but in fact there were significant differences among them. At the lowest end of the scale were the barbarian prisoners of war ordered to fight in the arena, but who might choose suicide over such a demeaning fate.[15] At a similar level were the criminals (*noxii*) condemned *ad gladium*, to the sword, i.e. to fight each other to death, without proper armour or training, as part of the *meridianum* or noon-time show that filled the gap between the morning's entertainment (usually a *venatio*) and the professional gladiatorial fights that took place in the afternoon.[16] At the next level up were the slaves, criminals, and volunteers (*auctorati*) who were given training in a gladiatorial school (*ludus*), showed some skill, took an oath to willingly suffer being burned, chained, beaten, and put to death, and who plied their trade in the provinces or in Rome as part of itinerant troops who could be hired to put on shows (Apuleius, *Metamorphoses*, Budé, 10.18).[17] At the top of the heap were the imperial gladiators, trained in schools organized by the imperial administration and who fought under standardized rules with standardized equipment. Having lost his Saxon prisoners, Symmachus (*Letters*, Budé, 2.46) tries to recruit by contract some selected gladiators with long experience who know how to put on a proper show ('longus usus…gladiaturae idoneos'). In short, the *munera* were not as deadly as popular legend would have it. For example, Junckelmann (2000a) has calculated that in the first and second centuries a gladiator's chances of survival on entering the arena were 9:1; if he lost, they dropped to 4:1; by the third century, the initial odds had fallen to 3:1, for the loser to 2:1. After 25 or 40 fights a gladiator might even request – and be given – a *rudis*, a wooden sword whose granting symbolized the gladiator's release from his oath. Gladiatorial fights were 'not war without weapons, but rather war games with weapons – deep and dangerous play indeed.…[Under Augustus they became] a national (and imperial) Roman "sport" – a brutal blood sport, yes, but a professional spectator sport nonetheless' (Kyle 2003: 13, 20; also Plass 1995: 29–45).[18]

Whatever their place in the hierarchy, gladiators were *infames*, disreputable, marginalized individuals with no civic rights. All of which is not to say that they were completely despised. Horace (*Satires*, Loeb, 2.7) alludes to life-like pictures of contemporary gladiators drawn on walls, thus indicating that they were celebrities. From inscriptions and other sources it is clear that many of them had long careers and became famous – Junckelmann (2000b: 194) lists the names of 180 of them – and many apparently exuded enormous erotic attraction for women of all ages.[19] This fact may partially explain why – like any modern athlete – a gladiator who was not chosen to fight by his team's manager (*lanista*) became angry (Epictetus, *Discourses*, Loeb, 1.29.34–9).

The standard classification of gladiatorial types was established by Friedländer in the nineteenth century (1908–13/1862–71). He was able to enumerate 17 different types of gladiatorial fighters according to their weaponry and armour, though more recent research by Junckelmann (2000b: 111–28) has refined that list and extended it by one. It was normally the case that matches opposed two different types of gladiators, sometimes on the basis of symbolism, sometimes according to popular demand (Seneca, *Letters*, Loeb, 7). A common pairing, for example, opposed the heavily armed *murmillo*, whose helmet was decorated with a stylized fish (see Ill. 1), and the lightly armed *retiarius*, whose chief weapon was his net and trident (also Juvenal, *Satires*, Loeb, 8.200–10). On the other hand, certain kinds of gladiators, e.g. the heavily armoured *equites*, fought each other (see Ill. 3).

It now seems clear, however, that these types evolved over time. Initially, gladiators were captured foreigners who fought wearing their traditional protection and using their national weapons. They were thus designated by their native names: Gauls, Thracians, Samnites, etc. Later, under the Empire, when integration rather than differentiation became the watchword, the foreign labels were replaced with terms that reflected fighting styles (Wiedemann 1992; Kyle 2003). Maurin (1984) has argued that whatever their real or supposed ethnicity, gladiators remained functionally barbarians within the Roman imaginary. Their armour and weaponry was characterized by disparity and dissymmetry, both with respect to each other – one too lightly armed, the other too heavily – and with respect to the civic and military norms of Rome. And since the seating in the amphitheatre reflected the distribution and hierarchies of Roman society, in fact was a microcosm of that society (Thuillier 1996b; Kyle 1998), within the confines of a gladiatorial show in the Colosseum, Rome surrounded the barbarians who were in the centre of the arena; whereas in the world outside, the barbarians surrounded Rome.[20]

The full assimilation of gladiatorial shows into Roman spectacle culture can be localized chronologically by the construction of stone amphitheatres specifically designed to house this type of contest – as well as the *venationes* that became associated with them. Traditionally, gladiators had fought in spaces that normally had other practical uses, e.g. one or another of the Forums where the city's business was transacted, or in temporary wooden structures that were dismantled after use. They were, in other words, intruders into the normal scheme of Roman life, like the Greek athletes who also competed in ad hoc settings. Beginning with the amphitheatre in Pompeii (first century BC), however, they had their own reserved venues that were not amenable for other purposes. The construction of the Colosseum in 70–80 AD resolutely confirmed that gladiators, and the *venationes* associated with them, had become a permanent fixture of Roman spectacle culture. The building of imitation Colosseums all over the Empire (Hopkins and Beard 2005) demonstrated that this confirmation was not simply a local phenomenon. Although not the first permanent amphitheatre constructed in Rome or in the Roman world, the Colosseum's enormous size and architectural beauty quickly imposed it on the contemporary imagination, and, like the Olympic Games in ancient Greece, it set the standard of construction for all the arenas built since, whether in Antiquity or in modern times. Certainly, by the early Middle Ages it had become the symbol of Rome itself for people on the edges of the former Empire.[21]

The siting of these amphitheatres is in itself not without controversy. In choosing to build the Colosseum on the drained bed of Nero's artificial lake, the emperor Vespasian seemed to be making a political statement: the Rome of the tyrant who had burned the poor quarters of the city in order to make room for his sumptuous palace was gone. In its place the Colosseum stood as the symbol of a new order that placed the interests of the citizens above those of the ruler (Bomgardner 2000: 4–5). But Vespasian may have been as much motivated by hard economic facts as he was by symbolism. The construction of an arena as enormous as the Colosseum required the availability of a large tract of reasonably priced real estate. Nero's unlamented death freed up such a tract in the heart of Rome itself, but in provincial towns – as in modern cities – unencumbered lots of the size needed could only be found outside the walls, as in Périgueux, for example, or at the extreme edges of the fortified area, as in Pompeii.[22] Georges Ville (1981: 464) has argued that amphitheatres were placed outside the walls because they were equated with cemeteries and thus with Roman attitudes towards corpses, but the symbolic distancing of the arena from normal civic life is only part of the explanation. Gladiatorial fights and their accompanying *venationes* would attract people from all over the area; it was definitely in the interests of the cities to keep these often unruly crowds outside the walls.

The *venationes* were originally staged as a postlude to the *ludi*. Their symbolic function was related to Rome's expanding empire, and hence the more exotic the animals shown and slain, the greater the spectators' supposed conviction that Rome was growing ever grander and that they were increasingly protected by the Empire against strange dangers (Kyle 1998). Many mosaics show scenes of hunting and animal collecting, and special arrangements were made to transport the animals to Rome (Jennison 1937). Although the mosaicists like to show their skill at portraying elephants and great cats – and although these remained an important part of the show – any kind of unusual beast was enough to excite the crowd. Symmachus, for example, hopes that the emperor will replace his original gift of Saxon slave gladiators with 'Libycae', North African animals (*Letters*, Budé, 2.46); he also reports that the crowd was astounded by seven Scottish dogs that his brother contributed to the show (*Letters*, 2.77).

Assimilated to gladiators once the *venatio* had become the prelude to the *munera*, the status of the professional hunters, the *venatores*, is not really clear. There seems initially to have been a distinction existing between them and the *bestiarii*, criminals condemned to the *Ludus matutinus*, the 'morning' school, so-called because that was the time of day reserved for the *venationes*. There they received a brief training in animal fighting, just enough in fact to make their fights with the wild beasts entertaining, but not enough to ensure that they would not be killed (Balsdon 1969;

Kyle 1998). Few names of successful *venatores* have come down to us – the most famous is Carpophorus, praised by Martial as another Hercules (*De spectaculis*, Loeb, 15.22, 27) – although some indeed did survive and go on to have successful careers. Wild beast shows, in fact, lasted much longer than either the *certamina* or the *munera*, and though Cassiodorus, a Christian, found these spectacles deplorably inhumane, he somehow advocated their continuation and gives a vivid description of how they unfolded, with poor wretches encased in wicker 'armour' trying to fend off ferocious foes (Cassiodorus 1973: 5.42).

In short, whether we speak of gladiators, charioteers, hunters, or Greek athletes, professional sports in Rome consisted – in the eyes of the Romans – of the under classes (coerced into) performing for the upper classes, often at the risk of their lives. Although this circumstance may initially make us reluctant to call these spectacles 'sport', it is still the case today that professional athletes in the major spectator sports generally come from a humbler social status than the spectators who can actually afford to purchase a seat in the arena. The Romans certainly appreciated athletic skill, even in practice matches (Seneca, *Letters*, Loeb, 80), which is why the names of so many gladiators, Greek athletes, and charioteers have survived. Professional athletes formed a distinctive class; they were paid and they generated secondary economic activity;[23] they played according to schedules and rules using standardized equipment; they trained rigorously and wore the uniforms that were specified for their teams and their specialty; and if, for some, the risk of serious injury and death was greater than what we find acceptable today, the difference in the odds was really just a matter of quantity and not quality.[24]

On the amateur level upper class and wealthy Romans trained and exercised in various ways and played several varieties of ball games. During the Republic and the era of citizen armies, these exercises were traditionally proto-military. In his biography of Cato the Elder (243–149 BC) the Greek biographer Plutarch gives us a glimpse of what these were, in his account of how Cato raised his own son: javelin throwing, fighting in armour, horseback riding, to strike with the hand clenched into a fist, i.e. to box, to withstand heat and cold, and to force his way by swimming through the eddies and rough waves of the Tiber (Plutarch, *Marcus Cato*, Loeb, 20). A similar version is found in Horace, who adds discus and wrestling and indicates that these activities were undertaken strenuously and often competitively, in front of an appreciative crowd that shouted approval of the winners (*Epistles*, Loeb, 1.18.52–4; *Odes*, Loeb, 1.8, 3.7, 3.12).[25] The usual place for these exercises was the Campus Martius, a large open field beside the Tiber, in which they would afterwards swim to cool down and clean off. Horace also hints that the young men of his time are abandoning the strenuous Roman exercises in favour of softer Greek ways (*Satires* 2.2; *Odes* 3.24).

It is in the light of this last remark that the games narrated by Virgil (*Aeneid* 5) can be best understood. The sporting events in the *Aeneid* are an imaginative recreation of a legendary but undocumented past. These competitions create a picture of the athletic pursuits that the Roman aristocracy should practice because they were practiced by their own ancestors – Virgil is at pains to point out that the competitors in these games were the founders of the great patrician Roman families. With the exception of the equestrian exercise, what characterizes them is that they are distinctly Roman adaptations of Greek proto-military models.[26] Although the book 5 games are not really Olympic, the participants are rewarded with both material prizes, like the heroes of *Iliad* 23, and with crowns of vegetation, like the winners of events in the 'crown' games of Greece. At a time when the Roman armies had become completely professionalized, and hence the idea of citizens exercising with a view to doing their military service had become irrelevant, Virgil is advocating a return to an older ethos, but under a new guise.

This new guise was very much an idea of Augustus himself, who – perhaps influenced by the prescriptions advanced by Plato (*Republic* 3, *Laws* 7 and 8) and the now moribund Greek institution of the *ephēbeia* – wanted to promote 'a return to the morality of old Rome coupled with the idealism of Greece' (Briggs 1975: 275). To that end he revived the Republican institution of the *Collegia iuvenum* and reoriented its program. Now open to young nobles of both sexes, 'l'activité caractéristique de ces clubs est, comme celle des ephèbes, d'ordre sportif' (Marrou 1981/1948: 2, 107–10); they were 'training grounds for male nobles who wised to appear in the arena' and girls too seem to have participated and received training as gladiators (Vesley 1998). The athletic activity of girls and women in ancient Rome is only now coming to be studied and documents previously misinterpreted, e.g. the bikini-clad girls in the mosaic at Piazza Armerina, are now understood to be representations of female athletes (Lee 1984). That said, much of what we know about the *Collegia* is based on inscriptions and hence on conjecture.

The one area where the historian is on solider ground is that of the *lusus Troiae* – also know as the labyrinth game (Heller 1946) – the convoluted equestrian display that marked the end of the games in *Aeneid* 5 and that was specifically practiced by upper-class Roman youths during the Republic. According to Plutarch (*Cato the Younger*, Loeb, 3.1) it was revived in the time of the dictator Sulla (138–78 BC), who called on Cato of Utica (93–46 BC) to take part in it when he was about 14. Caesar included it in his 46–5 games (see above) and Augustus ordered frequent performances of it. It seems to have been a reasonably strenuous sport, because two noble participants – still young boys – broke their legs and Augustus was forced to suspend it (Suetonius, *Augustus*, Loeb, 43).

To judge by Horace's poetry and the letters of Seneca and the Younger Pliny, physical exercise constituted a part of the normal day for upper-class Romans. Beyond mentioning a ball game on the Campus Martius (*Satires*, Loeb, 1.6.122–8), Horace is not very precise as to what he actually does, but Seneca speaks of running – with a young slave to set the pace – and swimming (*Letters*, Loeb, 83); in many other places he lauds the systematic use of exercise for health (Cagniart 2000). Although they were separated by only a couple of generations, the difference between Horace and Seneca in respect of exercise is striking. The latter used to swim in the Tiber, but now has a warm pool at home. As the Campus Martius was gradually urbanized, the places designated for exercise shifted to the public baths and adjoining *palaestrae*, or in specifically designed and appointed rooms at home – that is to say, in specially constructed buildings or spaces, just as was the case for professional sports. At the same time, these exercises changed from being distinctly Roman and proto-military to being more associated with hygiene and the ideals of the Greek gymnasium.

This becomes clearer in the Younger Pliny's letters. He owned two country houses, both of which possessed extensive facilities for exercise (*Letters* 2.17 and 5.6). His place at Laurentum, 17 miles from Rome, had a *gymnasium*, a heated swimming pool from which the swimmers could see the sea ('calida piscina…ex qua natantes mare adspiciunt'), and a *sphaeristerium* for ball games. Farther from Rome, his house in Umbria had an indoor cool swimming pool (*baptisterium*) and in the courtyard a heated *piscina* and three other baths to plunge into (*descensiones*).[27] Above the dressing room adjacent to the indoor baths was a *sphaeristerium* in which there was room for several kinds of exercise and several circles of ball players ('quod plura genera exercitationis pluresque circulos capit'). It also had a large and elaborate shaded *hippodromum* to practice riding and apparently enough land for hunting. These are the physical recreations of a gentleman who wants to keep fit, not the rigorous training of a man who anticipates being mobilized in time of war.

The ball games that Horace mentioned, that crop up in Seneca's writings, and for which Pliny provided space in his villas, were an important part of upper class Roman athletic life and were marked by a certain social prestige.[28] Horace recounts that Maecenas, the intimate friend of the emperor Augustus, relaxed after a tiring journey by playing a strenuous game of ball (*Satires*, Loeb, 1.5) and in another poem he links three-cornered catch (*lusus trigon*) to the leisure classes (*Satires* 1.6).[29] A century later, Petronius, the friend of Nero, depicts the *nouveau riche* Trimalchio showing off his newly-won status by playing ball at the baths, but not deigning to pick it up when he failed to make a catch (*Satyricon*, Budé, 15.26–7). Petronius' contemporary, Calpurnius Siculus, lavishes extravagant praises on the great aristocrat C. Calpurnius Piso for all his considerable talents; not least among these is his ability to play ball – apparently again *lusus trigon* – so spectacularly that people playing nearby stop their game to watch him (*Laus Pisonis*, Loeb, 185–9). Three centuries later the Gallo-Roman aristocrat (and later bishop and saint) Sidonius Apollinaris (430–86) claims to have been an avid player of ball games, limits the participation to students ('scholastici') and citizens of the first rank, and recounts the athletic (mis)adventures of a certain Philomathius who was of the highest senatorial class but was now too old and out of shape to play this strenuous game with men who were half his age (*Letters*, Loeb, 5.17). When in the sixth century Gregory of Tours compares his poor skills at writing Latin to a sluggish donkey running into the middle of a ball game ('asinus segnis inter spheristarum ordinem celeri volatu discurrat', Gregory 1922: 5), the clear implication is that ball play is the preserve of the intellectually refined.

Trying to understand the exact nature of Roman ball games, however, is another matter. As in other situations, the Romans seemed to care little for terminological precision, talking simply of *ludus/lusus pilae*, the game of ball, a term that referred indiscriminately to leisurely recreations, games played for exercise, and physically demanding team games, however much they might differ from each other. The writer always assumed that readers would know what was meant. In the sixteenth century Mercurialis (1672/1569: 2.5.126–35) attempted a classification based partially on the kind of ball used (*follis*, inflated; *paganica*, large, filled with feathers – probably like a modern medicine ball), partially on the kind of game (*trigonalis*, a kind of three-cornered catch; *harpastum*, a game of interception, 'pila, quam… alter alteri eripiebat').[30]

Harpastum is also described by Galen in a rudimentary way (Galen 1991/200) and more fully by Sidonius (*Letters* 5.17). Players stood in two lines or a circle and threw a ball at or over a 'middle runner'. He, in turn, attempted to either intercept it or avoid being hit by it, all the while struggling to break out of his encirclement by knocking the other players out of the way – Philomathius was repeatedly knocked out of [his] position in the ranks by the impact of the middle runner, 'de loco stantum medii currentis impulsu summoveretur'. If he succeeded, he would join the circle and the player whose throw was intercepted or who allowed the middle runner to break free would replace him as the target.[31]

Another game that seems to have been current at least in the second century was *episkyros* (described by Suetonius 1967: 2 and Pollux 1967: 103–7 and 1991).[32] Two teams of equal but indeterminate size played on a field marked out with centre and end lines. The former consisted of stone chips – that is the meaning of *skyros* – the latter were just scratched in the ground. The teams competed to get at a ball that had been placed on the mid-field line. The one that succeeded then threw it over the head of the other team and the point at which the ball was caught or retrieved marked the position of the return throw. There is no clear implication of physical contact between the teams, but at least the initial face-off could have been the occasion for some physical confrontation. Otherwise, the game see-sawed back and forth until one of the teams was forced back over its own goal line. It is not clear from the descriptions whether the game was finished at that point, or whether, as in some modern ball games, the teams returned to mid-field and started over, with a score-keeper keeping track of the game's progress. It looks, then, to be a game of throwing but with essentially territorial domination in mind; presumably the team that had the strongest arms won. In the sixteenth century Giovanni Bardi (1580) thought that *episkyros* was the ancestor of another territorial game, Florentine *calcio* (see below), whereas at the same time Mercurialis attributed this ancestry to *harpastum*, as did Gian-Battista Ferrari a century later (1688).

There is some slight evidence that *episkyros* may have been played in Italy for spectators, perhaps by professionals. Pollux says that another name for *episkyros* is *sphairomachia*, the ball fight, and Seneca, in a letter written from Naples around the year 60, mentions he has been left in peace all day because all the annoying people ('omnes molestos') have gone to see the exhibition of 'sphaeromachian' (*Letters*, Loeb, 80). The word occurs only twice in Latin – the other example occurs about 30 years later in Statius (*Silvae*,. Loeb, 4, prol.) – and according to which translation or commentary you read, it is taken to mean either boxing with reinforced gloves or a kind of non-competitive boxing for training purposes (Frère 1940) or a fencing match in which the weapons have been blunted with a protective button or knob (Statius 1988: 61). There is, however, an argument to be made for supposing that *sphaeromachia* meant in Latin exactly what it meant to Pollux in Greek: a team ball game that had enough physical contact and displays of throwing and catching skills to make it exciting to spectators, especially in Naples, still a Greek city.

Just how *lusus trigon* or *pila trigonalis* was actually played is similarly problematical. Beyond the fact that it involved three players standing in a triangle – at least that is what the name means, although Pliny's reference to *circulos* implies a more relaxed formation – it is not certain whether the ball was caught and thrown or simply struck by the hand. Ancient writers are more intrigued by the fact that the game was played ambidextrously, and it seems also the case that the score was kept by a *pilicrepus* (Seneca, *Letters*, Loeb, 56) who perhaps counted the number of times the ball struck the ground (Isidori Frasca 1980). Two ways of playing the game are expressed by the obscure adverbs *datatim*, giving alternately, and *expulsim*, driving away. The former suggests an orderly game whose purpose was simple recreation, but the latter clearly implies a more strenuous sport – although it is not at all clear whether *expulsim* means that the ball was bounced off a wall (Balsdon 1969) or that it was hit with a wooden implement (Isidori Frasca 1980) or that the players struck the ball in such a way as to make a return shot difficult (my view). In any case, *lusus trigon* was played in a variety of surroundings including both at the baths and on the Campus Martius, the army's original training ground.[33]

As far as any written or iconographical record is concerned, *episkyros*, *harpastum*, and *pila trigonalis* vanished from the athletic panorama of Western Europe during the chaotic and very warlike conditions that prevailed following the collapse of the Roman and Ostrogothic administration in the fifth and sixth centuries (Duby 1973b). Like the chariot races that had been a hallmark of Romanization in the western provinces of the Empire, organized ball play seems to have been almost forgotten. The memory of ball games did retain some aura of class superiority, however, as is clear from Gregory of Tours' remark quoted above, and from the ninth century *Historia Brittonum* in which the pre-destined fifth-century heir to the throne of England is described as a patrician boy playing ball (Nennius 1985: 92–5).

When a recognizable athletic ethos does emerge in the eleventh century, it owes nothing to the Roman past and it arises within the context of a new polity that was defined around the year 1000 and remained operative until the great peaceful and violent revolutions of the late eighteenth and early nineteenth centuries. The pragmatic social and political structures that had gradually materialized in the aftermath of the 'barbarian' incursions from the east and north were eventually theorized into a tripartite structure that did not replicate the three levels of Roman society – patricians, *equites* or knights, and plebes. Medieval society was composed of three mutually exclusive – but also mutually dependent – classes or estates of people: ecclesiastics that prayed, knights that fought, peasants that worked

(Duby 1980).[34] The new athletics became correlative to the new social structures. The knightly class took as its prerogative the military and equestrian sports, and left the ball games to the other two classes, where, in the twelfth and thirteenth centuries, documented evidence can first be found. From an athletic point of view, the Middle Ages thus finds itself in contradistinction to ancient Rome: the blood sports – tourneying, jousting, killing animals – are now practiced exclusively by the warrior caste, while ball sports – not the same ones, to be sure – have been split between the clergy and the farm boys.

In general terms, though, we can postulate a preliminary distinction. Non-contact games, e.g. *jeu de paume*, the 'palm' game, corresponding approximately to *pila trigonalis* in terms of exertion, were played by clerics in the confines of the cloisters and the monasteries (Mehl 1990; Gillmeister 1997).[35] The more strenuous sports, the ones that were analogous to *harpastum* and *episkyros*, came to be played in open spaces by the peasant, i.e. working class and by young men generally. Thus a twelfth-century reference to the ball game known in France as *soule* or *choule* simply says that it was played by 'rustici homines', country folk (Mehl 1990: 70), but such games might also be played in cities. In 1175 William Fitzstephen (1908) tells of all the youth of London going out to the fields 'ad lusum pilae celebrem', to play the famous game of ball, in a match that pitted the pupils from the various schools against the tradesmen. 'Celebrem' certainly indicates that the game was well-established and not to be confused with other games, but just how it was actually played is never made explicit.

Soule required a large leather ball about the size of a man's head, filled with feathers or hair, like the Roman *paganica*. The ball could be kicked or carried or, in a later development, might also be propelled with a *crosse*, i.e. the kind of heavy cudgel with a curved end that shepherds used to drive strays back to the flock. Rules seem to have been mostly *ad hoc*, but if the game was played with sticks, the notion of 'out of bounds' was applied. Played more in the north of France than the south, it was a team game in which nonetheless one individual player – the one who carried or propelled the ball to the designated goal – was the winner.[36] Subsequently – and this was the first step towards golf (and towards field hockey) – the stuffed ball was replaced with a small wooden sphere that would not become sodden and too heavy for the *crosse* to drive if it fell into water or if the ground was wet from rain (Flannery and Leech 2004). With respect to ancient practice, we are witness here to two technological innovations that are hallmarks of the early modern athletic ethos: the first is in the willingness to use new materials if the traditional ones are not really adaptable to the terrain and the weather; the second is in the notion that ball games might be played using sticks or clubs.[37]

Boisterous ball games studded with injuries and deaths were also noted in England in the thirteenth century (Carter 1988), but what is noteworthy is that from 1314 on, football ('pelotes de pee [pied], pila pediva, pila pedalis') is singled out by name and thereby distinguished from other forms of *ludus pilae*. Like *soule*, early football was certainly 'a rough and tumble, formless punting game, played by an indeterminate number of players' with no mention of rules or goals, though a late fifteenth-century text does mention boundaries (Magoun 1938: 14–6).[38] A decree of Edward III (1 June 1363) makes even further distinctions among football ('pilam pedivam'), handball ('pilam manualem', *jeu de paume*), and ball games using some kind of a club or stick ('bacularem et ad cambucam') (Rymer 1830: 704). This decree illustrates, among other things, that *jeu de paume* had spread out from the cloister to the general population and that games involving a ball and bat existed in at least two varieties and were commonly played.

There are certainly texts from before the end of the thirteenth century indicating that clubs for hitting balls were being specially fabricated – 'baculis ad ipsam pilam aptatis', sticks fit to play ball with; 'percuciendo in capud cum quodam baculo ad pilam', hitting him on the head with a kind of stick for playing ball (*Dictionary* 1975–97). In addition to games that required the players to hit the ball along the ground, there were other games involving a club and a ball that seem prototypes of cricket and baseball. Indeed the very first representation of an early modern ball game – an English manuscript illumination dated 1120 – clearly shows a pitcher/bowler, fielders, and a batter wielding a curved *crosse* (Flannery and Leech 2004: pl. 56). Thirteenth-century images from Montpellier and from Spain illustrate a similar configuration, though in the former a woman is holding a cricket bat (Flannery and Leech 2004: pl. 61), while in the latter a young man has the exact same stance and weapon as a modern baseball player (Alfonso X El Sabio 1979/1250: 61v°; see Ill. 4). A device somewhere between a cricket bat and a baseball bat shows up again in a fourteenth-century picture of monks and nuns playing a ball game (Flannery and Leech 2004: pl. 63) and a small baseball bat reappears in a fifteenth-century aristocratic Italian ladies' ball game (Barletta 1993: 244 and pl. 8). This last image appears to represent a simple form of recreation in a garden, but the text accompanying the Spanish picture – the only picture, in fact, to have an explanatory text – indicates that the game was played very vigorously by a large group of young city-dwelling males (Alfonso X El Sabio 1985/1250: 81).[39]

Medieval Italian cities were the theatres for other strenuous – and often dangerous – popular games that did not involve ball play. These usually took the form of confrontations between the inhabitants of different clans or neighbourhoods and were consequently expressions of territorial rivalry.[40] Occasionally they had a military function. Since the independent communes of central Italy needed an armed citizens' militia for defence, games like *mazzascudo*, club and shield, *elmora*, the helmet game, and the *battaglia dei sassi*, the battle of the stones, were both training exercises and often ceremonial celebrations of the city's autonomy. In their original thirteenth or fourteenth-century forms they often resulted in serious injuries and death, and so, under pressure from the communal governments and the church, they were abolished or they morphed into milder fighting games like the *gioco del ponte*, the bridge game, in Pisa (Giovannini 1906; see Ill. 7), the *gioco della pugna*, the fist-fight, in Siena (*cf.* Davis 1994), or a 'prisoner-release' game called *pome* in Florence (see Chapter 7).[41] Animals might be substituted for people, as in various forms of animal baiting, sometimes quite elaborate (Masi 1906/1478–1526; Boiteux 1982) or, most famously, in the various *palii* or horse races, of which the Sienese version still survives today.[42] Other cities went still farther in eliminating violence to living creatures. In Florence, the ball game of *calcio* articulated the competition between districts, while in Lucca they retained the military component by instituting a crossbow contest in 1443, to which was added harquebus shooting in 1487 (Angelucci 1863).[43]

Shooting contests in which the citizenry participated were widely encouraged in England (Ascham 1904/1545) and they existed elsewhere in Italy and in many other parts of Europe as well (Burgener 1982; Montaigne 1983/1580), but a clause in the Lucca harquebus contest rules introduced a new dimension. The only people who could compete were 'personas ad id instructas', i.e. trained shooters or, in other words, professionals. This is not the only text of the period that admits to the existence of lower-class people who earn their living practicing a sport. The diarist Luca Landucci (1883/1517) mentions that his brother Gostanzo was a winning jockey in 20 *palii* between 1481 and 1485 in a number of Tuscan cities. In his analysis of the varieties of ball games, Antonio Scaino describes the special individual talents of six famous international tennis pros who were certainly of humble rank, at least to judge by the fact that five of them had no last names, only geographical origins.[44] The duke in Shakespeare's *As You Like It* keeps a wrestler on his payroll and the French kings Charles X and Henri III had a stable of acrobats, chief among them the famous Arcangelo Tuccaro.[45]

Despite their closeness to the highest levels of nobility and even royalty, professional athletes were rejected in the Middle Ages and only grudgingly appreciated in the Renaissance, and then largely for their strength (Bascetta 1978: 1.xxxv–xli). The prince of Ferrara's tennis players were officially described as 'servants' and 'waiters', while the acrobats at the French court might be called away from a demonstration of their athletics feats in order to carry some nobleman's luggage (Tuccaro 1599: f. 168r°). In England Elizabeth I liked to watch servants 'stripped of their doublets' play five on five handball and in the seventeenth and eighteenth centuries it was the practice of the wealthy to hire domestic servants with athletic abilities, e.g. fast runners, and pit them against those of their neighbours, for the purpose of betting (Brailsford 1969).

Free-lance athletes were even more poorly regarded. The wrestler Charles in *As You Like It* is a brutal individual who, when competing for prize money, promises to break his opponent's limbs and has already brought three brothers who wrestled him near to death (*As You Like It* 1.1–2); his defeat by the upper-class Orlando is simply his just deserts. Professional boxers in the thirteenth century were equated with gamblers, the lowest of the low (Alfonso X El Sabio 1979: 112v°). In Rome in October 1581, Montaigne went to the Baths of Diocletian to watch an equestrian acrobat. This man, an Italian who had been slave in Turkey, put on a display of elaborate tricks that he had learned in captivity (Montaigne 1983: 492–3). Although Montaigne does slip a couple of laudatory phrases into his account – 'rare cose', 'grande agevolezza', unusual sights, great ease of performance – it is mostly a dry enumeration of a set of astounding athletic feats. Although a great admirer of good horsemanship, Montaigne thought acrobatic feats were part of another world, the world of underlings and of the wandering mountebanks that sometimes came to his château.[46]

Horse-vaulting and equestrian events in general are the point where two conceptions of sport clash. Castiglione (1972/1528) and Rabelais (1994/1534) thought of them as essentially noble activities, and that way of thinking persisted into the seventeenth century (Vaucelle 2004). But when someone of low social class performed these feats for money, the feats themselves became degraded. This clash was, in fact, the confrontation of the gentleman amateur and the common professional, a confrontation that would colour the recreation of the Olympic Games in 1896. This confrontation did not occur in tennis – the prince of Ferrara played against his own hired professionals – perhaps because it was a sport that had migrated into the upper-classes from the monks and monasteries through the daily life of the big cities. Indeed, in the fourteenth and fifteenth centuries the compartmentalization of sports among the three classes of society (see above) began to break down, particularly in the sense of the upper classes – royalty, nobility, the knightly class, university students – wanting to play lower-class *soule*, football, and ecclesiastical games. At the same time, the upwardly mobile bourgeoisie aspired to take part in tournaments, increasingly conducted with blunted weapons (Francioni 1993; Mallett 1974: 211–15) but the end of this trend was for the chivalric skill of jousting to be depreciated at the upper levels of the social scale and to descend finally into lower-class amusements (Brailsford 1969; Clare 1983).

Ball games not only migrated upwards to become the preferred sport of the aristocracy and the bourgeoisie, they also migrated in a geographical sense, from the countryside to the city. And this migration was accompanied by an increasing variation in the way the games were played – hence the need for the typology developed by Scaino. The earliest references to, and images of, ball games either speak of their being played between two towns – or in an open space, such as Smithfield, just outside the town; or remain silent on the matter; or indicate the game, e.g. *jeu de paume*, relied on a makeshift location. But by at least the middle of the fourteenth century the French King Charles V had a specially constructed tennis court built at his palace at the Louvre. Castles built, or renovated, in France in the fifteenth and sixteenth centuries – Amboise, Ecouen, Fontainebleau, Henri II's rebuilt Louvre – normally had one or more tennis courts incorporated into the fabric of the building (Du Cerceau 1988/1576), and the same was true in other countries – Hampton Court, the Castello Estense in Ferrara, the ducal palace in Innsbruck.[47] By the early sixteenth century municipal authorities were providing spaces where ball games might be played without interference. In Florence a wooden fence was built around the Piazza Sta Croce and a marble plaque inserted into the façade of a neighbouring building to mark permanently the mid-field line for *calcio*. In Paris an area called Braque was paved with tiles and designated as a place for ball games (Rabelais 1994/1534; Vives 1970/1540).[48]

Tennis in the sixteenth century evolved from being *jeu de paume* into a subtler game that might or might not use a net and in which the ball might be struck with racquet, a paddle, a wooden armguard, or a kind of bat called a 'scanno', though different conventions applied according to the implement chosen (Scaino 1555). At the same time, the rambunctious cross-country game, *soule à la crosse*, changed into a variety of less brutal, more refined contests that required specialized clubs for driving and putting or clubs with two different faces for straight and lifted shots. Some of these games retained a natural landscape as an essential element and in Scotland turned into golf. Others became city games, played either through the streets over a mutually acceptable course (Ricci 1978/1553) or on a long, straight, laid-out terrain that had a goal at one end. Both forms were called pall-mall in English – from the Italian *palla*, ball, and *maglio*, mallet – but the latter variant became intensely popular among the English and French upper classes, to the point of rivalling tennis as the national game in France (Estienne 1896/1579; Flannery and Leech 2004; McClelland 2006).

Another Italian city game was *pallone*, or large ball, that Goethe saw being played in Verona in 1786 (Goethe 1976: 60–1). This game used the armguards mentioned by Scaino and, when Goethe watched it, was played on the edge of town by nobles ('vier edle Veroneser'). However, in the sixteenth and seventeenth centuries it could also be played by semi-professionals in narrow straight streets that encouraged hitting the ball great distances – as much as 'ottanta passi', 80 paces – and using the building facades for ricochets.[49] This last feature proved to be too much of a nuisance and so, in 1596, the Florence city council banned the game at least from the Via del Parione (Dati 1596). Both the diarist Settimanni (quoted in Artusi and Gabbrielli 1976: 72–3) and the poet Chiabrera (1952/1625: 295–302) write of *pallone* matches the Florentine grand duke Cosimo II organized in 1618–19, bringing in seven or eight professionals from central and northern Italy. Settimanni records the names of four of the Florentine players – Chiabrera supplies one more – and the fact that they were paid 150 or 200 *scudi*, certainly a significant amount of money.[50]

Finally, the formless sport the Italians called *calcio* – certainly a candidate for being a country game, with its 27 players a side – became the Florentine urban contest *par excellence* and was submitted to rules and regulations. The earliest account of a *calcio* game (Frescobaldi (1973–5/1460) tells of its being played in the not-quite-rectangular Piazza di Santo Spirito and from 1530 onwards the Piazza Santa Croce, a perfect rectangle, was the *terrain de choix*. However, Filipono's 1518 description of how the game was organized and played (also Filopono 1518/1898) indicates that the normal playing space was the *prato* (meadow), an oddly-shaped plot of grazing land that also had a communal well and that was left undeveloped inside the southwest corner of the city walls on the northern bank of the Arno. One end of the playing space was the wall (*mura*), the other was a temporary moat (*fossa*) dug across the *prato* purely for the purposes of the game. The playing field thus duplicated internally the city's external defences, a gesture that possessed a rich symbolism (see Chapter 7), given the fact that the game served the contradictory purposes of bringing neighbourhood rivalries into the open and of celebrating Florence's internal, republican cohesiveness *vis-à-vis* external enemies (Boccalini 1910/1612).[51]

Calcio displayed all the violence that at the time was associated with lower-class *soule* and football, but was restricted, in principle at least, to honoured soldiers, nobles, lords, and princes up to the age of 45 (Bardi 1580/1978: 1.140). Bardi's concerns, however, were not limited to the social quality of the players. He had a clear idea of their physical requirements and set them out in his book:

> The halfbacks should be the strongest and physically largest of the players, and the biggest halfback and the one who can hit the ball the hardest will play on the wall side of the field.[52] On the other hand, the halfback who will play on the moat side should be very agile and very quick to get on the ball. For the fullbacks you need to ... pick the fastest runners, the ones with the most courage and who can hit hard ... Then choose five blockers per side, big, tough, strong guys who are both muscular and smart. The blocker who is to protect the wall side of the field should be the biggest-limbed and most powerful player on the team, while the one who plays on the moat side really needs to be agile, quick, and know just when to go after the ball. The blocker in the middle has to have good strong legs, and the two others ... must be especially ferocious. Finally, the forwards, fifteen on each side ... should be fast, strong-winded runners, and full of high spirits (1.142).[53]

Bardi's precision in these matters, like Scaino's before him, is unexpected by modern readers, but reveals that he took the game as seriously and had as good an understanding of tactics and position play as any coach of today – or as any Renaissance teacher of the potentially deadly art of sword and weapon play.[54]

Chapter 5

Tournaments, jousting and the game of death

The growth of the popularity of ball games among the upper classes almost exactly parallels the gradual demise of early modern Europe's longest-lived sport, the knightly tournament. In fact the two sports developed along opposite paths. From being an effigy of war in the Middle Ages, the tournament had turned into pure spectacle, an occasion for young and not-so-young knights to show off for the ladies. Ball games – *calcio* in particular – had gone the other way. Both Scaino (1555) and Bardi (1580) insist on battle array and tactics as the paradigm for *calcio* (and, in the case of Scaino, for tennis as well) (McClelland 2003a). As Richard Lassels' (1670: 212–15) account of the preparations for a match reveals, a *calcio* match came about when two groups of young men conducted mock negotiations with each other in the manner of autonomous states; when the negotiations broke down, they would 'resolve on a battle at *Calcio*'.

The tournament too had been a country game that migrated to the city. Up into the fifteenth century the French and English texts are categorical with respect to the fact that tournament locations should be away from built-up areas. For René d'Anjou (1986/1460) tourneying should take place in open fields outside a fortified town, while Olivier de La Marche's 1443 set of jousts was held away from Dijon, in a triangle formed by three châteaux, each a league from the other two (La Marche 1883/1500). The 1389 jousts at St Inglevert unfolded 'in a fayre playne' between that village and Calais (Froissart 1902/1523–5), while the thirteenth-century English tournaments listed by Matthew Paris (1880/1258) all take place 'apud', i.e. near – but not in – some town or other. And in the twelfth century, whether in the biography of William Marshall or the romances of Chrétien de Troyes, the same type of geographical designation arises almost insistently.[1] Even in fiction it seems a necessity to specify a rural location.

There were nonetheless significant exceptions. The fourteenth-century tournament at which the young Bertrand du Guesclin made his mark was held 'Ou plain marchié de Resnes', in the middle of the Rennes market place (Cuvelier 1990/1400). Contemporary paintings or wall decorations show tournaments taking place in the Piazza Sta Maria Novella in Florence or the Piazza Navona in Rome (Barber and Barker 1989) and the young Lorenzo the Magnificent was introduced to his Florentine subjects in a tournament at the Piazza Sta Croce in

1469 (see Chapter 6).[2] The tournament that cost Henri II his life in June–July 1559 was precisely one of those exceptions: a large-scale chivalric event that ought to have been organized in the suburbs of Paris or at the royal palace of Fontainebleau, but that was crowded into the wide western end of the Rue St Antoine, a venue for urban tournaments since the fourteenth century. The street's paving stones had to be dug up for the occasion, wooden grandstands specially built, and normal traffic diverted (the Rue St Antoine was the city's chief east–west artery at that point, leading from the Bastille gate to the Châtelet). Although Paris in Roman times had possessed an all-purpose amphitheatre – the so-called 'Arènes de Lutèce' – by the Middle Ages it had, like most ancient Roman arenas, fallen into disrepair and been built over; it was only rediscovered in 1869. In Paris as elsewhere, any athletic spectacle in the Middle Ages and the Renaissance, if it needed a crowd, had to displace some other activity.[3]

The reasons for the urban setting for Henri's tournament were both technical and political. The latter will be explored in a later chapter; the former derive out of the evolution of knightly sporting contests, which laid greater and greater stress on the individual being able to demonstrate his prowess. Jousting was the ideal means for achieving this, since it always pitted one knight against another in single combat, with a result that was perfectly clear. And although jousting is now usually imagined only as two lance-bearing horsemen trying to unseat each other, in the early modern period that might be only the preliminary encounter. The contest could and did continue, on horseback or on foot, with the two jousters fighting with swords, axes, pikestaffs, or other weapons, sometimes separated by a barrier, sometimes within a wooden enclosure.

The political consequences of Henri's accidental death were far-reaching, for shortly thereafter France split along Protestant–Catholic lines and a civil war erupted that lasted over three decades. But in their way, the athletic consequences were no less significant. Henri's fatal joust set in motion a process that would culminate in the disappearance of a chivalric sport that, as the Medieval sources made clear, had been a focus and even a means of livelihood for Western European nobility since the eleventh century. Jousting and tournaments would continue to be practiced through to the end of the sixteenth century and beyond, but the weapons became increasingly harmless, spectacle became more important than athletic achievement, and the display of masterful horsemanship eclipsed the display of handling sword and lance. Subsequent generations of royalty and aristocracy refused to put their lives at risk by playing at simulacra of warfare in order to demonstrate their virility.

To begin with jousting itself, the sport required two heavily armoured, lance-bearing horsemen to charge at each other along a course of about one hundred metres.[4] Each rider's goal was to strike his opponent in the head, or at least the upper part of his shield or body. In the early years the purpose was to knock the other knight off his horse without falling yourself, but later scoring systems awarded points for accurate hits, and unhorsing your adversary became less necessary. The lance could be anywhere between three and a half and five metres in length and was most often made of oak or some other hard wood. From at least the fifteenth century onwards each tournament set its own standard for lance sizes and each weapon used had to be certified as conforming to it. The horses were bred for the sport and were mostly identical: stallions weighing about a metric tonne and often highly-prized – harming your opponent's horse could be cause for disqualification. Saddles and shields were also regulated with respect to shape and size, again on an ad hoc basis, but there is evidence of at least embryonic international standards.

Jousting was a very cumbersome sport. The jouster was encased in about 25 kilos of armour and the horse was also protected with, at the very least, a heavy cloth. The saddle was thickly padded, to protect the horse, and high backed, to help the rider keep his seat when struck by his opponent's lance. Because of its weight, and because by far the longest part of it was forward of his grasp – and thus seriously imbalanced when aimed horizontally – the jouster held his lance upright at the start of the course, resting the butt on his stirrup, another essential feature of the equipment. About midway to the point of contact – the jousters covered the distance between them in seven to eight seconds – he would start lowering it into the couched horizontal position and, according to his strength and technical preferences, would support it or not on the horse's neck or on his own left hand or arm (Duarte 1944: 74).[5]

The lance was, to use a technical parlance, the delivery vehicle of a force easily strong enough to knock an inexperienced or unwary knight off his horse and onto the ground. Adding rider, shield, lance, saddle, and horse together, the total weight of the moving projectile came to as much as 1,200 kilos. When multiplied by the square of the horses' speed – the two riders approached each other at a rate of 25 kilometres an hour – this considerable mass generated on impact an enormous discharge of energy, all of which was concentrated at the point of the lance and from there to the target. At the same time it also produced a violent reverse reaction.[6] Taking all these factors into account, jousting clearly required of the knight a good deal of physical strength, training, courage, and *sang-froid* if he was to be able to 'instantaneously co-ordinate his attack and defense, his locked muscles and recoiling horse amid the shock of steel and splintering wood' (Malszecki 1982: 90). Denholm-Young's summary of late Medieval jousting as consisting of two riders trotting 'ponderously past' each other, able only to 'poke at each other at an angle' (1948: 240) is overly dismissive. An eye-witness account of Henri II's fatal encounter states that the king wanted to run a second joust against Montgomery because during the first, the young man's lance 'l'avoit faict bransler & quasi quicter les estrieux', had shaken him up and almost knocked him out of the stirrups (Vieilleville 1757/1571: 4.172). A jouster was supposed to withstand a jolt of considerable force without showing any apparent effect.

By the sixteenth century jousting and tourneying were highly organized and regulated events. Beginning in the 1460s, itemized rules had been drawn up in various places governing all the technical aspects of the tournament, including the scoring.[7] The rules for a 1465 tournament in Milan, for example, specified that if a jouster's lance struck the bottom third of his opponent's shield, it did not count; if he struck the middle third and broke his lance, it counted as a good hit; if he struck the top third and broke his lance, or hit his opponent's helmet and did not break his lance, it was a very good hit; striking the other jouster on the head and breaking your lance in the process counted as two very good hits; disabling him to the point of his not being able to continue counted for three; and knocking him out of the saddle or knocking him and his horse to the ground counted for four (Angelucci 1866; Rühl 2001). A quantitative system of keeping track of the score for a tournament lasting over several days had also been worked out in England – though not on the continent – and some of these have survived, showing a method of counting not unlike the box scores of modern baseball (Malszecki 1985; Rühl 2006).

The notion that tournaments and jousting had to be regulated derives partially from the fact that from at least the fourteenth century they were ceremonial affairs held in conjunction with some symbolic event such as a princely marriage, the signing of a treaty, or the first official entry of a sovereign into a city that owed him obeisance. It also derives from their essentially warlike nature (see Chapter 6). Whatever training function early tournaments may have had in preparing mounted knights to fight en masse, it was superseded by their transformation into little private wars whose only purpose was to capture knights and horses and hold them for ransom. Early attempts at regulation, therefore, e.g. Charny in the fourteenth century (Muhlberger 2002) or the *Statuta Armorum* first formulated around 1267 (Denholm-Young 1948), were aimed at curbing the excesses of knights and squires whose thirst for gain pushed them beyond the bounds of legality and convention.

Henri II's tournament was similarly bound by rules, which were published about three weeks before the tourney was due to begin (Du Bellay 1908–31: 6.72–4). They specified that Henri, the duc de Guise, the prince of Ferrara, and the duc de Nemours would take on all challengers, beginning on 15 June.[8] There were to be three *emprises*, or forms of competitive fighting: five courses of jousting on horseback with lances; sword fighting on horseback, one on one or two on two, the number of hits required to be determined by the field judges (the *maistres du camp*); and fighting on foot with pikestaffs (three hits; see Ill. 6) and swords (six hits).[9] The challengers, or *assaillans*, could choose to compete in any or all of these *emprises* and would select which of the *tenans* – all four if they wanted – they wished to fight. The determination of the winner in the jousts was partially a matter of numbers – 'celuy des assaillans qui aura le plus rompu [de lances]', i.e. whichever of the challengers had struck the most opponents accurately enough to break his lance – but in the main was to be settled qualitatively: '& [qui aura] le mieux faict', and who will have performed the best. As for the contests with swords and pikestaffs, it was left entirely to the judges to decide 'qui aura le mieux combatu', who will have fought the best.

The primacy of a subjective evaluation of the jousters was just one of the dimensions of Henri II's tournament that made it old-fashioned, a revival of a Medieval knightly ethos as it was embodied in Chrétien de Troyes' chivalric romances or as René d'Anjou (1986) enunciated it in his *Livre des tournois* of 1460.[10] But even René admitted that at the time of his writing the ideal tournament he was describing was something of the past and no longer practiced in France. Second, the fact that this event was to take the form of a *pas d'armes* in which the *tenans* proposed to take on any and all qualified challengers puts it into the same category as the internationally publicized jousts at Smithfield in 1467, near Dijon in 1443 (La Marche 1883/1500) or at St Inglevert almost a century and three-quarters earlier.[11] On those occasions the goal was to show the superiority of French knights over the English or vice versa. In other words, this was not just jousting for the sake of fun, as often occurred to celebrate princely weddings, but jousting that put those who had issued the challenge in the position of having to prove in single combat that they, individually, were better fighters than anyone who care to take them up on it. Henri's purpose in calling the 1559 tournament in the form that he did similarly had much to do with his personal and kingly prestige. Ostensibly, however, this tournament was, like all the other countless sets of jousts that had taken place since St Inglevert, simply an 'autotelic, ludic, physical contest' (Guttmann 1986: 4). To the extent that the prizes offered could not have been any real inducement to already well-off knights, it was an upper-class amateur sporting event of the kind that Coubertin would have approved.

Finally, Henri's participation in the jousting was also an anachronism. English kings had been enthusiastic tourneyers in the thirteenth and fourteenth centuries, though usually before they assumed the throne, and Henri's father François I had jousted against England's Henry VIII at the Field of Cloth of Gold in 1520 (Russell 1969) – but the two of them were 26 and 29 respectively, not 40. But by 1559 European customs and sense of propriety were changing as a new civility emerged (Elias 1939, 1969). The jurist and historian Etienne Pasquier (1529–1615), who was actually present at Henri's fatal joust, states the principle very clearly: 'plusieurs personnes de bon cerveau' – among whom he surely counted himself – found it strange that Henri should be one of the *tenans*, 'disans que la majesté d'un Roi estoit pour estre juge des coups, & non d'entrer sur les rangs' (Pasquier 1586: f. 85v°).[12]

It goes without saying that jousting was a very dangerous sport. Deaths and serious injuries were not uncommon, nor was Henri the first royal personage to meet his end that way. Geoffrey Plantagenet, fourth son of King Henry II of England, died as a result of tournament injuries in 1186, as did duke Leopold V of Austria in 1194. Jousting deaths might take a particularly brutal form. Arnaud de Montigny died in an encounter at Walden in 1252 when a lance severed his throat, trachea, and carotid artery (Paris 1880/1258: 5.318).[13] Or they might just as easily result from collateral circumstances: heat exhaustion, heart attacks, and suffocation. This was the case at Neuss in 1241 when some 60 to 80 knights and squires died that way in a single afternoon (Barber and Barker 1989: 54). Although the chroniclers do report these deaths, they do not fuss over them, whether the victim was a youthful member of a prominent Florentine family (Carew-Reid

1995: 35) or a couple of minor French knights (*Journal* 1854: 4 and 436–7) or three knights who died one right after the other in three successive jousts at Asti in 1555 (Brantôme 1864–82: 4.172–4). To be killed in a joust was not common, but it was not unexpected either. At the triumphal entry of France's Louis XII into Milan in June 1507, to amuse the king ('lui donner divers passe temps') there were jousts, tourneys, and prolonged axe fights; there were several injuries and one knight died (D'Auton 1889–95/1515: 4.303–24).[14]

Henri's death in 1559, however, seems to have been more of his own doing. As tourneying and jousting evolved from the thirteenth into the fourteenth century, it changed from being a simulacrum of battle and a means of acquiring wealth, and turned into a form of spectacle entertainment that allowed knights to show off individually in front of a crowd. English, French, and German knights and nobles continued to be uncouth soldiers used to the violence of war, but the increasing civilization of society meant that tournament spectators were less willing to tolerate the spectacle of death on what was supposed to be the field of sport. Consequently, from about 1300 onwards, innovations were introduced to improve the jouster's safety. Lances might be made of lighter wood and be tapered toward the point so as to break more easily at the moment of contact. The end could be adapted to a coronal or three-pointed tip that would facilitate shattering and thus a relative dissipation of the expended force. At the same time, the armour became stronger, better ventilated, and better articulated.[15] To prevent a collision between the horses, a median barrier – also called a 'tilt' – was usually constructed to separate the jousters, and a counter-barrier might also be installed in order to prevent the horse from swerving away – and concomitantly to reduce the rider's need to think about reining his horse in while other, more serious thoughts were on his mind.

Of course, these precautions were not always observed. At the tournament held to mark Henri II's official entry into Paris after his accession to the throne in 1547, the knights ran without a tilt – thus increasing the chances of a collision – and planned on finishing the tourney jousting with lances armed 'con deminino'. It is not quite clear what is meant by this term, but it seems to designate a long, hard, sharp point adapted to a heavy lance; it may be the same thing as the 'lanças con puntas de diamante' mentioned by Alcocer (1559: 288–9). The word is mentioned in connection with various fifteenth-century tournaments in Italy, where the jousters wore special armour and the horses were saddled differently whenever the *deminino* were used. The French, however, were more reckless and did not take the same protective measures. Hence the duke of Mantua in 1518 advised his son, in Paris at the time, not to joust with the French because he risked getting severely hurt (Truffi 1911: 71–2 and 218–25).

Despite all the normal precautions and the protection that the knight wore, the prospect of a violent impact was still unsettling. In the early fifteenth century Duarte of Portugal (1944: 82) commented on the not surprising fact that jousters often could not prevent themselves from closing their eyes or turning their heads away at the time of the encounter, and thus they failed to strike their target. This observation is confirmed by the statistics in La Marche's account (1883: 295–333) of the jousts in Burgundy in 1443. Although the jousters were all experienced – and one of them went on to make a career in the sport – the misses and near-misses exceeded the hits by at least three to one.

In the fifteenth century an improved form of head protection, the so-called frog-mouth helm (see Ill. 5), was invented and became generalized. It further reduced the risk of injury – the jouster's main target was, after all, his adversary's head – but it also complicated the crucial task of any athletic contest, keeping your eye on your opponent:

> The *veue*, or sight-line, was so designed that the jouster had full vision only when leaning forward. ... During that time he had to assess his opponent and train his lance for contact. Just before the actual contact he would sit upright again and that same movement would lift the helm so that the eyes were completely protected by the projecting lower lip. It would also render the jouster completely blind, so that he was unable to take further action without returning to the couched position.
>
> (Barber and Barker 1989:157)

But it was also the frog-mouth helm that was at least partially Henri's undoing. I have argued elsewhere (McClelland 1997a) that Henri expected Montgomery, who at that time was very much the king's protégé, to 'take a dive'. The middle-aged Henri, embattled on several fronts and tired by the afternoon's jousting (Haton 2001: 1.135–43), needed to show that he could defeat a much younger man. This, in turn, led him to an act of rashness not unusual in a sporting competition: he refused to wait for the armourer to attach the hook that would keep his visor closed (Tavannes 1838/1573; De Serres 1598). Montgomery, an inept jouster by some accounts (Matthieu 1631) failed to drop his shattered lance, Henri's visor popped open, and the stump of the lance drove some splinters deep into his eye and brain (Vieilleville 1757/1571: 174, Throckmorton 1863/1559: 347).[16]

I have dwelt at some length on the 1559 tournament because it represents the technological and cultural culmination of an athletic process whose ascent can be traced back beyond Nithard and Charlemagne. Its correlative degeneration can similarly be followed forward at least into the late seventeenth century, although that phase will not concern us here.[17] Potentially lethal encounters between members of the noble military caste were a staple of Renaissance chivalric literature, e.g. the two great Italian epics, Ariosto's *Orlando Furioso* of 1532 and Tasso's *Gerusalemme liberata* of 1581, and of the Medieval romances and epics out of which they grew – and thus of early modern society's ideal view of itself, so successfully mocked in *Don Quijote*. That in 1559 such encounters were intended to be mere replicas of the real thing is made explicit in the published program of Henri's tournament: the weapons of war, which have been used to shed blood, are now to become instruments of pleasure and utility for those who wish to test and train themselves in deeds both manly and praiseworthy.[18] Other sixteenth-century jousts were similar peaceful entertainments, often proclaimed in the name of love, as had been done earlier in literary texts, or having no real purpose other than mere spectacle, e.g. Messeri (1894), Cimilotti (1587).

Jousts and tournaments were not the only occasions where the general populace might watch their social betters fight with weapons. The invention of the light, easily handled, but deadly rapier meant that duelling – banned except when officially sanctioned – became increasingly common.[19] In July 1547 two French nobles, Jarnac and La Châteigneraie, fought a famous duel with Henri II's permission in front of the entire court; contemporary engravings show that special stands had been built to accommodate the spectators. Less deadly encounters might also be observed. At Henri II's official entry into Lyon in 1548 a 'combat à l'antique de douze gladiateurs' was organized, and though it was labelled as being 'à l'outrance', i.e. using genuine weapons, it was just a show. Apparently a very realistic one, because some of the spectators believed it was the real thing (Brantôme 1864–82: 3.250–6). Fencing masters also opened their academies to paying spectators (Montaigne 1983) and as the last scene of *Hamlet* (5.2) makes it clear, it was not unusual for fencing matches to take place in front of a relatively private audience. In earlier centuries, however, there were examples of young nobles fighting each other, without apparent animosity, and risking death in the process. Petrarch (1934: 5.6; also 1975) writes of attending an 'infamis gladiatorius ludus' in Naples in 1343 in which the aristocratic youth of the city – already, in his opinion, totally undisciplined – put on regular displays of all-out weapons fighting in full daylight, in front of the rulers of the city and the rest of the people; many were killed.

Knightly combat sports in the sixteenth century were only one of the many possible, i.e. socially acceptable, forms of physical games that a noble might practice. In his *Book of the Courtier* of 1528 Castiglione (1972) catalogued 18 competitive sports and forms of exercise that were suitable for a courtier – some on condition that the opponent was of the same social rank. Horse-vaulting and ball-games were especially good for showing off in front of a crowd. Three years later, Thomas Elyot's *Book of the Governor* (1962: 60 ff.) contained a list of similar length of 'exercises that are apt to the furniture of a gentleman's personage'. The two lists are not identical, though there is a good deal of overlap, but the point is the diversity of sports that had become available to the physically active noble in a short period of time. Humanistic research into ancient sport had validated as athletic pursuits running, swimming, wrestling, and long-jumping, heretofore restricted to peasants or to single-minded knights in training like Boucicaut (1985/1400).

The social ascent of ball games can be observed when we compare the names of the players taking part in the *calcio* match narrated by Frescobaldi in ±1460 with the names of the nobles who jousted in Lorenzo de' Medici's inaugural tourney in 1469 (Frescobaldi 1973–5/1460; Pulci 1986/1471). Many of them are the same, but if we go back a century earlier, there is no evidence of knights or nobles playing any sports other than military. The squire, and son, of Chaucer's knight can draw, compose songs, sing, dance, and play the flute, but his only sport is jousting; his father, for all his social reserve and learning, is a hard-bitten soldier who killed men in the lists and apparently had no time for play – their servant carries bow and arrows, a sword, a small shield, and a dagger; Chaucer 1958/1400: prol. ll. 43–117. Chaucer's slightly older contemporary, Bertrand du Guesclin, was ridiculed for wrestling and was appreciated only when he showed he could also joust superlatively (Cuvelier 1990/1400).

Chrétien de Troyes's knights and William Marshall seemingly did not lower themselves to play the bourgeois sports that Fitzstephen described (1908), but curiously enough, King Arthur's knights did, at least according to the way they were imagined by the early twelfth century (Geoffrey 1985–91: 5.197–9). Following the king's coronation, we are told, there was a kind of athletic festival in which the knights competed in physical exercises (*palestram*), military exercises (*tirocinium*), dice (*taxillos*), wrestling (*lucte certamen*), or foot-racing (*vincere cursu certat*).[20] But further back along the chain of history the range of athletic pursuits grows narrower again. In the eighth century Charlemagne rode, hunted, and swam (Eginhard 1967); in the sixth Chilperic just hunted (Gregory of Tours 1884, 1927), as did Theoderic in the fifth (Sidonius, *Letters*, Loeb, 1.2). Combat sport, at least as a sport potentially available to spectators, disappeared with the end of gladiatorial fights in the fifth century, not to reappear until the tournaments became popular in the eleventh.[21]

Superficially at least, chivalric sports as they can be reconstructed from Renaissance examples appear to be linked very largely to celebrations: princely marriages, peace treaties, the ceremonial entries of new sovereigns into their subject cities. In fact, on such occasions they seem to have been automatically expected, so that when England's Henry V refused to joust after his marriage to the daughter of France's Charles VI – he suggested that instead they should all show off their prowess by attacking the evil Burgundians who were holding the city of Sens – it took everyone by surprise (*Journal* 1975: 140). Otherwise, the chronicles, memoirs, and histories of the fourteenth, fifteenth and sixteenth centuries are filled with references to 15 days of jousting here, ten days there, and so on. Only the jousts narrated by Olivier de La Marche (1883) seem to have been organized out sheer high spirits and the wish to have a party, but perhaps there too there was an underlying political motive unknown to La Marche.

But in the thirteenth century and earlier the motivation was different and very much linked to the feudal organization of society and the state. Beyond their value as military training – now debated – tournaments were a means of establishing pyramidal hierarchies within the nascent states of western Europe, a spontaneous way of determining who was strongest and smartest, most likely to survive, and most suitable to belong to the inner circles of power. The career of William Marshall, who rose from relatively humble beginnings to become Regent of England is in this case emblematic. William, who was so poor he had to borrow a horse for his first tournament, ended up taking four from his opponents and so was on his way to fame and fortune. Later, William teamed up with Roger de

Gaugi to form a kind of tag team, and between the two of them they captured 103 knights plus assorted horses and equipment in the space of eight months (Marshall 1891–1901: ll. 3381 ff.). Tournaments and similar encounters were thus more than noble recreations and socially obligatory pursuits for the aristocracy. Because they were the equivalent of real battles, a knight could be just as much a hero through his athletic exploits as he could for his military ones – perhaps even more so, since he could be seen by a relatively large public when tourneying, but battles were necessarily secluded events, seen only by a few peasants or villagers and publicized only by the heralds who wrote them up later (Duby 1973a, 1984).

Tournaments were thus outlets for ambitions, especially for landless younger sons, and the knightly class was so eager to participate that 'an energetic knight-errant had the opportunity [in the thirteenth century] of attending about one a fortnight' (Denholm-Young 1948: 242). As a means of gaining wealth and position, they were the domestic equivalent of the earlier colonial, missionary, and military expansion of Latin Christendom into the under-populated areas of central and eastern Europe (Bartlett 1993). The principle of the feudal system had been established legendarily by Charles Martel (Charlemagne's grandfather) before the battle of Poitiers in 732. Needing heavy cavalry, he 'massively and systematically secularized the church's property which he then conceded … to his faithful followers in exchange for mounted military service' (Contamine 1984: 179–81). Whether or not this legend is true – Contamine goes on to give the evidence against it – Geoffrey of Monmouth's story of Arthur's coronation games certainly confirms the principle. When the winners have been declared, the king rewards them with cities, castles, archbishoprics, bishoprics, and abbeys (Geoffrey 1985–91/1136).

Arthur's athletes are of course seasoned soldiers whose prizes come to them less for their sporting achievements than for their service to the king during the battles that brought him to the throne. As in *Iliad* 23, victory in non-military contest is not so much a foretaste of their warlike prowess as a confirmation of it. More importantly, Arthur's fighting men are present in the text collectively as *milites*, soldier-nobles, or more commonly, knights. Scaglione (1991: 17–18) dates the recognized creation of this class from 980, when the *milites* became an intermediate order between the *rustici* and the *nobiles*; they started to merge with the latter around 1150. As in the *Iliad*, then, the sports of Arthur's knights are the normal pursuits of a class of people and not just of superior individuals.

Since knighthood was initially not hereditary, it involved solemn commitment to one's feudal lord, hence the process of dubbing or initiation. And since social classes were defined ecclesiastically as well as sociologically and politically, the church's definition of a knight's commitment extended down as well as up: protection of the weak and vulnerable was as important as fulfilling one's military duty. In the twelfth century John of Salibury expressed it thus:

> What is the justification of knighthood's existence? To protect the Church, to
> fight infidels, to honor priesthood, to protect the poor from iniquity, to pacify

the land, to shed one's own blood and, if necessary, to give one's life for his brethren.

(quoted in Goetz 1993: 179)[22]

On the one hand, the knight was to be a selfless individual, a Christian warrior serving both his inferiors and his superiors, but on the other hand he was motivated by self-interest and the traditions of his caste to acquire by violent means – whether in battle or not – whatever goods and property he needed to secure his security and social ascension.

From the late eleventh century onwards the rapaciousness of the knights was a subject of concern and their general failure to live up to knightly ideals continued to be a preoccupation into the fifteenth century, even after 'civilizing influences' theoretically began to be felt. The Heilbronn tournament regulations of 1485, for example, list the various moral and criminal lapses that would cause a knight to be excluded from tourneying (Rühl 2006). In the sixteenth century Vieilleville, one of the king's closest friends, at age 18 killed the *maître d'hôtel* of Louise de Savoie, the king's mother, because he had insulted him. At age 54 he had lost none of his youthful impetuosity, cutting off the arm of a fellow noble because they had quarrelled (Vieilleville 1757/1571: 7–8, 337–8). 'Knights were indeed the privileged practitioners of violence in their society', and they often practiced that violence in the name of prowess (Kaeuper 1999: 130).

Prowess was a legitimate quality for knights to display, indeed it was part of the chivalric ideal to which Henri II tried to conform. In his bilingual Latin–French obituary of the king, the poet Joachim du Bellay (1522–60) praised Henri for thinking it shameful to 's'exercer en un jeu, s'il n'estoit/Digne de sa vertu, & son Mars ne sentoit'.[23] Medieval literary versions of what knights were like usually mention the show of prowess as the hero's purposes in tourneying, while attributing the baser motives only to the villains or lesser individuals. Chrétien de Troyes's Erec, for example explicitly disdains to capture horses or their riders; his only goal is to be seen as a skilful and valiant jouster.

> Erec ne voloit pas entandre
> a cheval n'a chevalier prandre,
> mes a joster et a bien feire
> por ce que sa proesce apeire
> (Chrétien 1955/1160–70: ll. 2159–62)[24]

Others of Chrétien's heroes, Gawain and Lancelot, both give away the horses they have taken from defeated opponents, while the biographer of the fourteenth-century French marshal Boucicaut (one of the *tenans* at St Inglevert) emphasizes that his only motivation in tourneying was to enhance his reputation for valour and prowess (Boucicaut 1985: 66–7).

Tournaments – understood in their original form as massed *mêlées* of knights fighting in teams – were the ideal place to acquire material wealth in the form of ransomable horses and riders, but not for displaying prowess, since they were often scattered across wide stretches of countryside and valiant deeds might pass unobserved. Hence the emergence in the first half of the thirteenth century of the so-called 'round table', a form of tournament in which knights fought each other with blunted weapons, serially and individually, i.e. jousted (Denholm-Young 1948; Jackson 1985: 279). The model for this form of combat may well have been pseudo-historical, leaving aside the obvious reference to King Arthur's Round Table of knights. The earliest Old French epic, the *Chanson de Roland*, recounts in literary form the defeat of Charlemagne's rearguard at Roncesvaux in the Pyrenees in 778. According to the poem, prior to the main battle the chief Saracen and French knights fight each other in single combat and the word 'josterez', joust, is explicitly used (*Chanson* 1924: ll.1188–337). Whether that was the model or not, jousting became part of tournaments in the thirteenth century, usually on the first or last day, and then in the fourteenth century more or less supplanted the massed combat entirely in northern Italy, France, and England. On the other hand, in central Italy the two tended to co-exist into the early sixteenth century (Castiglione 1972/1528) while in Germany the 'tournoi de masse' persisted as the principal articulation of chivalric sport (Rühl 2006).

Whatever the literary sources say, a knight's motive for tourneying was to capture valuable prizes. At the beginning, jousting retained that motive, since a successful jouster acquired the horse of the knight he had defeated (Muhlberger 2002). But once the material reasons for playing the game disappeared, jousting became the ultimate sport, in the same way as gladiatorial fights had been: two men, with no prior mutual animosity and without provocation, confront each other fully armed, with the certainty that only one – or perhaps neither – will walk away unscathed, and with the knowledge that death is one possible outcome. Even protective armour and breakaway weapons were no guarantee, as Henri II demonstrated. There were competitive substitutes for jousting – running at the ring, quintain, *saracino* – that required greater skill in riding and aiming your lance; but if they were done badly and there was some accident, the spectators ended up laughing, not gasping in admiration or horror or pity (Dissennati 1982; Clare 1983: 27). And so, even if the death of a monarch signalled that jousting's days were over, the image of virility it projected and the difficulty in mastering its techniques could still prompt the publication in the early seventeenth century of a book – Villalobos (1605) – that, in the style of Duarte (1944), explained how it all was done.

The question arises, of course, as to whether tournaments, jousting, and other forms of weapons fighting in the early modern period deserve to be called sports at all. They certainly fit the distinctive-feature definition I have elaborated in Chapter 1, but the fact that the players could be killed has been a stumbling-block for the historian, as it was for gladiatorial fights. We accept serious harm as a possible result of a sporting event, but are shocked by death, perceived as qualitatively different from being hurt and not just the next step in the total spectrum of injuries. Even if tournament deaths were in theory accidental, jousters were using the implements of war, or imitations thereof, and jousting in 1559 was still a far riskier business than any other contemporary sport.

At the same time, the sport conformed closely to the varieties of play as defined by Caillois (1967/1958: 60–83), although the progression was different. Jousting – and the tournament in its later stages – began with *mimicry*. The players donned special armour and helmets adorned with often extravagant decorations, see the illustrations in René d'Anjou 1986 or Barber and Barker 1989. Sometimes they wore satirical costumes or disguises aimed at disorientating both the athletes and the spectators by the evocation of worlds fabulous or exotic (Clare 1983: 71).[25] *Agon*, competition, was, of course, the stated purpose of the event, but there was a considerable degree of chance, *alea*: which challenger would choose which *tenan* to fight with which weapons; how skittish would the horse be; would the opponent joust according to accepted practice (Montgomery did not). Finally, there was *ilinx*, vertigo, produced by the speed of the horse, the sudden jolt to the head from the adversary's lance and the recoil of one's own, then the, possible, fall from the horse and the concussion of striking the ground while still moving forward. Caillois has argued that what he calls *ludus* – disciplined, calculated play, as opposed to *paidia*, spontaneous, exuberant play – is incompatible with *ilinx*, but though jousting was a very regulated sport, it seems as if *ilinx* was in fact its goal. Its anticipation undoubtedly induced an adrenalin rush for the jouster and his successful and rapid recovery from it, coupled with his adversary's inability to do the same, surely conferred on him the same magnetism that it had on ancient gladiators. Jousting was thus a progression from *mimicry* to *ilinx*, from one form of disorientation to another, via the combination of *agon* and *alea*. Its disappearance from the set of noble sports in the latter half of the sixteenth century was not simply an after-effect of a king's death.

As the increasing trend after 1250 towards tournament regulations and quantified scoring systems demonstrates, numbers, logic, and reason were enjoying a growing prestige as determinants of modern comportment, including all forms of athletics (McClelland 1990). In other words, judgment and calculation were supplanting spontaneity and impulsiveness, the mind was mastering the body. Instead of escaping from an imperfect world by changing oneself – this is the procedure accomplished by *ilinx* and *mimicry* – one constructed a perfect, parallel world where *agon* and *alea* were subject to rules and confined to their own space. This is what the Greeks had done with their athletic festivals, what the Romans had done by isolating sports in arenas, stadiums, and circuses, and what the modern world would learn to do – gradually – after the death of Henri II had brought it to its senses. The emergence of a class of professional athletes from the sixteenth century onwards, especially ball players, gymnasts, and fencers, meant that rulers and nobles no longer had to perform as athletes in public contests, as Castiglione had advised them to do and as Henri II found it necessary. Instead, they could hope to garner the same glory by becoming patrons and sponsors.

Illustration 1 Gladiatorial helmet, first century AD, Royal Ontario Museum, Toronto

Illustration 2 Roman oil lamp decorated with a scene from a chariot race, Royal Ontario Museum, Toronto

Illustration 3 Frieze showing two types of gladiators from a gladiatorial school in the eastern Mediterranean, Royal Ontario Museum, Toronto

Illustration 4 Ball game, from the *Cantigas de Santa María*, Biblioteca de San Lorenzo el Real de El Escorial, Spain

Illustration 5 Jousting helmet, Royal Ontario Museum, Toronto

Illustration 6 Pikestaff, Royal Ontario Museum, Toronto

Illustration 7 Helmet worn in the Gioco del ponte, Royal Ontario Museum, Toronto

Illustration 8 Playing ball and tilting at the ring in the sixteenth century. Wall painting from the Château d'Orion

Illustration 9 Geometric gymnastics. The backward *salto* from a platform. Tuccaro, *Trois dialogues de sauter et voltiger en l'air*, 1599 (personal copy)

Illustration 10 Starting formation in a *calcio* game. Giovanni Bardi, *Discorso sopra il giuco del calcio fiorentino*, 1580 (personal copy)

Chapter 6

Sport in the service
of *res publica*

The joust in which Henri was mortally wounded on 30 June 1559 was organized as part of the celebrations connected with the ratification of the Treaty of Cateau-Cambrésis – named for the town in present-day Belgium where it was negotiated the previous April. The French invasion of Italy in 1494, ostensibly to exercise an ancestral claim to the kingdom of Naples, had touched off a European war that was subsequently complicated by the Protestant Reformation in the 1520s. By the 1550s it had largely bankrupted most of Europe's ruling families and so some kind of permanent peace had become a necessity (Elliott 1968: 11). The treaty putting an end to so many decades of war would naturally be a cause for festivities, especially since it also involved the marriages of Henri's daughter Elisabeth to Philip II of Spain and of his sister to the Duke of Savoy.

Despite all this, Henri could not have been deriving much satisfaction from the ratification process. The defeat of his armies at St Quentin in 1557 – by the very men to whom he was now going to marry his daughter and sister – and France's precarious financial situation had obliged him to negotiate this treaty that deprived him of the territories in Italy he either possessed or laid claim to. It obliged him to pay enormous dowries to his daughter and sister, and alienated his chief army commanders, among whom was the very popular duc de Guise. On 8 January 1558 Guise had captured Calais, the last English possession in France, and that victory had redounded more to his credit than to Henri's.[1] Theoretically Henri still had other cards to play. His daughter-in-law Mary, wife of the dauphin François – she was also the niece of the duc de Guise – was simultaneously queen of Scotland and pretender to the throne of England – a pretension she proclaimed very publicly.[2] If things worked out as they were intended, Henri's successors would rule both France and Britain and would dominate both Spain and the Holy Roman Empire. However, the return of the Protestant leader John Knox to Scotland had very seriously weakened Mary's position there, and Elizabeth I's popularity did not bode well for the future of Henri's projects. In short, in June 1559 Henri II looked to be the only European ruler who was incapable of imposing his will on any of his neighbours.

Domestically, things were no better. Unlike his father François I, Henri was a conservative in matters of religion and was determined to stamp out the Protestant heresy. Yet the Huguenots seemed to be growing stronger. In March 1559 some liberal members of the Parlement de Paris had openly defied the king and the cardinal de Lorraine by treating Protestants accused of heresy with some indulgence. In April the Bishop of Nevers had spectacularly gone over to the reformed religion and fled to Geneva. In May the Protestants had held a national synod right in Paris, and some 50,000 persons in the west and southwest of the country had reportedly 'subscribed to a confession in religion comfortable to that of Geneva'. Finally, on 10 June, in the presence of the king himself, Anne du Bourg, counsel to the Parlement or supreme court, had criticized the licentious behaviour of the 'greatest persons of the realm', a statement that was taken to be a reference to Henri's ongoing adultery with Diane de Poitiers. At the same sitting, the Parlement had demanded, by a vote of 95 to 15, that the Church be reformed, starting from the top down. Henri was so incensed that he had one of his guards immediately arrest Du Bourg and another councillor (Throckmorton 1863/1559: 255–6 and 308–10).

Obviously, then, Henri had to make some sort of a gesture that would re-establish, however symbolically, his power at home and his image abroad. The tournament he had proclaimed on 22 May – rather too close to the event itself, scheduled to begin on 15 June – seemed to provide a ready-made occasion. Thus then his decision that it be conducted *à l'imitation des anciens tournois*, as an old-style tourney that hearkened back to the *pas d'armes* or 'guard-the-gate' contests of the thirteenth and fourteenth centuries when France was the leading country in Europe. As I have suggested, Henri's own rashness undid his intentions, and to a greater extent than he had imagined. His sickly teenage son and successor died shortly after and France, divided along Catholic-Protestant lines, became the scene of a civil war that did not end until the 1590s.

It was no secret at the time that for Henri's gambit to succeed politically, he had to impress the foreign powers that had forced him to sign the humiliating treaty or that were ready to profit from it. As Pasquier (1586: f. 85vº) put it, he wanted 'to demonstrate to the foreigners how skilled he was in handling weapons and experienced in controlling a horse'. The memorialist Claude Haton (2001) insists in several places on the care that was taken to impress foreign ambassadors and other envoys. It is perhaps ironic that on the day of the accident only one ambassador was actually present, the Englishman Throckmorton, who represented a country not ready to be impressed by Henri's show.

However unfortunate the results, Henri had had both a certain body of theory and a prestigious example to guide him in his quest to demonstrate his personal political power through success in manly sports. Florence had been successfully ruled, *de facto* if not *de iure*, for 30 years by Cosimo de' Medici (1434–64), but Cosimo's son and successor Piero was not in good health, so it became necessary to prepare the way for his teenage son, Lorenzo – later known as 'il Magnifico' – to inherit control of the city. In April 1468 Piero had negotiated an end to hostilities that had been threatening Florence since 1465, and it seemed to the Medici appropriate to celebrate the truce with a show of jousting in which the young Lorenzo would participate. Retrospectively, the cynical Machiavelli thought that the Medici's sole purpose was to give people something to think about that would distract them from politics, but André Rochon is closer to the mark in saying it was to 'renforcer durablement ... [le] pouvoir' of the ruling family (Ricciardi 1992: 167–8; Rochon 1963: 80–6, 96). Jousting was particularly associated with the feudal and military culture of northern Europe and the cities of the Po valley – Milan, Verona, Padua. By introducing the Medici heir to the city and the world in such a context, the family would signify its social ascension from the banking trade to feudal dynasty in the style of the Visconti, the princes of the German empire, or the kings of France and England.

The joust was held on 7 February 1469 in the city's largest open space, the Piazza Sta Croce, thus ensuring the presence of a maximum number of spectators. Lorenzo was seen to have important foreign support – King Ferdinand of Aragon and other non-Florentine rulers contributed horses to the event – and the judges not surprisingly declared him a winner, though he later admitted in his memoirs that 'd'armi e di colpi non fussi molto strenuo'.[3] His shield proclaimed the family's dynastic intentions in the motto it bore,in French: 'Le tems revient', which, in the literary monument erected to the event, was interpreted to mean 'tornare il tempo e 'l secol rinnovarsi', to bring back the good old days and make the world renew itself, a reference seemingly not only to the authoritarianism of Cosimo's rule, but also, in a humanistic vein, to Virgil's fourth *Eclogue*.[4]

Despite all these efforts and precautions, the Medici's plan was not immediately successful. Jousting as a spectator sport was not wide-spread in central Italy, but it had been a part of medieval Florentine culture up to Cosimo's accession in 1434, though purely on a local basis (Barber and Barker 1989: 84). It has been argued that it remained fundamentally foreign to the city's customs, and that the way the Medici appropriated it to their own ends turned a competitive sport into an essentially meaningless spectacle.[5] There are however two points to be made about the Medici's effort to impose the young Lorenzo on a not altogether willing citizenry by showing him off in a sports contest. First, the notion that the technical skill with which you played a sport could demonstrate both your attractive physical form and your moral fibre and decisiveness to a crowd of spectators, and thereby win their support, became a commonplace in a number of sixteenth-century Italian books. Castiglione's *Libro del cortegiano* (1972/1528), Camillo Agrippa's *Trattato di scienza d'arme* (1553), Antonio Scaino's *Trattato del giuoco dalla palla* (1555), and Arcangelo Tuccaro's *Trois dialogues de l'exercice de sauter et voltiger en l'air* (1599) all express that idea. In 1572 the French king Charles IX attempted to put it into practice by obliging the English ambassador to watch him play tennis before privately seeking the support of the English in his bid to be elected Holy Roman Emperor (Nichols 1823: 1.303). The Medici may well have intuited the concept before it was actually articulated.

Second, tournaments were organized to coincide with the signing of peace treaties and pacts of mutual assistance, and as such were enactments of battles that might have taken place if there had been no pact or no treaty. But just as Von Clausewitz advanced a famous proposition about war being 'the continuation of the political process by the adjunction of other means',[6] the function of the sham battles that the Medici and Henri organized can best be understood by taking that dictum and adding a codicil to it: 'tournaments are the continuation of war by other means'. That is, tournaments were also symbolic of battles that might still take place if any of the signatories failed to live up to the terms of the agreement (McClelland 1997b). Not so much war without weapons as weapons without war, at least for the time being, as in the ancient epics. There is evidence that as much as two years before his fatal joust, Henri had envisaged a chivalric spectacle in which his eldest son, the frail François II, would perform as a worthy successor to his father, commanding – symbolically – significant bodies of soldiers and enjoying the support of his potential rivals.[7] By displaying his military prowess in an athletic context, young François would demonstrate that France, despite its reverses, was still a country to be reckoned with on the field of battle. But as it happened, that role fell to Henri himself. The 15-year old François was not physically able to joust with grown men, and Henri needed to demonstrate that he was France's strong man and able to deal with his foreign enemies.

Although Lorenzo was eventually able to control Florence by virtue of his other, non-athletic qualities, both his family and Henri II might have found in antiquity a model more exemplary for using sport politically than was afforded by Medieval chivalry. Upon becoming virtual emperor in 31 BC Augustus had to face and overcome at least two problems: his age – at 32 he was still not old enough to enter the Senate – and the fact that for the first time the vast territories that Rome had conquered were under a single government. He solved the first problem at home by monopolizing the sponsorship of large-scale sport spectacles and thus winning the support of the general populace, as he made clear in the *Monumentum Ancyranum*, his testimony to his own accomplishments (Augustus 1923/14). The purpose of these shows was to arouse 'sentiments of loyalty and adoration toward the *person* of the emperor', who was seen by virtue of his place within the scheme of the spectators to be raised 'far above the level of ordinary mortals'. Conversely, the venues for spectator sports were the only places where the citizens might have direct access to the ruler and express to him their feelings, not only as to whether a particular gladiator should live or die – the emperor in these cases had to obey the wishes of the crowd – but on all matters of individual concern. Thus it was the games, rather than any instituted political process, that visually established the ruler's exalted position and that at the same time were the channel that linked him to his subjects (Cameron 1976; Wiedemann 1992; Beacham 1999, 2005). Further, seating plans in the circus and the amphitheatre determined the places that the various classes of society and the constituent bodies of the state would occupy. Anybody present could actually observe a microcosm of the Roman state assembled in one place according to a fixed hierarchy, and thus see him or herself as part of a total social and political order.

Augustus also solved the age problem politically by basing his power on the constituency of the youth and young adults. The idea undoubtedly came from Plato. Although the philosopher rejected professional athletes as badly-nourished slobs who slept too much, he saw considerable advantage in using competitive sport – under the guise of *gymnastikē*, comprehensive physical education – to train the militia that would guard the state in the event of an attack (Plato, *Republic*, Loeb, 3.404*a*, *Laws*, Loeb, 7 and 8). Augustus was fairly quick to adopt this Platonic dogma. He created clubs for young nobles – the *collegia iuvenum* – to encourage the practice of the proto-military exercises that had been part of Roman upper-class life up to the time of Cicero. As Horace in his poetry (*Epistles*, Loeb, 1.18; *Odes* 3.7) and Vegetius (1995/fourth c.: 1.9 and 2.23) in his art of soldiering make clear, these exercises had a competitive dimension. Not surprisingly, the *collegia* later branched out in the direction of sports such as gladiatorial contests (Vesley 1998) and chariot racing, which was historically a sport that nobles could perform for spectators without becoming *déclassés*. It is thus normal that in the film *Ben Hur* the eponymous hero and his Roman antagonist Massala – young nobles both – should have the skills necessary to drive a four-horse chariot. Four centuries later, Sidonius's noble friend Cosentius displayed a similar courage and mastery of tactics in winning a race at Ravenna (Sidonius, *Poems* 23, Loeb). By emphasizing competitive athletics in the program of these aristocratic sports clubs, Augustus was reconstituting an age-old Roman dichotomy that opposed the *iuniores* and the *seniores*, and thus locating his power base in the class of men who were under 35 or 40. Older Romans still exercised, but were no longer in adequate physical shape to compete (Seneca, *Letters* 83, Loeb).[8]

Outside Rome and its provinces, Augustus's problem was not generational but cultural. Augustus' defeat of Antony in 31 had the effect of eliminating the division that had previously made the Greek-speaking Hellenized eastern Mediterranean distinct from the Latin West. The extension of citizenship to the non-Roman residents of these 'Asiatic' territories was one way of promoting unity, and spectator sports were another. Augustus deliberately encouraged eastern governors to mount Roman-style chariot races and gladiatorial games, and similarly facilitated the spread of Greek-style athletic competitions in the west. Although the latter never really became popular beyond the 'areas which had long been part of the Mediterranean world', they could seem to the residents there 'to be one of the bonuses of being part of a multicultural empire, ... another example of the ways Greek culture could be put to the services of Roman needs' (Newby 2005: 140). On the other hand, chariots and gladiators were a great success in the eastern provinces (Robert 1940), much to the disgust of modern historians such as E. Norman Gardiner, who were offended at the idea that Greeks might like to see armed men kill each other (Gardiner 1910: 172). At all events, a citizen could now travel throughout the length and breadth of the Empire, attend the same sports events everywhere, and be convinced that the territories ruled by Rome were 'one and indivisible' (Wiedemann 1992: 45–6, 61). In so doing, he established a model that his successors seem eagerly to have followed. In his encomium of the blessed state of the world under Rome's domination (155 AD, during the reign of Antoninus Pius), the Greek orator Aristides twice mentions the abundance of organized competitive athletic festivals as a sign of the benefits and progress that the Roman emperors had conferred on Greece. At the time of his writing, the number of such festivals had increased to over 300, and expensive physical improvements had been made to the facilities at both Olympia and Delphi (Aristides 1983: §§ 99 and 105; Swaddling 1999).

Augustus's political exploitation of Roman youth and his monopolization of Roman games created a new paradigm for the conduct of Roman sports both on the private and the public level.[9] They were given voice by a prestigious literary text – Virgil's *Aeneid* 5 – that established a pseudo-historical model for his policies, gave them a justification, and laid out a program to follow. Unlike the games in *Iliad* 23, which are both a break from warfare and an act of reconciliation among rival Greek generals, Virgil's games are a prelude to the first positive actions the Trojans will take since the destruction of their city. In book 4 Aeneas has been commanded by Jupiter to renounce the essentially passive life he has been leading as paramour of the Carthaginian queen Dido and to sail for Italy to found a successor city to Troy. En route, his ships are forced by a storm to interrupt their voyage in Sicily, as it happens at the very place where just a year earlier his father Anchises had died. Like Achilles in *Iliad* 23, Aeneas announces quite unexpectedly to his followers that to commemorate his father, there will be eight days, i.e. a *nondinum*, a Roman 'week', of animal sacrifices to the gods, followed by some athletic competitions. Although these last only one day, the amount of space devoted to them in the poem (500 lines) is quite disproportionate to the space that retails the eight days of religious observance (32 lines).[10]

The fact of this disproportion indexes a number of things, only one of which need concern us here: through Aeneas' promise that these festivities would become a yearly event (*Aeneid* 5.59–60) and the statement that his son Ascanius taught the early Latins to continue the tradition of these contests (5.596–601), it establishes the importance of sport as a phenomenon that will define Roman culture. The origin of the competitors also has political significance. By virtue of the fact that the competitions are not limited to the Trojan exiles, but that their Sicilian hosts also take part, they foreshadows Augustus' policy of political unity by instituting the same sports spectacles from one end of the Empire to the other. And finally it creates a picture of the athletic pursuits that the Roman aristocracy ought to practice because they were practiced by their own ancestors. Virgil is at pains to point out that the competitors in these games were the founders of the great patrician Roman families.

The competitions that Aeneas announces are both reminiscent of Patroclus' funeral games in the *Iliad* and quite distinctly Roman. The boat race with which they begin is surprising. The *Iliad*, Virgil's model here, had used a chariot race as the premier event, and chariot racing is generally thought to have been the *ur*-sport of ancient Rome. Among the spectator sports of imperial times, it alone could be practiced by the nobility without any loss of social status, as I have said, and would have been the logical way to start off these games – except for the fact that in their escape from Troy they had not been able to bring their chariots with them. But Virgil's motivation may have been at least equally political. Augustus was a noted Hellenophile and owed his imperial position to a naval victory over Mark Antony. The Greek-style athletic festival, the *Actia*, he had instituted to mark this event, may have included a boat race among the competitions (Harris 1972; Caldelli 1993; Thuillier 1996b) and Julius Caesar, Augustus's revered predecessor, had included a *naumachia*, a mock naval battle, as part of the games he staged in 45–4 BC (see Chapter 2).[11]

Three other events in these games – the footrace, the archery contest, and the boxing match – imitate the events in the *Iliad*, but the last of them has a distinctly Roman stamp, since the boxers evoke, but do not wear, the steel-reinforced *caestus*, the boxing 'gloves' that supposedly distinguished heavy Roman boxing from its lighter, more agile Greek equivalent (Lee 1997). Finally, Aeneas' son, Iulus/Ascanius, leads the other Trojan boys in a previously unannounced event: the complicated equestrian display called the *lusus Troiae* that seems to owe nothing to any Greek model.[12] The fact that the athletic competitions of *Aeneid* 5 finish up with this youthful display is not merely a matter of the parents showing off their children. What is significant in this and in the other competitions is Virgil's insistence on youth. Terms like *puer* (boy), *pubes* (young adult), and the cognates of *iuvenis* (youthful) abound, and only Aeneas, his venerable host Acestes, and the victorious boxer Entellus are designated by other terms denoting a more advanced age. Equally importantly, the vocabulary of the *lusus Troiae* is distinctly military, while the *lusus* itself 'underlines the martial significance of the Sicilian games ... by substituting military manoeuvres for the Phaeacian dancing, etc. [in *Odyssey* 8], activities antithetic to fighting' (Cairns 1989: 229, 247).[13]

After the games end, the reader learns that not all the exiled Trojans had moved from the seashore to the pseudo-arena where the field events were held. A sizable remnant composed mostly of older people had stayed behind to concentrate their energies on continuing the religious observances that had preceded the games, and these people were disheartened at the prospect of the further hardships that would be entailed by the attempt to create a new Troy in Italy. They are thus easily convinced when Aeneas's enemy, the goddess Juno, appears to them disguised as a Trojan woman, and urges them to burn the ships so that the quest can go no further. They are only partially successful. Aeneas and his men put out the fire, but instead of punishing the culprits, he resolves to accede to their request not to continue but to stay in Sicily – he even creates a city for them to inhabit – and takes with him to Italy only the active young who had taken part in the games or who had furnished the crowd of spectators. Virgil's narrative thus predicts or replicates what was in fact Augustus' policy: reform the state by shifting the balance of power away from the Senate (Eder 2005), a word linked to *senex*, an old man, i.e. a man over 40, and towards the class of young, i.e. under 40, men who had been formed in the *collegia iuvenum*, the sports clubs for young nobles. Still, the fact that some Trojans remain in Sicily was also politically significant, since during Augustus's reign Roman citizenship was gradually being extended to certain Sicilian cities and the island itself was gradually being incorporated into Italia and ceasing to be a *provincia*, i.e. a conquered foreign territory.

The competitions in book 5 are bracketed by two shorter but no less significant descriptions of sporting activity in books 3 and 6. Before reaching Sicily – and prior to that, Carthage – the Trojans make various attempts to land and start a new colony on Mediterranean islands, but were thwarted by danger, illness, or divine command to continue on. The only place the refugees are unexpectedly able to come ashore in safety is Actium, on the west coast of Greece – modern Preveza – where Augustus had defeated Mark Antony and where he had created an athletic festival. It is here that Virgil introduces the first instance of the Trojans taking part in athletic activities.

Aeneas and his followers briefly occupy the place, ritually purify themselves, build altars, sacrifice to Jupiter, and hold gymnastic games and exercises in the nude, i.e. after the fashion of the Olympics. In the text, however, these games are referred to as the *Iliacis ludis*, the games of Ilium – another name for Troy – and also as *patrias palaestras*, ancestral wrestling exercises. By literally juxtaposing, in two and a half lines, Actium, Troy, the Latin word for ritual games, gymnastic exercises, the practice of athletes rubbing their bodies with oil, and naked participation, Virgil has melded into one sentence Greek athletics and the principle that competitions of this sort were as much Trojan as they were Greek, and were therefore authentically Roman (3.280–2).[14] More importantly, this short episode also establishes an ancient genealogy for the *Actia*, the Greek-style athletic festival that Augustus – the heir and descendant of Aeneas[15] – had grafted onto an existing athletic festival at nearby Nicopolis in order to commemorate his victory.

In book 6 Aeneas and his comrades descend through Hell into the Elysian Fields, where they see the mythical heroes of Trojan history, including Assaracus, Aeneas's own great-grandfather. These blessed souls are enjoying themselves in an idyllic pastoral setting, and part of their enjoyment consists of physical exercise on grassy training grounds, competing in field games, and wrestling on yellow sand (6.642–3).[16] Again, the reference is unmistakable: these kinds of games are not the exclusive purview of the Greeks, but have been part of Trojan culture since time immemorial. As in the earlier passages, these Trojans seem to be Greeks in disguise, but from the point of view of Augustan politics, the argument is that the Romans ought to adopt athletic competitions because they are part of their primordial heritage, not some foreign import. Seen in this light, the *Aeneid* is a piece of political rhetoric masquerading as imaginative literature. Unlike the *ludi* and the *munera*, it teaches that the basic disciplines of Greek sports – running, jumping, throwing, and bare-hand fighting – can be practiced with some degree of proficiency by everyone. Taking an active or passive interest in these sports, according to Virgil, is not an act of diversion but of participation in the building of the new Augustan empire. Within the overall framework of Augustus's use of sport to promote certain of his imperial policies, Virgil's *Aeneid* plays the same role as Cicero's essays and legal orations did during the last years of the Republic: establish standards of moral – even self-sacrificing – behaviour and attitude that will further the interests of the state. But it brings those standards down from the level of theory to the level of the individual, who is moved by the poem to identify with the epic heroes.

In the centuries following Augustus there are many examples of emperors, barbarian kings, feudal monarchs, and communal governments using sport to promote the interests of the state, the local polity, or their own dynastic ambitions – these latter often taken to be synonymous with the former two. Vespasian built the Colosseum and his son Domitian the stadium on what is now the Piazza Navona. Trajan enlarged and improved the Circus Maximus and in the third century Caracalla (211–17) and Diocletian (284–305) constructed enormous public baths where all forms of exercises and athletics could be practiced. The Ostrogoth Totila held games in Rome in 549 and the Merovingian Chilperic in Soissons and Paris in 577 in an effort to shore up support among the population at a time when they were politically and militarily vulnerable, but these remain isolated instances. The first generations of barbarian kings usually came to power through sheer brute force and relied on that force to maintain their rule. They were willing to demonstrate the physical strength that was their claim to kingship through displays of certain athletic feats (Sidonius, *Letters*, Loeb 1.2). But these kings were also in constant danger of assassination and overthrow, and did not relish the idea of any form of physical competition, even symbolic, that might reveal some weakness. To the extent that in Rome and Byzantium victorious or defeated charioteers came to be linked to the emperors who supported their factions (Cameron 1976), the Gothic and Frankish rulers of the dismembered Empire would have been reluctant to be seen as backing a losing horse.

The first ruler in a position to overcome this reluctance was Charlemagne, who in the eighth century tried to appropriate elements of the Latin past to create a system of order in the administration of his vast empire. Despite his own fondness for sport, however, his revival of Roman culture ignored ancient athletics entirely. There was no sense of reviving the past, only of using its ways of thought and modes of expression for modern practical purposes (Reynolds and Wilson 1974; McKitterick 1995). In the twelfth century England's Henry II seems to have found it to his political advantage to be tolerant of the sporting activities of Londoners that William Fitzstephen (1908/1174) described in his encomium of the city, but his attitude may owe at least something to Geoffrey of Monmouth.

If we assume that the *History of the Kings of Britain* is as much a work of political theory as it is a history book, then the role of Arthur's coronation games takes on new importance. In one way these sports contests are Medieval replicas of *Aeneid* 5 and of the kinds of games Roman emperors staged to celebrate their accession to supreme power. The twelfth century was increasingly aware of the Roman past and wished to emulate it, as in king Philippe II of France (1180–1225) taking the nickname 'Auguste'.[17] More significant for our purposes is the order of events as Geoffrey presents them: a series of battles in which his knights played an important role brought Arthur to the throne; he was crowned; a banquet took place; then the knights spontaneously played strenuous competitive games. Winners were determined and the king rewarded them generously with – according to one version – cities, castles, archbishoprics, bishoprics, and abbeys, which is to say, with prizes that gave them lands, agglomerations, and institutions over which to rule (Geoffrey 1985–91: 1.112; 2.151; 5.157–9). Arthur thereby fixed the political hierarchy and territorial organization of his feudal kingdom and guaranteed the fidelity of his knights by ensuring them a source of income. Clearly, the prizes given for athletic competition are actually rewards for past services, and, presumably, for future assistance. But by interposing sports victories, Geoffrey shows Arthur to be downgrading military might – and the threat that that might pose to his rule – and to be making the distribution of largess dependent on his judgment rather than on a recognition of debt.

From the fourteenth through the sixteenth centuries examples can be found of kings and cities encouraging and discouraging certain sports, usually with some military goal in mind. After the beginning of the Hundred Years War (1337), both English and French kings sought to encourage the lower orders to practice archery by forbidding them – without much success – from playing football and the like (Magoun 1938; Elias and Dunning 1972; Mehl 1982, 1990). A century later a Scottish king most famously tried to ban golf in favour of archery, with the same success – or lack thereof – as his predecessors in other countries.[18] These attempts to legislate the sports that people could play lacked one thing: a reward for devoting one's time to proto-military sports. Had actual prize competitions been created, some interest would have been sparked. Otherwise, the archery training must have been little more than sheer drudgery. In Italy, the city of Genoa was giving prizes to the best target shooters as early as 1386, while in 1443 the municipal government of the Tuscan city of Lucca had the bright idea of creating a crossbow competition as a way of training their militia and turning sport to politico-military advantage – they added a harquebus contest in 1487 (Angelucci 1863). Cities in Switzerland and southern Germany did the same and enlivened the competition by building attractive covered stands to accommodate spectators (Burgener 1982; Montaigne 1983).

However, the most pertinent Renaissance examples of putting sport at the service of the *res publica* come from late sixteenth-century Florence and early seventeenth-century England. In 1537 the Medici had at last achieved their goal of becoming the undisputed ruling dynasty of Florence in the person of Cosimo I. Cosimo was anxious, nonetheless, to elevate his status, and by 1560 was wooing both the pope and the Philip II to change his title from duke to either grand duke or archduke (Carcereri 1926). As part of that initiative, in 1563 he instituted an annual chariot race in the style of the ancient Roman circuses, constructing two wooden obelisks in the Piazza Sta Maria Novella to replicate the *spina* that had separated the up lane from the down. The vehicles – modern carts or coaches, not real chariots – and their drivers were adorned with the colours of the Roman circus: blue, green, red, and white. More sensible than Henri II, Cosimo and his duchess watched the race from the Loggia di San Paolo, thus emulating Augustus himself, his 'favourite spiritual ancestor' (Hale 1977: 141) in the imperial box at the Circus Maximus. The extent to which the creation of the chariot race was an overt political act can be gauged by Cosimo's actions the following year. The painter Vasari had been charged with redecorating the Palazzo Vecchio with scenes depicting Florentine history. Cosimo judged that the space allotted to the representation of republican institutions was excessive and so he reduced it, thereby, as John Hale (1977: 143) has said, 'subordinating the whole history of Florence … to his own fame'.

We have two sixteenth-century descriptions of the race, the first from the diarist Settimanni:

> On the 23rd of June [1563], St John's Eve, the grand duke organized a carriage race on the Piazza Sta Maria Novella, at 5 o'clock in the afternoon, the prize being a *palio* of red damask lined with taffeta and having a multi-coloured border. Each carriage and its driver circled the full length of the Piazza three times, turning around two wooden obelisks, one set near the church and the other near the Hospital of St Paul, without touching the rope that was stretched from one obelisk to the other. And he ordered that the race be held every year on St John's Eve.
>
> (quoted in Gori 1926: 232; my trans.)[19]

In 1581, during his long stay in Italy, Montaigne arranged his itinerary so as to be in Florence at the time of the St John's Day celebrations, and gave this account of what he saw:

> About the 23rd they had the chariot race in a beautiful large *piazza*, rectangular, longer than it is wide, surrounded on all sides by beautiful houses. At each end was placed a square wooden obelisk, and a long rope was attached from one to the other, so that people could not cross the square; and some men placed themselves across to reinforce the said rope. All the balconies crowded with ladies, and in one palace the grand duke, his wife, and his court. The populace along the square, and on a kind of grandstand, as I was too.
>
> Five empty coaches raced. They were assigned their places by lot at one side of one pyramid. And some said that the outside one had the advantage, because it could make the turns more easily. They started at the sound of trumpets. The third turn around the pyramid they started from gives the victory. The grand duke's coach was ahead all the way until the third lap. Here Strozzi's coach, which had been second, with the horses given free rein, putting on greater speed than before and closing in, placed the victory in doubt. I noticed that the silence of the people was broken when they saw Strozzi coming close, and with shouts and applause they gave him all the encouragement possible under the eyes of the prince. And then, when this dispute and altercation came to be judged by certain gentlemen, and those favouring Strozzi referred it to the opinion of the populace present, there immediately arose from the people a universal shout and a public consensus in favour of Strozzi, who finally had it – contrary to reason, in my opinion.

The prize would be worth a hundred crowns. I enjoyed this spectacle more than any other I had seen in Italy for its resemblance to the ancient type of race.

(Montaigne 1958: 1004; I have altered the translation slightly in a few places)

Beyond its technical and archaeological interest – and beyond what it tells us about Montaigne's preoccupations – this description reveals that the Florentines were not duped by the grand duke's propaganda, any more than they had been a century earlier by Lorenzo's joust. Whether they relied on medieval chivalric models or on those that had proved successful in imperial Rome, the Medici were not really able to win over the population by using spectator sports as symbols of their power within the state. Curiously, however aristocratic and oligarchic the government that ruled Florence, somehow the citizens continued to think of themselves as living in a republic. And the sport that incarnated the ethos of that republic was the ball game known as *calcio*.

Although the *calcio* matches we have on record were played by nobles – to borrow a phrase from the English, *calcio* was a 'hooligan's game played by gentlemen' – the game seemed to both the players and the spectators to represent the city rather than its rulers and to assert a pro-republican, anti-noble stance. This paradoxically 'grass-roots' character of the game – which differentiated it from other forms of contemporary noble spectator sports – comes out in the spontaneous way the games were organized, replete with fancy uniforms, referees, and a marching band. In 1530, when the pope and the Holy Roman Emperor were trying to re-impose militarily the Medici family as rulers of the Florentine republic, 50 young men staged a *calcio* game at Sta Croce, in full sight and range of the besieging artillery. Their explicit purpose was to mock the enemy, and to guarantee they were observed, they put the band on the roof of the church; a shot fired at them missed its mark (Varchi 1838–41/1565: 2.295–6). In another vein, Michelangelo Tenagli recounts in his *Ricordi* how 'i giovani di Firenze' wanted to honour the duke's new son-in-law, and did so by staging an elaborate *calcio* match at Sta Croce on 29 July 1558. Another group of young men who had been left out of the game decided to mount a rival match three days later, at Sta Maria Novella. They built a new fence around the square, hired all new referees and musicians, and bought uniforms that were even fancier than their rivals. In all this there was no intervention on the part of the state, not even, as far as we know, in the form of monetary assistance (Tenagli 1538–66: f. 10rº–vº).

I would argue that it was the genuinely popular nature of *calcio*, the fact that it was not dominated by the Medici, that inspired the humanist Giovanni Bardi to write his *Discorso sopra il giuoco del calcio fiorentino* (1580) as a patriotic tract and to dedicate it to the grand duke Francesco. Although he makes no explicit reference to the chariot race, Bardi does remind Francesco that Florence had been founded by the Romans in republican times and that the city is the natural heir to the model of republican sport. This includes, in the first instance, sports used to ensure physical fitness:

> As long as the Romans did physical training in the schools and gymnasiums they were so robust that they … extended their limitless Empire beyond all limits. … Because this city [i.e. Florence] has held to the same ways as the [ancient] Romans, it has never failed thus far to occupy young people in the most noble exercises.
>
> (Bardi in Bascetta 1978: 1.134–5)

Bardi goes on to specify what these most noble exercises are: ball games, *pome* (see Chapter 7), swimming, hunting, horse vaulting, wrestling, *calcio*, jousting, tournaments, and equestrian games.[20] He also claims that the ancient Romans played *episkyros*, and that *calcio* is the descendant of that game. Bardi's tactic here seems to be this: suggest to the grand duke an antecedent sport that is just as Roman as the chariot race, that is genuinely Florentine, and that has the enthusiastic support of a wide segment of the population. His argument is both patriotic and nationalistic: '[il] calcio … è proprio giuoco nostro fiorentino', *calcio* is our genuine Florentine game, and so the grand duke ought to act in such as way that 'Fiorenza sua … faccia questo [giuoco] utile al mondo', Florence should make this game useful to the rest of the word (1.135 and 162).

The utility of *calcio*, in the first instance, lies in the fact that the game has been structured to serve the art of war, as it accustoms us to both its fatigues and its rewards (138). Chief among the men allowed to play *calcio* are 'soldati onorati', soldiers recognized for their valour (140). The team is referred to as a 'battalion' (142) and its disposition on the field at the beginning of the game is derived from the ancient Roman battle formation. The forwards are equivalent to ancient 'slingers' or to modern 'riflemen' and are organized into three 'squads' (143); their job is to 'besiege' the 'enemy' players (148). The winners are 'victors', and the player that scores a point receives as much 'gloria e applauso' as would a soldier who had managed to capture an enemy king (150). The 'sconciatori', the blockers who play in the second line, are like the field commanders who determine the overall course of the battle (153). As in warfare, each team tries to capture and destroy the battle flags of the other (161). In short, by encouraging *calcio*, the archduke Francesco would be gaining trained soldiers to put at the service of the state.

Calcio is also useful on a more peaceful level because the matches bring foreigners to the city and they are impressed with what they see on the field. *Calcio* played by Florentines elsewhere – the Italian community in Lyon, for example, played a game of *calcio* in honour of the French king Henri III when he passed through the city in 1575 (Artusi and Gabbrielli 1986) – would similarly redound to Florence's prestige. Despite the game's republican, anti-elitist character – at least in Bardi's eyes – it would be in the interest of Florence's Medicean rulers to support it. To organize a *calcio* game was after all an expensive procedure, since it required a fence to be built, covered stands to be erected for the judges and the VIP fans, a pre-game parade, uniforms, and – since the matches were frequently the source of a lot of crowd violence – heavy security. The important thing to note is that Bardi had absolutely nothing to gain from his advocacy of state support for *calcio*. His little book is one of the few modern texts that really and selflessly puts sport at the service of the *res publica*.

When James VI of Scotland became James I of England in 1603, he found himself at the head of a country that was deeply divided along religious lines. He was titular head of the established Church of England, whose theology was still too close to Catholicism to please people of a puritan, Calvinistic bent, the 'non-conformists', and too revolutionary for those who chose to remain in the church of Rome, the 'recusants', despite the exclusion from society that that decision implied. The former group were more of a nuisance than anything else – James said he would make them conform or 'harry them out of the land', and he did – but the latter constituted a real political danger. Catholics were often regionally based, and of course they enjoyed the support of exiled recusant groups and various catholic kings on the continent. James' problem was to find a way to accelerate the conversion of the Catholics to Anglicanism while at the same time reducing the austere influence that the puritans exercised within the official church – they were still Anglicans because as yet, in England, there did not exist any organized 'protestant' churches to which they might belong (Parker 1988: 139–60).

In 1617 James came up with an expedient that would achieve just that, marginalizing the puritans at the same time as it demonstrated to the Catholics that Anglicanism could be an attractive alternative. This expedient was a text commonly called *The King's Book of Sports* (James I 1982), although the real title of the 1617 text – it was reissued in 1618 – was a *Declaration to His Subjects, Concerning Lawfull Sports to be Used*. It acquired the *Book of Sports* label when James' son Charles I republished it 1633. For country people Sunday was the only day of the week they did not have to work, although church attendance was virtually compulsory. The puritans considered that to practice any form of amusement in the free time following services was a profanation of the 'Lord's Day', which the fourth commandment forbade. Some Lancashire magistrates with puritan leanings had even gone so far as to prohibit by decree certain forms of recreation on Sunday.

Catholics, on the other hand, had a less formalistic view of what was allowable in this area, and might easily be persuaded by their priests – or so James feared – 'that no honest mirth or recreation is lawfull or tollerable in Our Religion', and so would be less eager to convert to Anglicanism. The purpose of the *Declaration* was thus to encourage and facilitate the practice of certain sports on Sunday afternoon: 'dauncing, either men or women, Archerie for men, leaping, vaulting, or any other such harmlesse Recreation, … and the setting up of May-poles and other sports therewith used' – *inter alia*, bowling was forbidden. The text also specifically prohibited Catholics from taking part in this 'benefite and libertie', for the only people who might participate were those who had attended Anglican worship services in the morning. But by the same token, the *Declaration* foiled nonconformist attempts to regulate the behaviour of the entire population, since the king's writ clearly overrode the decrees of a few local magistrates (Lee 1990; Lockyer 1998).

The *Declaration* also had some other, more utilitarian goals that it did not hide. Like countless temperance leaders after him, James believed that if the common people remained idle on Sunday after church, they might indulge in 'filthy tiplings and drunkennesse', and that that might lead in turn to 'idle and discontented speaches in their Ale-houses'. And, like ancient emperors and medieval kings, he was quick to imagine – and articulate – the notion that sport could be turned to military training and thus produce soldiers ready to serve their king: 'This prohibition [issued by the puritan magistrates] barreth the common and meaner sort of people from using such exercises as may make their bodies more able for Warre, when Wee or Our Successors shall have occasion to use them'.

The essential element of the *Declaration* is to be found none the less in its implicit stipulation that, between the polarized positions of the puritans and the Catholics, Anglicanism offered a balanced middle ground where citizens could improve their moral and corporal well-being at the same time that they were ensuring the salvation of their immortal souls. In return for conforming to the tenets of the established religion, the religion that would come to define England, Anglicans reaped the reward of being able to practice healthy, useful, and pleasurable sports on Sunday afternoon. While it is impossible to say just how much the *Book of Sports* contributed to solving England's political problems, James' goal was achieved: the puritan influence was diminished, and those who could not live with Sunday sports brought their dogma to North America; the Catholics were marginalized, and the re-establishment of the papal religion in England – Philip II's chief goal with the Armada of 1588 – became a fantasy that was finally destroyed at the battle of the Boyne in 1689. Modern sports historiography often refers to England as the 'land of sport', but this label usually designates developments that occurred in the nineteenth century. The *Book of Sports* requires us to push the date back 200 years.

The two events with which I began this chapter represent failed attempts to turn sport to the service of the state, as Henri II and Lorenzo de' Medici defined it. In the first case, the time was out of joint; in the second it was the place, but in both the motivation was misguided. The three texts that have been set in contrast to those events – the *Aeneid*, Bardi's *Discorso*, and James' *Declaration* – have this in common: all three writers imagine sport as an enterprise of collective political empowerment. After the funeral games for Anchises, the heretofore wandering Trojans – athletes and spectators – become focused on the task building the new Troy. Bardi's Florentines are healthier for playing *calcio*, they acquire skills useful for the defence of the state, and they enact for themselves and their audience the very nature of the republic: settling mutual differences through a medium that is not warfare, Even James' 'common and meaner sort of people' are raised above those who do not practice sport, or who – because of misleading allegiances – are excluded from it. By virtue of practicing Anglicanism, they become full-fledged English men and women.

Chapter 7

Athletics within the social fabric

Augustus's new paradigm that would determine how sport would be organized, practiced, and understood within the Empire did not meet with universal acceptance. In the famous 'bread and circuses' passage of his tenth satire, the second-century poet Juvenal emphasizes that in republican times power in Rome flowed upwards. It was the Roman people that with their votes bestowed commands, consulships, legions, and all else on the ruling classes. Now, under the Empire, the populace does not care any more. It has abdicated the power it once had, holds back from politics and longs eagerly for just two things, bread and games (Juvenal, *Satires*, Loeb, 10.79–81).[1] The implications of this passage are far-reaching. Spectator sports – *ludi* – had been an essential element of the religious festivals that punctuated the secular year. They were primarily events conducted for the benefit of the entire community, which would gather to watch them as an act of civic cohesion.[2] Now they have lost that purpose, are reduced to being mere chariot races – *circenses* – and have no more spiritual, cognitive, or collective dimension to them than do the mere necessities of life. The spectacular games that have become a staple of imperial politics have in fact destroyed the social contract.

Juvenal's contemporary, the younger Pliny, presents an opposing view. Praising the emperor Trajan (98–117) who had recently restored and enlarged the Circus Maximus, partially destroyed in Nero's fire of 64 and which now held close to 150,000 spectators, he says this:

> In addition, the seats of the people and the emperor are on the same level, since along the entire length there is one single uninterrupted, undifferentiated façade. There is no private accommodation provided to Caesar the spectator, no private show. Your citizens are free to contemplate you as you them. [The reconfigured Circus] will allow them to recognize not an emperor's box, but the emperor himself, in public, sitting among his people.
>
> (Pliny, *Letters and Panegyricus*, Loeb, 2.438)

The Circus Maximus, like the Colosseum and Domitian's stadium built in the last years of the first century, possessed an inverted conical shape that, during the games, configured the onlookers into a single entity, arranged hierarchically to form a microcosm of Roman society.[3] The amphitheatre, the circus, and the stadium were the places where the ruler came into direct contact with his people and they with him, and thus the social contract was maintained.[4] Beyond that, the immense size and architectural beauty of these buildings were monuments the Romans had erected to themselves. As Pliny says of the Circus, it was a structure that deserved to be seen not only for the shows that were mounted there, but also as 'a throne worthy of a people that had conquered the nations'. The games were occasions for the Romans to renew their confidence in their own power and the colossal arenas they built for spectator sports were not simply large-scale devices for crowd manipulation. They were also ongoing *lieux de mémoire*, as it were, that brought the citizenry together as one,

Admittedly, positive or negative beliefs concerning the social value of professional sports were not independent of attitudes towards the athletes themselves. Cicero, certainly the most influential Roman thinker, expressed the quandary that most educated Romans must have felt. As a Stoic, he finds it inappropriate to utter noises at moments of extreme emotional tension, but stresses that utterances of grief or despair are not to be confused with the actions of runners, boxers, and track and field athletes. They shout loudly or groan at the moment of greatest effort, not because of pain or faint-heartedness, but because it helps them concentrate their strength, strike harder blows, and produce more forceful results. Slightly earlier in the same book – it is his last and most important philosophical work – he contrasts the strength, courage, and endurance of veteran soldiers with the self-indulgence of athletes who cannot stand to go a day without food and who value the false glory of an Olympic victory. Cicero then goes on to praise the courage and indifference to pain that he has observed in gladiators; they are the dregs of society, but they offer a model of behaviour in the face of suffering and death that others could imitate (*Tusculan Disputations*, Loeb, 2.23.56–7 and 2.16.37–2.17.41).

In another book that dates from the same period (*Orator*, Loeb, 68.228–9), he introduces a lengthy comparison between public speakers on the one hand and gladiators and *athletas* – here meaning boxers – on the other. The latter two do not make any moves, whether parrying or attacking, that are not graceful, i.e. do not show the signs of proper training ('non habeat palaestram'), so that whatever is useful in fighting ('utiliter') is also agreeable to look at ('venustum').[5] Orators must do the same, and they can achieve this through imparting the proper rhythm to their speech. Otherwise, says Cicero, they resemble those that the Greeks call 'apalaistrous', untrained in gymnastics, i.e. awkward. The metaphor is based on an image of Greek athletic practices, but Roman gladiatorial fighting styles are explicitly described as possessing the same qualities. The gladiator, the boxer, and the athlete in general are held up as Stoic examples for the rest of the population. The goal or end-result of these sports may be trivial or horrific, but the practitioner is shown to be a model of determination, someone willing to undergo long hours of training to achieve his goals and to tolerate injury and even death without complaining.

Between the two polarized attitudes of Juvenal and Pliny, but more decisive than Cicero, the games of *Aeneid* 5 – and the Greek-style athletics that they seemed to promote – offered a middle way. There were social and qualitative differences between the traditional Roman spectator sports practiced by professionals (the *ludi* and the *munera*) and the attempts of amateur upper class Romans to imitate them. However these same distinctions did not apply to the *certamina*, in which the sports that were practiced seemed mere extensions of the physical exercises the Romans did in private: running, jumping, throwing, weight-lifting, and wrestling.[6] Insofar as it represents competitive athletic activities as an intrinsic element of the lives of their ancestors, the *Aeneid* has created an heroic Greco–Trojan model to be imitated by upper class Romans.[7] This was a model to which the Romans enthusiastically took. Physical exercises, whether competitive or not, had been part of Roman life during the Republic (Plautus, *Rudens*, Loeb, 2.1; Plutarch, *Marcus Cato*, Loeb, 20) and during imperial times they continued to form an important element in the rhythms of daily life (Balsdon 1969). The very fact of practicing regular exercise, even if, like Seneca, one did it in the privacy of his country villa, contributed to social solidarity.

On the other hand, although writers like Quintilian extolled intense physical activity as a model for intellectual life (Grodde 1997), it is clear that those who practiced it did not always have Virgil in mind. Seneca (*Letters*, Loeb, 15 and 56) condemns professional athletes' obsession with their own muscular bodies and those who are overly fond of developing their physique. His depiction in the latter letter of the bathhouse over which he lives (see Chapter 2) implies that those who frequent it for exercise and massage are not exactly the flower of Roman society. A similar picture emerges from Petronius's *Satyricon* and St Augustine admits (*Confessions*, Budé, 1.9–10) that his motivations in playing competitive games were not always wholesome or beneficial.

Although it was written almost at the end of the Empire, Sidonius's account of *harpastum* (*Letters*, Loeb, 5.17) illuminates the way in which private sport both encouraged social cohesion and perpetuated class distinctions. In September 469 the 39 year old Sidonius was part of a group in Lyon that went before dawn to a church service commemorating St Just, the city's bishop almost a century before. Following the service, and while awaiting the time for mass, the different social classes ('varia ordinum corpora') each went their own way, but the leading citizens of the town ('consulis civium primis') chatted together before deciding to do something to fill up the time. The older members of the group wanted to play board games, but Sidonius – who proclaims himself an avid athlete – preferred to play ball. Accordingly, a game was organized involving, apparently, some men Sidonius' age and some students, presumably younger. Two points are to be made. The first is that, at 39, Sidonius still considered himself young enough to play a ball game with students, thus he was still a *iuvenis* in the sense imagined by Augustus. Second, in Sidonius's social system ball games are the prerogative of the ruling classes, and the lower orders are not invited to participate.

Sidonius's description is to say the least idyllic and not quite in keeping with contemporary realities. By his time, what is now France had been overrun by 'barbarian' Goths and Franks with whom the Romanized Celtic population lived in a state of uneasy tension, yet his description of leisurely play evokes the practices of carefree noble Romans of an earlier age (cf. Horace, *Satires*, Loeb, 1.5). Sidonius may simply be trying to 'convince himself that … the world he knows is still intact and in place' (Percival 1997: 287), but whatever his real preoccupations, his letter presents the sports historian with an accurate picture of a Roman game neither physically nor socially unlike the touch football played by the New England upper-classes on fall holiday weekends.[8]

Antiquity thus bequeathed to later centuries a complex understanding as to how sport might fit into the social fabric. It can somehow be both degrading and edifying, socially destructive and socially constructive, inspiring and pleasurable on the personal level but annoying when someone else is doing it, an instrument of class solidarity and of class distinction. These complex instrumentalities were lost on the Goths, Franks, and other barbarians who came to rule sections of Western Europe after 476. Athletic prowess for them – to the extent that we can discern it – meant nothing more than demonstrating their physical superiority to their underlings. The Augustan paradigm of public sports and private athletics no longer corresponded to the mentalities of a largely uneducated, very warlike, yet Christian ruling class. Charlemagne – the first emperor in over 300 years – was both emblematic of this class and yet innovative with respect to the function sport might play within the social system. His physical presence commanded respect, as did his display of outstanding athletic ability. But by inviting his vassals to swim with him, he made sport into a new, cohesive sociability and integrated it into the feudal system. Eginhard's biography (1967/828) publicized these innovations, thereby establishing a paradigm to at last replace the imperial Roman model. It proposed a revived, ultimately chivalric function for athletics in the emerging European polity and a new place for it within the imaginative system of Latin Christendom.

The first evidence of Charlemagne's paradigm taking hold is found in Nithard's *Histories* (Nithard 1926/843: 110–13) where he recounts the mock warfare frequently played out between the armies of Charlemagne's grandsons, Louis the German and Charles the Bald, when they met to sign a treaty of mutual assistance. The foot-soldiers pretended – reciprocally – to attack and retreat, and then the two kings rode in and, as pre-arranged, broke up the game. Sport was thereby demonstrated to be a form of sociable behaviour that overcame potential enmity, while at the same time the rulers were understood to be the arbiters of the game and the masters of the players. The paradigm is also visible in the tournaments of massed knights that emerged in the eleventh century out of the private wars among knights of the Carolingian period (Parisse 1985). As in these wars the purpose was to capture horses, men, and other booty, and though in one sense it was every knight for himself, the knights did fight in teams organized by their feudal lords and grouped by geographical origin. The young William Marshall's first tournament pitted knights from Anjou, Maine, Poitou, and Brittany against teams from the Ile-de-France, Normandy, and England (William 1891–1901/1220: 44–5, ll. 1201–12). There was no sense of animosity in these encounters, only the inter-regional rivalry everyone is familiar with and that has been an acknowledged staple of sport since the seventeenth century. But at the same time, the exhibition of superior individual prowess could mark a successful knight for future advancement within the system, as it did for Marshall (Duby 1984). In other words, tourneying promoted, paradoxically, both team solidarity and individualism.

The further implementation of Charlemagne's paradigm was not without obstacle. The violence that was a necessary side-effect of tournaments and later jousting, even if it was accidental, led the Church to ban such encounters in 1130. This position was, of course, consistent with the early Church's condemnation of gladiatorial fights. As a Christian institution it could not tolerate any kind of sport in which, as Alcocer put it much later, there was 'peligro probable de muerte', probable danger of death (1559: 286). By the beginning of the twelfth century secular authorities in England had already prohibited – in vain – participation in these sham battles, though the king of France did not join forces in the ban until 1260, perhaps because tournaments were a source of revenue for northern France. However, all attempts to render tournaments illegal proved fruitless. The nobility was so attracted to these dangerous sports as opportunities both to show off their knightly prowess and gain rich prizes that they paid little attention to the prohibitions.

Richard the Lion Heart was the only monarch wise enough to realize that, if he could not stop his knights from tourneying, he ought to draw some advantage from it. In 1194 he authorized tournaments in five very precisely delimited regions in the centre and south of England. Any English noble or knight could purchase the right to tourney or even to organize a tournament in these areas by paying anywhere from two to 20 marks, according to his rank – foreigners were excluded lest the tournaments turn into wars.[9] Richard's policy was actually double-edged. It brought revenue to his treasury and it limited some potential domestic problems. Since tournaments covered wide swaths of territory, they laid waste to the fields and villages belonging to peasants and monasteries and to the forests that belonged to the king. By confining them to well-defined districts, Richard reduced the damages they caused and the lawsuits that might also result. Despite the apparently obvious advantages of his licensing system, no contemporary or posterior ruler imitated him. As knights gradually metamorphosed from being an exclusively warrior caste into a landed aristocracy that still owed military service to the king, the capturing of men and booty became less important and tournaments became more occasions for displaying obsolescent military skills. Collectively, the knightly sports had gone beyond the stage of being replicas of real warfare into being spectacle entertainments of no military use, but the mania with which they were pursued remained a source of conflict between the nobles and the king.

In fact even as early as the fourteenth century Philippe IV in France 'had tried to prohibit or limit tournaments, which [he] considered dangerous and vain exercises, a waste of energy, which worked to the detriment of proper military activities' (Contamine 1984: 216). He may also have feared the dynastic ambitions – and consequent social upheaval – that tournament success could nurture in barons not overly heedful of their feudal obligations. This possibility certainly pertained in Renaissance England (Gunn 1990).

In addition to the value or detriment that tournaments brought to the knights that participated in them and to the rule of civil and ecclesiastical law, tournaments – when they could be held in or in proximity to large towns or cities – had other social functions. As Chrétien and later writers depict them, they were very showy occasions – contemporary pictorial images confirm this – a chance for townspeople to see celebrities and be dazzled by the colours, the costumes, and the excitement of the action itself.[10] When jousting became the main feature of these knightly sports, it often went on for two weeks or more. Streets were blocked off, temporary spectators' stands were built, and the cities took on an air of festivity. The middle-class memorialists (e.g. Sardo 1845; Del Corazza 1894; *Récits* 1887; *Journal* 1854; *Journal* 1975) mention these events because they were unavoidable as they went about their daily life. As in ancient Rome, spectacle sports intruded into the lives of late Medieval city-dwellers and became a normal component of the way they conceived the world. Some of them, e.g. the 1389 jousts at St Inglevert, were in a sense monumentalized and came to occupy an uncommon place in the contemporary imagination. The verbal record of this event was composed by an experienced eye-witness, the chronicler Jean Froissart; but the pictorial record is found only in the lavish illuminations to a manuscript of Froissart's work produced many years after his death (Barber and Barker 1989). While the former attested that the spectacle took place and provided concrete details, the latter – executed by an artist who was not present – elevated it to legendary status.

Chivalric sports after 1300 became principally celebratory occasions and were usually organized in conjunction with treaty-signings and princely weddings. Leaving aside the former, which was dealt with in Chapter 6, the connection of tournaments to weddings would appear to be linked to mating rituals. In his account of Arthur's coronation games, Geoffrey of Monmouth (1985–91/1136) narrates the presence of a group of appreciative ladies watching the knights compete from the battlements of the castle. Each had her favourite (one version of the *History* speaks of 'furiales amores'), though none committed herself unless her champion had won three contests. The erotic dimension of sport, omnipresent in the ancient world, is here reborn and will become a commonplace of the Medieval tournament.[11]

With the *History of the Kings of Britain*, a new parameter is added to the paradigm of the tournament. Masculine sport has become a courtly endeavour, a means of showing off one's virility and of confirming a knight's right to substantial rewards and the love of a lady. Athletics have become an ineluctable dimension of the nobleman's comportment and thus one of his defining characteristics. They have also become an expected component of all ceremonial occasions and as such require an audience to observe that the ceremony has been accomplished. Now redefined, this paradigm will pertain into the seventeenth century and after, but it will not be theoretically defined until the publication of Castiglione's *Book of the Courtier* in 1528.[12]

The necessary presence of spectators, especially female, is confirmed by fictional literature as well. Chrétien de Troyes describes tournament spectators crowding to the windows and galleries in *Cligès* (Chrétien 1957/1176: ll. 2845–50) or trying to secure a place as high up as they can in *Perceval* (1959/1180: ll. 4956–58). However, if the tournament was held away from any built-up area, beautiful spacious wooden loges might be constructed for a queen and her ladies as in *Lancelot* (1958/1177–81: ll. 5580–5). In the fourteenth and fifteenth centuries it became standard practice to construct elevated covered stands to accommodate spectators, as pictorial representations of jousts and tournaments are always careful to show. This would include, most obviously, the knights' wives and lady friends and older knights appointed as judges. The latter decided which knight had fought best and one of the ladies would be selected to formally bestow the prize (René 1986/1460; Rühl 2006). However symbolically, it amounted to the lady granting her sexual favours to the knight with the most prowess.

Other spectators, however numerous and however willing to be impressed, seem to have been considered more of a nuisance than anything else. René d'Anjou is unambiguous on this point. He specifies that the field of play is to be surrounded by a double fence – the outer one four paces from the inner one – in order to separate the noble tourneyers from ordinary people, 'la foule du peuple'. Curiously enough, although the accompanying illustration shows that elevated stands are to be built for the judges and the aristocratic female spectators, the text itself makes no mention of their construction. Accommodations for nobles are thus a given; the second fence whose purpose is to keep the 'meaner sort' of spectators out of the knights' way has to be specified as a necessity.[13] Nonetheless, tournaments continued to be an exciting spectacle for city-dwellers. An engraving contemporary with Henri II's tournament shows large numbers of people on raised platforms, at the windows of neighbouring houses, and perched on slanted rooftops overlooking the scene.[14] In social terms, chivalric sports had two clear functions: as an intra-class event for the nobility, they were occasions for the alpha-males to strut in front of the females and any potential rivals; as an inter-class event that brought all strata of society together in the same place, they re-affirmed through physical display what was written in the legal texts: the right of the nobility to rule the lower orders.

Tournaments were not the only sport characterized by potential danger and brutality and that drew people away from what were, in the eyes of the authorities, safer activities, less detrimental to their practitioners, their surroundings, and the social compact. With the exception of *jeu de paume*, the earliest records of lower class games, in the cities and the countryside, indicate that serious injuries and deaths were not uncommon (Heywood 1969/1904; Carter 1988, 1992; Mehl 1990). Whether football in England, *soule* in France, or *mazzascudo* and the *giuoco del ponte* in Italy, such games were thought generally to be harmful to the common weal. London's Lord mayors tried to outlaw football – singled out by name and thereby distinguished from other ball games – because of the 'rageries' that accompanied its playing and the damage done to property (Magoun 1938).[15] Educational theorists like Mulcaster (1994/1581) decried its violence, while still recognizing that it was good exercise. James I did not even agree with that assessment: 'Certainly bodily exercises and games are very commendable. … But from this count I debar all rough and violent exercises, as the football, meeter for laming than making able the users thereof' (James I 1996/1599: 166–7).

In Italy popular sports provoked interventions on the part of late Medieval legislators, not only to shelter private individuals from the dangers that these activities entailed, but also to channel the existing ludic passions and energies toward the sports or other outward displays that would be more in harmony with the interests of the community and the image that it wanted to project of itself (Rizzi 1995: 89).[16]

These interventions were not always as successful as the municipalities had hoped. The history of Italian cities from the thirteenth through to the seventeenth centuries consists at least partially of repeated laws and prohibitions against street games, to which the citizens paid little attention. In Florence, for example, as late as 2 April 1669 the municipal government found it necessary to erect a plaque in the tiny Vicolo de' Cavallari, reminding passers-by that playing any kind of ball game would be punishable by a fine and two days in jail. These prohibitions were at least partly a matter of social class. A sixteenth-century political theorist, Ludovico Zuccolo, advocated the principle that the offspring of noble and bourgeois families should be taught to play tennis, *calcio*, pall-mall, games using a small ball, running, jumping, wrestling, and other strenuous physical activities because these are useful for civil defence and contribute to good health (quoted in Rizzi 1995: 163).[17]

In France and England interventions against popular games, ostensibly on moral grounds, took place on the national level. Edward III consistently tried to ban football, handball, ball games that used some kind of a club or stick, and cock fights as 'ludos inhonestos et minus utiles et valentes', indecent, useless, unworthy games (Rymer 1830: 704, quoting a decree of 1 June 1363). His aim was to replace them with militarily useful physical exercises and weapons practice, particularly archery, long considered the key to England's military superiority.[18] The French Kings Charles V and Charles VI tried similar measures in 1369 and again in 1393 (Tuchman 1978; Mehl 1990) and in the 1520s Henry VIII was still trying to force archery practice onto the English, even though it had long been superseded by guns (Hall 1997).

The lack of success municipalities and other governments experienced in attempting suppress, replace, or otherwise control popular sports was owing in part to the pleasure they gave the participants. Most of these games involved running or other physical exertion and must have afforded the players a gratifying exhilaration, even when, as in *soule à la crosse*, they risked being hit by the cudgel of an irate opponent (Mehl 1990). Sermini's text on the *gioco della pugna* (1968/1425) conveys the excitement felt in anticipation of an encounter in which injury and disfigurement were real possibilities. Henri II's eagerness to play any kind of rough sport, including – possibly – the peasant game of *soule*, is another case in point (Brantôme 1864–82/1614). Archery practice, on the other hand, required a lot of patient hard work (Ascham 1904/1545) and towns like Lucca were forced to offer rich prizes if they wanted the citizens to take part in the militia training that masqueraded as shooting contests (Angelucci 1863).

Pleasure and exhilaration are, however, not the whole explanation as to why these games persisted in spite of government intrusions and prohibitions. Most often it was because they possessed some ritual significance linked to specific dates on the calendar or to specific places, and had in addition some symbolic content. In England by the late Middle Ages, students in the best schools and universities adopted football, historically a game associated with commoners, despite official attempts to discourage them (Magoun 1938). This in itself is not surprising. Both Sidonius's 'scholastici' (*Letters*, Loeb, 5.17) and Fitzstephen's 'scholares' (1908/1174) played rough ball games enthusiastically. What did endow football with greater significance, however, was the fact that university students made winning football games a matter of college pride (Brailsford 1969). In another register, *soule* and football were played at Christmas, Epiphany (6 January), and *Mardi gras*, times when the customary social constraints were relaxed (Mehl 1990).[19] Similarly, one of the reasons the Florentines invoked as a reason for playing *calcio* during the siege of 1529–30 was to show the enemy that they were powerless to prevent the city from carrying on its normal Carnival routines (Varchi 1838–41/1565). For large segments of the population, sporting encounters were part of the rhythmic cycle that gave reassuring meaning to their lives. Authorities might find that these games comprised socially undesirable elements, but they could not suppress them without risking serious popular repercussions. As Fitzstephen stresses in his portrait of London, he has felt constrained to mention the leisure pursuits (*ludi*) of the bourgeoisie, because a city has to be 'pleasant and cheerful' as well as 'useful and serious-minded'.

Golf and *jeu de paume*, along with the latter's tennis-like derivatives raise social issues of another order. Roman society had functioned economically on the basis of slave labour and the exploitation of a largely foreign proletariat, and hence freeborn Romans scorned physical work (Schiavone 2000). Christian monasticism, on the other hand, conferred absolute value on all work, even the most servile, independently of any goods that it might produce (Ladner 1966), and so leisure pursuits like sport and games lay outside the legitimate concerns of any chronicler or thinker. When it came to athletic games in particular, from the early middle ages onward churchmen, like bureaucrats and sovereigns, thought them to be useless or even immoral. One of the most telling accusations leveled against the catholic Mary queen of Scots by her protestant enemies was that she played 'palmall and goif [*sic*]' within a few days of her husband's murder in February 1566 (Flannery and Leech 2004: 258).

On the other hand, the Church had to recognized that the sedentary life of ecclesiastics had to be compensated by some form of exercise, but it must not be pleasurable. At the same time, it had to be morally justified (Körbs 1938). This was achieved by a kind of semantic trick: the physical effort expended in playing could be assimilated to the taming of the flesh through the double meaning of the Greek word *askētikos*, which was used in classical times to mean both athletic and industrious. In late Latin, its latter meaning referred only to monks, who subjugated their physical desires to their calling. Since by definition they were *ascetici*, their athletic practices were part of their particular form of industriousness.

They also benefited from having at their disposal spaces – the cloisters that were annexed to monasteries and cathedrals – that by their rectangular shape and covered walkways replicated the *palaestras* and *xystus* or running tracks that were part of Roman athletic facilities. In any case, St Malo had shown that it was permissible for a future saint to run (Bili 1979/875) and small ball games that could use the cloisters' sloping roofs came to be associated with churchmen. The earliest references date from about the middle of the twelfth century. The first concerns an out-of-body experience by a young monk who temporarily died and went to hell, where the devils played a 'similitudinem ludi pilae', a kind of ball game, with his soul. The second is a text that expresses disapproval of the practice of certain high ecclesiastics who play games, and even 'ludum pile [pilae]' with other clerics 'in the cloisters' (Gillmeister 1997: 1–2).

Throughout the remainder of the Middle Ages there are many documents, usually municipal or ecclesiastical ordinances, that attest to monks and other young men – pupils in the cathedral schools run by religious orders? – playing ball games in the open courtyards and even in cemeteries that were part of, or adjacent to, churches and monasteries. Historians usually equate these games with tennis, i.e. real tennis, or with its pre-racquet version, *jeu de paume*, though these terms replace the indeterminate Latin *ludus pilae* only in the fourteenth century. The notion that tennis was originally a monks' game is well-attested in the archives and in literary and historical sources. Morgan (1995: 1 and 20 ff.), however, disputes this, arguing on grounds that are archaeological and anthropological that, while no medieval cloisters are suitable for playing real tennis, there is ample evidence from existing folk ball games that it was in the beginning a game played in the open country that later moved into urban spaces.

Whether monkish or rustic, the point is that tennis quickly moved beyond the cloisters and became very popular among royalty and the nobility, who built specially constructed courts, roofed or unroofed, or who renovated existing spaces to resemble the features possessed by cloisters. Morgan (1995: 28) records a private tennis court built in Valencia in 1285 and another in Paris before 1308. Another index to the mania that tennis became – and to its economic importance – is Mehl's discovery of 13 registered makers of tennis balls in Paris in 1292. By the fifteenth century the game had spread to the bourgeoisie, who played the game in public courts especially built for that purpose. These continued to multiply, to the point where there were reputedly 250 *jeux de paume* in Paris in 1596 and 7000 people living off the avails of tennis (Mehl 1990: 34 and 262). A fifteenth-century Parisian bourgeois (*Journal* 1975: 222) famously records the appearance in Paris in 1427 of an expert woman tennis player from southern Belgium named Margot. She played both forehand and backhand shots with such strength, cunning, and skill that she beat all but the most powerful men. The author goes on from there to mention which of the many tennis courts in Paris was the best, a detail that suggests both that he had more than a passing acquaintance with the game and that it was so popular that neophytes needed some guidance as to where they might best play. Tennis also took on symbolic value for the French. In 1572 Charles IX played tennis to impress the English ambassador (Nichols 1823: 1.303) and a few years later the Italophobic Henri Estienne tried to demonstrate that French tennis was in all ways superior to Italian pall-mall (Estienne 1896/1579: 135–6).

Despite the game's secularisation, however, the link with Christian ecclesiastical architecture survived. As Mehl describes it,

> if it is open to the sky, the tennis court reminds us of the cloister with its gallery running along two or three of its sides. If it is roofed over, its height and the way it is lit [by windows placed near the top of the walls] evoke the nave of a church.
>
> (Mehl 1990: 42, also 261)

This, in turn, brings us back to another social dilemma connected with games. Almost the only time that people could play was on a Sunday, and that of course conflicted with both the obligation for Christians to attend mass or other religious services and with the general requirement to observe the fourth commandment. If the seventh day of the week was ordained as a day of rest, and physical play was assimilated to physical labour – and useless physical labour at that – then obviously any kind of Sunday sport was a bad thing. But the Church was no more able to enforce its prohibitions in this area than were the secular authorities, and so history is dotted with decrees that remained ineffectual (Mehl 1990: 237–40). In this respect the solution finally devised by James I's *Book of Sports* is exemplary.

The problem of compatibility between participation in sport and religious observance was not restricted to Christians. European Jews enjoyed playing tennis, but their rabbis thought of it as a Christian game and in any case had an ancient tradition of being suspicious of gentile sports. Both *Books of the Maccabees* (1.1.13–15 and 2.4.9–15) equated the practice of Greek games with resorting to heathenism, and Josephus (*Jewish Antiquities*, Loeb 15.268, 273–5, 341 and 19.130) records the reluctance with which Jews greeted the games instituted by Herod the Great at Jerusalem in 8 BC. Rabbi Moses Provençalo of Mantua in 1560 was asked to write a *Responsum* on whether Jews could play tennis on the Sabbath. For him, the issue rested on motivation and whether or not a racquet was used. As long as the purpose of the game was for exercise and not for gambling – gambling seems to have been endemic among Mantuan Jews and they bet heavily on tennis games (Simonsohn 1977) – and that they played with their bare hands and did not venture too far out of the 'private domain', i.e. the rented tennis court, to chase balls that had been hit out of the windows, it was permissible to play on the Sabbath after the public sermon in the synagogue (Rivkind 1933; Simri 1973).[20] In short, Jewish and Christian authorities, ecclesiastic or civil, had to do some complicated thinking in order to keep the inevitable playing of games on Sunday or the Sabbath within the constraints of their religion.

Sport in the early modern period was condemned, in a sense, for the same reasons that led Juvenal to condemn it, although the condemnation was not articulated in the same terms, for obvious reasons. It was also a condemnation that came from the top down – hence from interested parties – and not from an ironic bystander like the Roman satirist. Whether the games were violent or just a waste of time, whether they were noble or rustic, they diverted the energies of both the individual and the collectivity away from what the authorities at whatever level thought ought to be the true purpose of the members of the state and the Church: the maintenance of Christian order.

Out of the chaos attendant on the incursions of non-Latinized peoples from the east and north that had destroyed the Roman empire, a new polity was defined around the year 1000. It theorized into a tripartite structure the pragmatic social and political organizations that had gradually materialized in the preceding centuries. Medieval society was henceforth composed of three mutually exclusive – but also mutually dependent – classes or estates of people: ecclesiastics that prayed, knights that fought, peasants that worked (Duby 1980). A new athletics emerged, correlative to the new social structures and generated by the fusion of the 'barbarian' ethos that privileged the strong man with whatever reminiscences there were of Roman sporting practices. The knightly class took as its prerogative the military and equestrian sports, and left fitness exercises and the ball games to the other two classes. From an athletic point of view, the Middle Ages thus found itself in contradistinction to ancient Rome: the blood sports – tourneying, jousting, killing animals – were now practiced by the nobility, while ball sports, not the same ones, to be sure, were divided up between the clergy and the peasantry.

It is, of course, hazardous to imagine that the equilibrium of this tripartite order could remain unchanged throughout the five centuries of the Middle Ages. Cities grew larger and became autonomous entities not envisaged by the original theory, undergoing along the way a vertiginous growth in the centuries immediately following the year 1000.[21] They and the schools and universities created ever larger bodies of merchants, students, and other secular intellectuals who were neither knights nor churchmen nor peasants (Crosby 1997: 51–2). The society produced by these changes challenged the existing order, and the barriers between the classes became permeable. One can hardly blame sport for bringing these changes about, but the migration of sport up and down the social scale and into the new urban class was certainly symptomatic of much larger transformations. Since popular and chivalric sports were more concrete, more visible, and apparently more manageable than other manifestations of change, they were more readily the targets for blame and concomitantly prohibition.

Two examples of Florentine games from the late Middle Ages that aspired not to upset the status quo but to maintain it will lead to a conclusion. The first of the games is called *pome*, a word whose origin and meaning are obscure; the *Grande Dizionario Italiano* can go no farther that to say it refers to an 'antico gioco', an old game. There are only two descriptions of the game. The first (Dati 1824/1600: viii–x) equates *pome* with the Latin word *pomum*, a piece of fruit, and says that the game began by throwing *pome* – apple-like objects made of stone, lead, or iron – and then degenerated into wrestling. The other description is more detailed and more reliable, since it comes from the mid-sixteenth century encyclopaedia of sports and games provisionally entitled *Ammaestramenti* (1550: 20r°).[22]

Pome was played by two teams of seven naked men, with one man on each team being the captain, apparently not an active player but rather one whose role was to direct the strategy of the others.[23] The field was large, ±120 metres long, and was delimited at either end by two square safe zones ('bombe') that were prescribed to be large enough to accommodate the seven members of the team standing in a row with each man having 50–60 cm of space. The 'bombe' were thus about four metres square. The game began when one member of each team met at the exact centre of the field where there was a mark called 'mezzo pome', mid-*pome*. One of the two then asked the other for 'mezzo pome', which here appears to mean something different from the previous occurrence, whereupon the first, aided by another member of his team, tried to chase and catch him before he got back to his team's safe zone (Bascetta 1978: 1.135, n. 1). If he was caught, the opponent won a point. The captured player must have then gone to the opposing team's 'bomba', because the description simply finishes by saying, 'et cosi seguita insino che sieno nelle Bombe giucatori', and so it continues until the players are in the safe zones. Presumably, however, the player who effectuated the last capture is still on the field and his team is declared the winner. But then again, perhaps not.

Although *pome* seems related to other games, now played only by children but three or four centuries ago by adults (*cf.* Willughby 2003/1672), the description leaves things unsaid that cannot always be supplied from our modern experience. It is not indicated, for example, whether or not an uncaptured player can try to free his imprisoned team-mates, although that is a feature of similar games elsewhere. Nor is it explicitly mentioned that the game is played reciprocally, although the fact that the description specifically invokes *calcio*, a reciprocal game, as a point of reference, suggests that it is and that after the first player is caught and the first point won, the teams change roles. As Foucault (1966) forcibly reminds us, we stand on the other side of at least one, if not two, epistemological divides separating us from the thought patterns of the Renaissance. It may be that in *pome* there is not a real winner, in our sense of the term, and that the point of the exercise is that the game is played, not that one team beats the other.

Pome appears to be a very symbolic – or more precisely iconic – sport whose meaning can best be understood by looking at three peculiarities in the description. The first is the nudity of the players, one of only three details that are mentioned twice in the description. The second is 'mezzo pome', again mentioned twice but with different referents; the first time it denotes the mid-field mark, the second it is the object of the request that puts the game in motion and may mean half the field or, more abstractly, simply a meeting to negotiate. The third is the 'bombe' or safe zones, to which the description devotes an unusual amount of space. We are told, in fact, more about the safe zones than we are about the field itself, and particularly their shape and the fact they are large enough to hold the players comfortably. As for the word 'pome' itself, it seems inescapably connected to the playing surface and its most likely derivation is from *pomerium/pomerio*, terms that in Latin and Italian denoted a sacred open space within, but adjacent to, the city walls. It symbolized the city's beginnings and was kept free of buildings; in Florence the space called the *Prato* fulfilled that function.

That being the case, we can read *pome* as a ritualistic game whose referent is the beginnings of civil society. Players emerge one at a time from an organized, secure space peopled by a regulated society – the team members are standing in a row and there is a captain. They appear naked, without any weapons or identifying accoutrements – hence are harmless and classless – and ask to share equitably a defined space, or at least enter into negotiation with a society similar to their own living at the other end of that space. The request is denied, a conflict ensues, but ultimately the game ends with each team occupying the other's 'bomba', though not as a result of aggression. In the same way as baseball, with its precise inner geometry and its ill-defined outer contours, re-enacts the founding American myth of settlers imposing form on a shapeless wilderness, *pome* re-enacts the creation of the city. Two already civilized groups of equals meet in a neutral space intermediate between their respective territories. The first encounters lead to hostility, but at the end a resolution is achieved through the two groups bringing about an exchange. The space – the *pome*, the Prato – remains unoccupied but is not a cause for rivalry; rather it is a place to settle differences. *Pome*, for all its violence – the supplementary description at f. 58 of the *Ammaestramenti* indicates that capture and avoiding capture involved tackling and other moves – was both a re-enactment of the founding of civil society and, ideally, a way of healing past conflicts through confrontational physical exertion. That by the mid-sixteenth century the game could no longer be played in Florence had less to do with nakedness than with the fact that it seemed archaic to sophisticated Renaissance Florentines. Its unsophisticated nature exiled it from polite society, but its place as a socially cohesive sport was taken by *calcio*.

Although *calcio* was played in other parts of Italy, in his 1580 *Discorso* on the game Giovanni Bardi (1978: 1.140) proclaimed it as 'proprio giuoco nostro fiorentino,' our very own Florentine game. And it was not just Bardi who held that opinion. A 1612 essay by the Venetian writer Traiano Boccalini (1910: 1.159–61) confirmed that others also thought that *calcio* was particularly emblematic of Florentine society and of the city's republican character. In his *Voyage of Italy* (1670: 212), Richard Lassels says that *calcio* is 'a thing particular to Florence [that therefore] deserves to be described'.

Bardi's apparent goal in writing the *Discorso* is quite explicit: he fears that the ill-effects of the passage of time may cause *calcio* to be forgotten, hence he wants his book to be a monument that will preserve the memory of the game (1580/1978: 1.135). His real goal, however, is less descriptive than prescriptive in two different ways. Bardi's account of the game is not so much a report on how the game is actually played as it is a set of rules, tactics, and practices dictating how it ought to be played, less a monument to the past than a text that he hopes will be actualized in an ideal match. Like René d'Anjou in the *Livre des tournois* (1986/1460), he even strives for a level of abstraction that would free the game from any contingencies, specifying, for example, that the site of the match ought to be a 'piazza principale' large enough to contain a playing field that is 172 *braccia* by 86, i.e. 100 m. by 50, when in fact there was only one such site in Florence, the Piazza Sta Croce (1580/1978: 1.139).[24]

Second, Bardi is clearly trying to persuade the grand duke Francesco to give *calcio* a more important place in the city's festivities than is presently the case, suggesting that the *calcio* season ought to return every year, like the sun, at the same time (1580/1978: 1.140). Although he makes no explicit reference to the grand duke's chariot race, he appears to see that manifestation as the real obstacle to the blossoming of *calcio*. Hence he reminds Francesco that Florence had been founded by the Romans in republican times, and that the city is the natural heir to the model of republican sport. He also claims that the ancient Romans, i.e. republican Romans, played *episkyros*, and that *calcio* is the descendant of that game. Bardi may be stretching things a bit, since the earliest descriptions of *episkyros* are in Greek and date from the mid- to late-second century AD, but the principle remains the same: propose to the grand duke an antecedent sport that is just as Roman as the chariot race, but that has become genuinely Florentine. As Montaigne's account of the chariot race a year later would demonstrate (see Chapter 6), this pseudo-Roman *ludus* was actually divisive of Florentine society rather than cohesive.

However, the civic symbolism of *calcio* may have eluded Bardi himself. When counselling future *calcio* captains on the qualities they should look for to fill the different positions on the team (1978: 1.142), he refers to the two sides of the *piazza* or playing field as the wall (*muro*) and the moat (*fossa*). Since the space that Bardi envisioned had neither wall nor moat but did have a fence (*steccato*) around it (see Ill. 10), his reference verges on the incomprehensible. Earlier documents reveal it to be a holdover from a previous playing space. The *Ammaestramenti* (1550: 21vº) specifies that the game cannot be played in any formless 'piaza, *prato*, o campo' (my italics) but in such spaces as are bound by 'fossi, muro[,] argini[,] stecchato, o corde', moats, a wall, barriers, a fence, or ropes. The various terms that signify limits to the playing space are thus more or less synonymous and may be substituted one for the other.

Filopono's letter of c. 1518, however, makes the sense even clearer and helps link *calcio* to *pome*. Writing to a friend unfamiliar with Florence, he first specified that there was at the west end of the city a 'pomerium' called the Prato that backed onto the wall and whose shape was 'quasi figura quadrangula perfecta'. It was bounded on the south by another wall and on the east and north by private houses. When young nobles came there to play ball games, however, a ditch ('fossa') was dug some 300 feet from the west wall, and the wall and the ditch together constituted both the goal lines and the enclosing boundaries of the game, which thus unfolded 'between the wall and the moat'.[25]

In the late fifteenth century another Florentine, Angelo Poliziano (1976/1475: 1.17.1–3) had used the moat and the wall together as symbols of the city, but before him the same symbolism, and in a more telling formulation, can be found in Dante's *Purgatorio* (6.82–4). There the Mantuan poets Virgil and Sordello lament the sad state into which Italy has fallen. Civil war wracks even cities and sets against each other 'quei ch'un muro e una fossa serra', those who are bound by the same wall and moat. In Medieval cities the wall and the moat were the double, parallel lines of defence and so were concrete images of the municipality's inner cohesion against attacks from outside. By transposing the moat symbolically onto the Prato and playing *calcio* between it and the wall, the young Florentine nobles were performing a re-enactment analogous to *pome*. Although the game was often played between rival neighbourhoods (Frescobaldi 1973–5/1460) its goal was not to accentuate social differences but to sublimate them. This exemplary character of *calcio* may be one reason that Bardi wanted the matches to be attended by large numbers of spectators (1580/1978: 1.140).

Bardi's retention of the *muro* and *fossa* terminology, even if it was transposed from the ends to the sides of the playing surface, emphasized the ongoing symbolism and signifying purpose of the game. But even he had to admit that that purpose was not always achieved. Players let their anger get control of them and fist-fights broke out (1580/1978: 1.159). Worse, since *calcio* teams were pseudo-military formations, they had battle flags. And since the practice was to change ends after every score, as the two teams passed each other, the team that had scored tried to tear up the opponents' flags and thereby provoke violent reactions (1.161–2). Bardi saw *calcio* as a game that had and could again promote Florentine republican ideals and civic solidarity, but human failings risked making it into something less than the weapon against divisiveness that he thought it might be.

The question posed at the beginning of this essay was whether or not sport contributed to the good functioning of ancient society, but the answers given were contingent on opposed views of the polity – the voice of the people vs the voice of the emperor – and the differences between spectator and participatory sports. To some extent Charlemagne's paradigm resolved the conflict: spectators watched the monarch or other noble individuals participate and society – defined in a limited way – could be united in admiration of a charismatic hero who was actually demonstrating his right to rule at some level of the feudal system. Over the long run, the succession of tournaments replicated the pyramidal structure of feudal society in the sense that it generated a hierarchy of nobles whose rank corresponded to their degree of success. Despite their humble origins, the great tourneyers could go on to be regents of England or constables of France, though they would have to add military success to their athletic victories.

This model could remain operative as a cohesive element in early modern society, however, only as long as the knights winning jousts in the public square could be imagined as doing the same thing on the field of battle. Once technology had made the knight in armour militarily obsolete, the panoply of the tournament and the clash of horses and weapons certainly retained their spectacle value. On the other hand, the knights and nobles who jousted had no more right to the fealty of the spectator public than did the charioteers and gladiators who had excited the Roman populace. What Henri II failed to realize was that contemporary sensibilities had moved beyond the ethos of the 'anciens tournois', and that demonstrating his physical prowess in front of spectators would neither impress foreign ambassadors nor encourage the social solidarity that the Protestant reformation was threatening to split.

Cosimo's pseudo-Roman chariot race was a similarly misguided, though less disastrous, effort to unite Florentines. It impressed Montaigne who, like other humanists, had his head filled with images of ancient Roman glory, but for it to achieve the kind of salutary effect on the general population that the Younger Pliny described, the charioteers would have had to be the same marginalized semi-slaves that raced in the Circus Maximus. In Rome support of the Green or Blue Factions did not threaten to topple the emperor if he supported the wrong side. In Florence the races were on one level simply Juvenal's *circenses*, distractions from involvement in the political process; but since the Florentine chariots were sponsored by both the Medici and by families that rivalled them, on another level they divided the city rather than uniting it.

Non-violent sports had a divisive social effect in a different way. Thought of as harmless pursuits by their practitioners, they were often perceived by religious and secular authorities as materially and morally deleterious, incompatible with Jewish or Christian principles, or at least as undesirable diversions from more edifying and useful pursuits. To the extent that governments and ecclesiastical institutions tried to regulate the games and the players, they were perceived as ineffectual if they failed and as despotic if they succeeded. In either case a wedge was driven between the rulers and the ruled that ultimately undermined the formers' power over the latter. James I's solution of uniting sport and religion was ingenious, but as later events proved, not in the end successful.

Sports of the more violent sort, which had tended to migrate upward from their peasant origins into the highest social classes, might have served to meld the citizenry into a community in the way that Aeneas's Trojans became united in purpose by watching their leaders compete in sports (*Aeneid* 5). Bardi never enunciated the principle in quite that way, but he certainly would have subscribed to it when thinking about how *calcio* could contribute to the social betterment of Florence. *Pome*, at least in its ideal form, showed how sport could be an archetype for resolving conflicts arising out of competing desires. But in the last analysis, the early modern period learnt – as Constantinople had learnt in Nika riots of 532 – that the passions and rivalries aroused by sport in both players and spectators prove contrary to any aspiration to use it as a device for social engineering. A century after Bardi's *Discorso, calcio* still risked provoking public animosities and social disruption in Florence. Arrangements for the matches started off peacefully enough, as did the game itself. After that, however, the players sometimes began 'to fall to it in deed and cuff [each other] handsomely: but upon payne of death, no man must resent afterwards out of the *lists*, what ever happened here; but all animosities ariseing here, end here too' (Lassels 1670: 215). The field of sport must not become the field of life, games are separate from society and cannot be used to cure its ills. In 1580 the *Prato* could have houses built on it because it was no longer a consecrated space where rival neighbourhoods resolved their mutual differences in sport. By 1670, if not before, matches were now played exclusively at Sta Croce because the *piazza* had the right dimensions; and they were organized not by city districts but by factions, like the Roman *ludi*. It was *panem et circenses* all over again.

Chapter 8

Body and mind

After the Renaissance

Act 3, scene 1 of *Romeo and Juliet* (1595) is both formally and dramatically the central scene of the play and one of its most crucial. The henchmen of the Capulets and the Montagues meet sort of by chance in the street, a fight ensues, Tybalt kills Mercutio, Romeo kills Tybalt, and from that point on the world of the star-crossed lovers falls apart. In the midst of that tumultuous scene, there is one brief utterance that is particularly puzzling. The mortally wounded Mercutio hurls a string of insults at Tybalt: 'Zounds, a dog, a rat, a mouse, a cat, to scratch a man to death! A braggart, a rogue, a villain that fights by the book of arithmetic'.[1] Given Tybalt's character and Mercutio's awareness of impending death, the seven epithets are both understandable and justified, but why is a sword wound described as a cat scratch? And what paradoxical link does Shakespeare see between the purely mental art of arithmetic and the purely physical art of swordplay? And just what is 'the book of arithmetic'?

Shakespeare's dislike of arithmetic is evidenced in other places (*Hamlet* 5.2, *Othello* 1.1) and will not concern us further here, except to say that he equates it with dull thinkers and Florentine shopkeepers.[2] Tybalt's techniques in sword-fighting, on the other hand, do preoccupy the good characters in *Romeo and Juliet* and deserve some attention. In his first appearance in the play, Tybalt is described by Benvolio as a blustery, ineffectual swordsman striking aimlessly about:

> …in the instant came
> The fiery Tybalt, with his sword prepared;
> Which, as he breathed defiance to my ears,
> He swung about his head and cut the winds,
> Who nothing hurt withal, hissed him in scorn.
>
> (*Romeo and Juliet* 1.1.104–8)

By this description Tybalt seems to be an undisciplined fencer, using his sword to try to slice at his adversaries, but not succeeding. A few scenes later, however, his skills in this area are enumerated in quite different terms (*Romeo and Juliet* 2.3/4):[3]

MERCUTIO. More than Prince o' Cats. O, he's the courageous captain of compliments. He fights as you sing prick-song: keeps time, distance, and proportion; he rests his minim rests, one, two, and the third in your bosom; the very butcher of a silk button, a duellist, a duellist, a gentleman of the very first house, of the first and second cause. Ah, the immortal *passado*! the *punto riverso*! the *hay*!

Taken together, the three passages from *Romeo and Juliet* sum up the evolution of sport from being the spontaneous muscular activity defined by Ingomar Weiler (1981: xi) into a carefully calculated pursuit using implements of refined manufacture and conducted according to principles and method rather than intuition. Of the three, the last cited deserves the closest attention.

'Prince of cats' is a premonition of the scratching cat of Act 3, scene 1. Tybalt is very adept at wounding an adversary with minimum of means. The thrust with which he kills Mercutio produces a barely visible mark. Benvolio can see nothing ('What, art thou hurt?'), while to Romeo the wound seems superficial ('Courage, man; the hurt cannot be much'). Mercutio knows, however, the full extent of the internal damage it has caused. 'Ay, ay, a scratch, a scratch', he answers ironically, 'No, 'tis not so deep as a well, nor so wide as a church door. But 'tis enough, 'twill serve. Ask for me tomorrow, and you shall find me a grave man'. As Grassi puts it, 'thrustes, though litle & weake, when they enter but iij. fingers into the bodie, are wont to kill' (Grassi 1594/1972: 40).

Second, he is the 'captain of compliments', a designation that is at odds with the act of fighting or duelling, but that reveals another dimension of the evolution. Like the elaborate palavers before *calcio* games recounted by Lassels (1670: 212–15) or the ceremonial tone of Henri II's tournament call, early modern sports were increasingly surrounded with protocol. This was particularly true of duelling, since of all sports it alone needed an appearance of a legitimacy that would differentiate it from street brawls. This too is the sense of the epithets 'a duellist, a duellist' – Mercutio is emphasizing that Tybalt fights from premeditation – and 'a gentleman of the very first house, of the first and second cause'. The reference to 'house' is unclear, but Mercutio is clearly mocking his supposed social standing, while the last of these expressions denotes a certain legal punctiliousness related to the legitimate reasons for resorting to arms. Mortal combat and the judicial duel were serious matters, and from at least the fifteenth century lawyers and moralists had been trying to determine when they were admissible. Shakespeare's contemporary, William Segar had reflected on these issues in his *Booke of Honor and Armes* (1590), declaring there to be only two causes, the first involving accusations of capital crimes, and the second to be honour. If Tybalt is going to fight, he wants to have a good reason that will not get him into trouble with the law.

The most significant element of Mercutio's speech is, however, the developed analogy between duelling and singing 'prick-songs', by which he is referring to part-songs, i.e. four-voice madrigals composed in imitative counterpoint. Since the singers of this kind of music – it was composed for amateurs – had only their own part in front of them and since bar-lines had not yet been invented, when playing or singing in ensemble pieces musicians had constantly to count, both in order to perform their own part correctly, thus 'keeping time', and to correlate what they were doing with the other players or singers – 'keeping distance and proportion, resting their minim rests'.[4] In other words, singing too was performed 'by the book of arithmetic' and the rhythms you learned there – 'one, two' – were the same as the rhythms of fencing – 'and the third in your bosom'. What is more, these rhythms allowed the fencer to be very precise in his gestures – 'the very butcher of a silk button' – assisted undoubtedly by the fact that he was using a light modern weapon, the rapier.[5]

Finally, the Italo-Spanish terms with which Mercutio ends his tirade are indicative of something else. They are all technical words that denote specific fencing gestures. A *passado* was an attack movement in which the fencer rapidly advanced ('passed') his rear foot in front of the other, so as to suddenly force the opponent back and off balance. This was a delicate movement to execute because it also temporarily deprived the attacking fencer of his equilibrium, thereby rendering him vulnerable. The 'punto riverso' was an attack or thrust delivered from the executant's left; sixteenth-century fencers normally circled counter-clockwise, i.e. to the right, but, to gain an advantage, might suddenly shift left and then thrust. 'Hay' (= tu lo hai) is the Italian for 'you have it', uttered presumably at the moment of thrusting – perhaps with the added aim of conferring on the utterer some psycho-physiological impulsion, as in karate.

The exact meaning of the terms, however, is less important than what is implied by them and than the sarcastic tone with which they are delivered. Tybalt has clearly received some technical training from a foreign fencing master and the impetuous Mercutio – in this play Shakespeare's mouthpiece – is obviously deriding it. Unfortunately for him, it is more successful than his own untrained style of combat. Tybalt's very cool, intellectual way of duelling wins out because he knows when to observe a pause and then resume the fight at precisely the most opportune moment, according to the rhythm of his opponent. Tybalt is able to 'thrust Mercutio in' when Romeo tries to interrupt the fight because, unlike his opponent, he has not broken his sequence of movements (*Romeo and Juliet* 3.1).[6]

The fighting style that Tybalt has acquired derives out of an Italian tradition of fencing manuals that have been thoroughly analyzed by Sydney Anglo (2000) and discussed here briefly in Chapter 3. From Manciolino (1531) to Vincentio Saviolo (1595) they teach a geometrical method combined with a discourse founded on musical arithmetic. They are very sensitive to bio-mechanical principles – fencing/duelling is an activity in which the whole body is implicated – and to recognition of the fact that fighting always involves an adversary. The swordsman cannot act as an isolated individual, but must move in dialectical concert with his opponent, whose personality and style will be different from those of his other opponents. Finally, their teachings were articulated in a new vocabulary that signalled a different way of conceiving the actions of the fencer. Not only the technical terms that Mercutio mocked, but words that denoted more general concepts: 'leggiadria' and 'grazia', lightness and grace;[7] terms like 'scienza' and 'ragione', science and ratio/reason, which imply an intellectualised approach to what had been theretofore a strictly physical endeavour; 'tempo' and 'misura', time and measure, which denote rhythm, precision, and control in the fencer's movements; 'armonia', 'compositione', and 'proportione', gestures that are related to each other in a manner that is both purposeful and well-balanced. Camillo Agrippa, a mechanical engineer, summed it all up: the actions of a sword-fighter 'are governed exclusively by points, lines, tempi, measures, and so on, and derive, so to speak, from mathematical considerations, or more precisely, from geometry' (1553: iiir°). The mind's conceptual control of the body as both stasis and kinesis can be grasped and enunciated by the mathematical procedures that would later be called calculus.

Mercutio's characterization of Tybalt's new fencing style, which he has learned from the 'book of arithmetic', is emblematic, however, not only of developments in swordplay but of the direction in which sports in general were going as the Renaissance gave way to the Age of Reason. The culmination of this evolution can be observed rudimentarily in the schematic drawings with which Francis Willughby illustrated his encyclopedia of games (2003/1672) but most fully in the complex engravings published in Girard Thibault's *Academie de l'espée* (1628) – analyzed by Anglo (2000: 73–82 *et passim*) – and in Arcangelo Tuccaro's explication of how an acrobat conceives and practices his art:

> BAPTISTE. A backward salto is nothing other than a *perfect circle* drawn in the air. Its *circumference* begins and ends at the point where the gymnast left the ground…The *centre of this circumference*…is thus necessarily at the mid-point of the space occupied by the gymnast's body.…In the frontward salto the gymnast's head always describes a *perfect circle*. The *area of that circle is bisected by the straight line drawn through the centre* from the point where the gymnast first placed his feet prior to the jump.…

> FERRANDO.…Who doesn't know that it is impossible, when executing a salto, whether front or back, to describe a *perfect circle?*…The head does not describe a circle at all, but rather various *intersecting arcs*.…

> BAPTISTE. I did not mean that we should teach a young gymnast by resorting to *mathematics*, although…we are obliged to borrow from mathematics most of the terms we apply to our art,…such as *circles, half-circles, lines, ovals*, etc. But the difference between longer or shorter, well done or badly done, derives from the degree of attention the gymnast pays to controlling his body according to the *proportions stipulated by mathematical measurements*.
>
> (Tuccaro 1599: 66v°–68r°, my italics)

Throughout this passage, as elsewhere in the *Trois dialogues*, Baptiste – who is Tuccaro's spokesman – emphasizes the principle that, for gymnastic movements to be aesthetically successful and physically possible, the gymnast has to conceive them in terms of the basic geometrical figures and in the light of harmonious proportional relations. To the objection that the gymnast's head cannot describe a perfect circle when performing a salto, and that therefore the analogy between gymnastics and geometry is a false and the mathematical analysis of acrobatic feats not really possible, Baptiste replies in sum that the gymnast has to think that it does, and that the only way to grasp intellectually this form of athletics is through geometrical models. In other words, the acrobat has to have in his mind a two-dimensional image of an abstract figure of geometry and then try to make his three-dimensional body describe that figure (see Ill. 9). In his treatise on horse-vaulting Giocondo Baluda goes farther, analyzing the wooden horse as a set of 11 tangential circles, each of which is a support point for his athletic feats (Baluda 1630/1978: 2.49–106).

In another passage of Tuccaro's book, Baptiste reveals that an acrobatic show is not nearly so spontaneous as the public might believe. Knowing where he is going to perform, he paces off the space in advance without anybody noticing and then, using the ratio of two paces to one salto, he is in a position to know exactly where any sequence of moves will actually take him (Tuccaro 1599: 84r^o–v^o). An analogous revelation is made by Scaino in his analysis of ball games. The walls of real tennis courts were not flat surfaces. Openings, overhangs – the penthouse – and columns were frequent and these features were not symmetrically distributed in the two halves of the court. Scaino is pleased that 'so many lovely accidents' can occur during a game as a result of these irregularities, chance effects that cause the spectators 'astonishment and pleasure'. But they are not chance effects at all, but events that are completely under the control of the 'discerning and skilful player' (Scaino 1555/1978: 1.297–9).

Like Tuccaro's application of proportional stable geometry to the practice of a kinetic sport, Scaino's book bristles with mathematics, in this case arithmetic: dimensions of the small and large tennis courts, sizes of the various types of racquets and paddles, diameters and weights of different kinds of balls. He describes tennis as 'ragionevole', i.e. reasonable, but a reasonableness that is based on ratios and numbers. Numbers are also ubiquitous in Bardi's *Discorso* (1580). He specifies – as the *Ammaestramenti* did for *pome* – the distances that must separate the players (see Ill. 10), the dimensions of the ball and the field, and the fact that winning the game is a matter of numbers: the team wins that gets the ball over the other team's goal three times if their opponents only manage to do so twice. The purpose of all these numbers and measurements, of course, is to eliminate unpredictability by standardizing, or at least by knowing in advance, the exact size of the playing area, the kind of implements that will be used – Medieval tournament lances had also been standardized on an ad hoc basis – and the scoring system that will be in effect. The game or the sport will be as far as possible under the complete intellectual control of the athlete.

As I have suggested in an earlier chapter, the beginnings of this process can be observed in Frederick II's *De arte venandi* (1955/1250). That book and its successors

(Crescenzi 1957/1305; Gaston Phoebus 1998/1387–9) demonstrated that by analyzing hunting into its component parts and then applying to them scientific and empirical reasoning, the aleatory sport of hunting could be transformed into a methodical pursuit with greatly improved chances of success. The subjection of tourneying and jousting to a similar form of analysis in the *Statuta armorum* in the thirteenth century (Denholm-Young 1948) and Charny's *Demandes pour la joute* (Muhlberger 2002) in the fourteenth aimed at the same effect, albeit in legal and moral terms. The tournament rules and scoring systems that were developed in the fifteenth century and the encyclopaedias of sport like the *Ammaestramenti* (1550) in the sixteenth century and Willughby's (2003/1672) in the seventeenth are prolongations that simply broaden the same analytical process. Its culmination can be observed in the actual itemizing of the rules for pall-mall in 1655 (Flannery and Leech 2004: 159, pl. 161) and for *calcio* at about the same time (Bini 1688).

To itemize the rules is in fact to negate the kind of humanistic discourse of sport that Renaissance writers imitated from Cicero and to place sport in the realm of science and mathematical proof. Crosby (1997: 49) has characterized it as the fundamental change that put Western European practical thinking ahead of the rest of the world: 'an acceleration after 1250 or so in the West's shift from qualitative perception to, or at least toward, quantificational perception'. What Robert Klein (1970: 333) called, speaking of pictorial perspective, 'la mathématisation de la nature', but which – according to Crosby – was based on the material concerns of the commercial and legal bourgeoisie.

Sport in the early modern period, as I have argued elsewhere (McClelland 1984) became assimilated to intellectual and artistic pursuits. The vocabulary and syntax of the fencing manuals, the books on tennis, on *calcio*, on acrobatics – number, measure, proportion, rhythm, tempo, harmony – are identical to those of contemporary books on painting, musical theory, the principles of architecture, the art of poetry, and so on.[8] All of them suppose that the basis of what they are doing is to be found in arithmetic and geometry, in other words is rational, regulated, predictable, and hence objectively comprehensible and superior to intuitive, qualitative methods. Henri II's decision to revert to an old-style tournament that gave more weight to the judge's qualitative opinion and less to adding up points scored, reveals a suspicion of arithmetic that puts him in the same camp as Shakespeare, a nostalgic for the good old days in sport.

The rivalry between Mercutio and Tybalt portended the conflict of two incompatible modes of being and playing, the old way of physical action versus the new way of mental reflection and calculation, of mind over body. The latter, seen in the description of Tybalt's precise actions when fencing and in his reported use of compliments and resorting to legal niceties, is also the way of a civility that avoids abrasion (*cf.* Della Casa 1994/1555 and, of course, Elias 1939, 1969). Although the duel is a mortal game, it is conducted through exchanges of courtesies. Tybalt is the villain of the play, in Act 3, scene 1, but he plays by those rules; it is actually Mercutio who does not and who provokes the fight. Shakespeare's fighting-singing analogy pursues this fundamental fact of concerted performance as it was conceived in the Renaissance. Whether the relationship is adversarial, as in sport, or collaborative, as in the performance of part-songs, it is also dialectical: all the participants have somehow to deal with the other as other in such a way that the performance – game or song or duel – actually accomplishes what it set out to do.

The civility that was supposed to govern such relationships was, however, all on the surface. Taken together with 'Prince of Cats', the sarcastic mention of 'compliments' and 'first and second causes' denotes a studied approach to human relationships that masks intentions under a set of superficial forms, whether these are verbal or gestural. Mercutio's speech castigates an entire mode of modern behaviour that is ruled by protocols obliging individuals to keep their distance from each other. The impetuosity Tybalt displayed in the opening scene of *Romeo and Juliet* has been replaced in Act 2, scenes 3/4 by gestures that are carefully controlled. In that sense Tybalt is modern man and the modern athlete, but he is still is the villain of the piece. Our sympathies are all with Mercutio and his impulsive, poetic style of living and dying.

The Renaissance was heir to several sports traditions, Roman and Medieval, private and public, chivalric and popular. For a while it seemed to accommodate them all and to integrate them into a new ethos that was quantifying, civil, and meaningful. Animosities and violence could cease because sports contests were conducted according to objective measure and proportion that defined both the appearance of the contest and its outcome. The sports signified a cultural continuation with the immediate past and a connection to more remote, but very prestigious, antecedents. Through a certain homogeneity of practice, they seemed to demonstrate a social levelling whereby the class barriers that had previously segregated sports appeared to dissolve. The matches and encounters were preceded and followed by festivities that brought the players together in a show of fellowship. But this was in fact just a show, as Bardi's injunctions against tearing the other team's flags and Lassels' reminder of possible capital punishment for post-game violence make clear. The passions generated by competitive physical exertion do not just dissipate, any more than do the resentments for blows received and play that has seemed underhanded.

The sports of the Renaissance gradually died out in the age of reason (*cf.* Eichberg 1978). The single exceptions were golf and duelling, one a new invention – and still at that time confined to Scotland and Scots expatriates – and the other a revitalized version of gladiator fights that both instilled and expressed the new decorum of self-control. The remainder were victims, perhaps, of too much quantifying and the reduction of style, emotion, and sheer physical exuberance to numbers, geometrical figures, and regulated constraints. Playing by the rules is never much fun. Or perhaps they could not survive the new civility. Montaigne's father, an old soldier from the Italian wars and the first of the family to move from the bourgeoisie to the nobility, willingly demonstrated his athletic prowess; Montaigne himself, a lawyer, eschewed doing so, claiming to have no talents in this area (Montaigne 1965: 2.2 and 2.17). Being prince of cats and captain of compliments requires both constraint and decorum. Neither one of these belongs on the field of sport.

More importantly, perhaps, the sports of the Renaissance died out from sheer semiotic inadequacy. Despite Cosimo's hope to emulate Augustus, chariot races and other Roman *ludi* could not be resuscitated other than as curiosities. The social, political, and religious conditions of the countries and city-states of Western Europe were simply not amenable to considering shows like the *munera* and the *certamina* as sophisticated adult entertainments. Competitive running, throwing, and jumping became the province of boys, peasants, and servants, as did all forms of fighting in public. The chivalric sports of the Middle Ages were dependent for their meaning on their resemblance to warfare. When technology rendered the armoured knight obsolete, the jouster became a mere mountebank. And the ritual games like *soule* and *pome* and *calcio* that had acted out rivalries and their resolution in an unsettled Europe became redundant in an increasingly urban, secure environment. Neighbourhood animosities faded away in the larger cities because social life was less a matter of forced mutual dependence and more the result of common commercial and familial interests. Untrammelled young men might still play football and similar games against competitors from different districts, but the 40-year old 'honoured soldiers' that Bardi thought would play *calcio* had advanced into the fifth age of man:

> In fair round belly with good capon lin'd,
> With eyes severe and beard of formal cut,
> Full of wise saws and modern instances
> (As You Like It, 2.7)

They had neither time nor inclination for rough sports and games.

Notes

1 Timelines, historiography, definitions

1 These games were also called by the traditional Latin designation of *ludi*, and not *certamina* or *agōnēs*, the usual labels for Greek games. Caldelli nonetheless argues that the program was essentially Greek in nature.

2 Writing in the first century AD, the Judaeo-Hellenic historian Josephus thought of the *Actia* as marking the beginning of a new starting point for recording time, replacing the manner by which the Greeks dated historical events in terms of Olympiads (*Jewish War*, Loeb, 1.398.4; ancient Greek and Roman authors whose works are available in standardized modern editions – Loeb Classical Library, Association Guillaume Budé – are not listed in the Bibliography; similarly, for the sake of clarity, in the case of ancient and early modern writers whose work I have read in a modern edition other than Loeb or Budé, the parenthetical reference will normally give both the date of the edition used and the original date of publication or composition). Shakespeare's plays are simply referenced by title, act, and scene. The parenthetical date for multi-volume books published over several years will indicate only the first year.

3 Before his fatal joust Henri II had been advised that it was unseemly for a king to take part in a tournament. It was rather his role financially to underwrite and preside over such events and gain glory from them in that capacity. In 1571 Andrea Bacci, physician to pope Sixtus V, complained that that monarchs no longer wanted to exercise, 'ob decorum, ac amplissimi ordinis maiestatem', because of the decorum and majesty of their exalted rank (Bacci 1622/1571: 378).

4 On this see Brailsford (1969) and Vaucelle (2004).

5 For a bibliography of these, see Krüger and McClelland, 'Primärliteratur' (1984: 133–60). Before the 1530s such books – they are concerned almost exclusively with the martial arts – relied almost completely on pictures.

6 Modern Sremska Mitrovica, on the Sava River, west of Belgrade.

7 Johann Joachim Winckelmann (1717–68) was the decisive proponent of the superiority of things Greek over things Roman (see Honour 1977: 57–62). On the Victorian Englishman's blind infatuation for Greek culture, especially in the areas of athletics and empire-building, see Jenkyns (1980: 210–26 and 331–46); also Turner (1981). On the attraction of Sparta for the Prussians, see most recently Kustrin and Mangan (2003). In *Les misérables* (1862) Victor Hugo succinctly summarized the twin (and disparate) attractions that nineteenth-century Europeans felt for Greece and Rome: 'La France … est athénienne par le beau et romaine par le grand'. Athletics having been conceived at least partially as an aesthetic spectacle in ancient Greece (Guttmann 1996) and not at all that way in Rome, Hugo's remark establishes *avant la*

lettre what would be one dimension of Coubertin's attitude towards sport in recreating the Olympic Games.

8 The pervasive view that the ancient Romans had fallen into decadence may possibly have stemmed from Edward Gibbon's *Decline and Fall of the Roman Empire* (1776–88). Thomas Couture's painting, *Les Romains de la décadence* (1847, Paris, Musée d'Orsay) is a very striking representation of modern attitudes towards Rome in its later stages.

9 Grant Dunlap in his unpaginated preface to the 1970 reprint of Greek *Athletic Sports*.

10 'Lange Zeit herrschte unter Altertumswissenschaftlern und Sporthistorikern die Ansicht, daß eine intensive Beschäftigung mit dem römischen Sport überflüssig sei' (Reis 1994: 11). Junckelmann (2000b: 12–13) echoes this position by saying that traditional ancient sports historiography marginalized the Romans and treated them as unworthy corrupters of the sublime example of the Greeks ('In den meisten klassischen Darstellungen des antiken Sports werden die Römer nur am Rande behandelt, als unwürdige Verderber des hehren griechischen Vorbilds').

11 'D'une certaine maniere, le sport moderne procéderait des Grecs. Aussi, pour le grand public (et, peut-être, pour une majorité de sportifs?), entre la disparition des compétitions athlétiques de l'Antiquité et leur rétablissement à l'orée du XXᵉ, l'éducation physique n'a pas d'histoire'. In *Athletics of the Ancient World* (1930), Gardiner does have a chapter on 'Roman sport', but it seems that at that time, very late in his life – he died the year of the book's publication – he had become disenchanted with the way money had come to dominate sport. The historians' neglect of sport over so many hundreds of years is what led me to borrow the title of my second and third chapters from the late Eric Cochrane's *Florence in the Forgotten Centuries* (1973, Chicago: University of Chicago Press). Like sport after the ancient Greeks, Florence after the Renaissance was over seemed to be devoid of interest.

12 Auguet (1970: 165–7) paints a very vivid picture of chariot collisions and of horses with broken legs and charioteers dragged to their deaths. On the killing of gladiators and wild animals, see Kyle (1998).

13 'Apres qu'on se fut apprivoisé à Romme aux spectacles des meurtres des animaux, on vint aux hommes et aux gladiateurs. Nature, à ce creins-je, elle mesme attache à l'homme quelque instinct à l'inhumanité. Nul ne prent son esbat à voir des bestes s'entrejouer et caresser, et nul ne faut de le prendre à les voir s'entredeschirer et desmambrer'. Montaigne added this passage to the original essay after he had been to Rome. The last sentence may refer to animal baiting, more common in England than elsewhere, but nonetheless practiced sporadically on the Continent (Davis 1994). Robert Laneham, a minor Elizabethan court official, describes as a 'sport very pleasant to see' a spectacle of thirteen bears baited by dogs presented for Elizabeth I in 1575 (Madden 1897: 369–70).

14 Chaucer's 'verray, parfit gentil knight', described in the prologue to the *Canterbury Tales*, had been in effect a mercenary soldier all over Europe, the Near East, and North Africa. Although he had fought in 15 'mortal batailles' and must have been a very hardened individual, Chaucer still says of him that 'he loved chivalrie, / Trouthe and honour, freedom and curteisie' (Chaucer 1958/1400: 2–3).

15 In Florence, in the tiny Vicolo de' Cavallari, there is still a plaque dated 2 April 1669 that warns citizens that ball games are prohibited there. Infractions will be punished by fines and imprisonment.

16 Davis reports that when he mentioned to a colleague that he would like to write a book about the quasi-institutionalized street fights in Renaissance Venice, the colleague asked 'Why? Who would ever want to read about such a tasteless topic' (Davis 1994: v).

17 Guttmann's seven defining characteristics of modern sport are very well known and do not need repeating here. For Vigarello (2002: 51–2) early modern sport was not

commensurate with its modern cousin by virtue of being socially and collectively determined. Kidd's argument (1996: 12–13) is very eloquently formulated and deserves being quoted here:

> The term 'sport' is used today in both broad and historically limited senses. In the first case, it refers to any form of competitive physical activity, without regard to place, period, rules, or meaning ... But most scholars today ... reject the naturalization of 'sport' as an unchanging, transhistorical, and universal cultural form performed and understood essentially the same way by all people in all societies. They argue instead that 'sports'—as a plurality—can be understood best as distinct creations of modernity, fashioned and continually refashioned in the revolutionizing conditions of industrial capitalist societies ... Scholars are equally careful to distinguish modern sports from the game forms of pre-modern Europe ... To be sure, sports have something in common with these other practices, but none of them can be fully understood if they are all assumed to be the same.

18 See 'Sekundärliteratur' in Krüger and McClelland (1984: 160–80).

19 Since the appearance of Grant's book, at least 35 others have been published that deal wholly or in part with gladiators.

20 These compilations are not nearly so extensive as Stephen Miller's anthology of Greek materials on sport (Miller 2004). It is not quite true that the Romans wrote nothing on the subject of sport, as Charles Homer Haskins once stated (Haskins 1929), but they certainly wrote less than the Greeks.

21 *Cf.* also the three volumes of papers edited by Jean Jacquot (1956–75) under the general title of *Les fêtes de la Renaissance*.

22 Weiler (1981: xi) explicitly denies the charge that it is an anachronism to apply 'sport' to ancient cultures. Borrowing his definition of the term from Hajo Bernett – sport is a spontaneous muscular activity driven by a playful impulse; its goal is measured achievement and regulated competition ('Spontane motorische Activität aus spielerischem Antrieb, die nach meßbarer Leistung und geregletem Wettkampf strebt') he argues that it is a constant of human behaviour. Taking a different tack, Thuillier (1996b: 12–13) maintains that while Roman sport and modern sport are not absolutely commensurate, the similarities between the two are not insignificant and that the 'spécificité de certaines pratiques [romaines]' justifies labelling them as sport.

23 Thus P. Parlebas, quoted by During (1984: 103–4), claims that the popular games catalogued by Rabelais in his 1534 novel *Gargantua* (1994/1534: 58–63) and portrayed by Pieter Breughel (*Children's Games*, 1559–60, Vienna, Kunsthistorisches Museum) are the Renaissance's social equivalent of modern sport ('le sport est à notre société actuelle ce que les jeux de Breughel et de Rabelais furent à la société de la Renaissance'). In fact, Rabelais condemns these games as a waste of time and sets them against more purposeful, more modern forms of athletics (1994/1534: 65–9), while Breughel was certainly seeking to amuse his aristocratic patrons, not hold up to them a mirror of their own lives.

24 The Roman poet Ovid was not really interested in chariot races or other sporting events but described them as a good opportunity to meet and begin the seduction of female fans (*Art of Love*, Loeb, 1.135–76). On erotic arousal as a by-product of sport, see Guttmann (1996), Guttmann *et al.* (2002).

25 For example, in the pair 'black/white', 'white' is contrary to black in the sense that it is another colour, but the contradiction of 'black' is 'non-black' since it excludes all possibility of blackness. To proceed conceptually from 'white' to 'black' one must pass through 'non-black'.

26 *Cf.* Roger Caillois (1967/1958: 7–8): 'le jeu ne produit rien: ni biens ni oeuvres. Il est essentiellement stérile . ... Cette gratuité fondamentale du jeu est bien le caractère qui le discrédite le plus' (playing is sterile and produces neither goods nor good works. It is discredited because it is fundamentally gratuitous).

27 An earlier version of what follows here appeared as the entry 'Sport' in the *Encyclopedia of Semiotics* (McClelland 1998).

2 Sport in the forgotten centuries (1)

1 The authors point out that 'the majority of medieval chronicles were written by members of religious orders, who could not take part in [tournaments], and in most cases might never have seen one' (Barber and Barker 1989: 10). I do not share their mistrust of the chivalric romances as sources of information. Poets lived at court, attended tournaments, and – needing to fill up their lines – often inserted technical details absent from more 'reliable' historical sources.

2 Horace's prescriptive advice on writing for the stage (*Art of Poetry*, Loeb) begins by telling the would-be dramatist to be realistic. François Rabelais could with good conscience advise his readers that his apparently fanciful comic novel *Gargantua* contained important serious insights into religion, politics, and economics (Rabelais 1994/1534: 7); he might have added, and with good reason, athletics, as I pointed out in Chapter 1.

3 These inscriptions have been published in the several volumes of the *Corpus inscriptionum latinarum* and the *Inscriptiones latinae selectae*, both originally published in the nineteenth century but frequently reprinted.

4 *Cf.* Harris (1964: 29–30). He is referring specifically to athletic scenes painted on Greek vases, but his point is valid for later sports paintings as well.

5 In his *Ten Books on Architecture*, the first-century BC architect-engineer, Vitruvius, prescribes the manner of designing and constructing an exercise space and running track in a public bath, and specifies that these should connect directly to a stadium used for Greek-style games (Vitruvius, *Architecture*, Loeb, 5.11.1–4). Russell Sturzebecker (1985) has provided a pictorial atlas of virtually all of the public buildings used for ancient sport across the full extent of the empire, but see Roos (1989) for a review indicating the book's omissions.

6 The Villa del Casale is of particular interest to the sports historian because it was decorated with mosaics depicting various athletic activities. In his *Letters* the fifth-century Gallo-Roman aristocrat Sidonius Apollinaris almost unwittingly reveals the state of dilapidation and decrepitude into which roads, private houses, and public and ecclesiastical administration had fallen in the late Empire (Percival 1997).

7 Dates given for private individuals are for their lives; for emperors, kings, popes, and the like, for their reigns.

8 H. A. Harris (1972) points out that Plautus's and Terence's plays were based on, or even translated from, Greek originals, but thinks nonetheless that the athletic allusions must have been readily understood by his Roman audience (Harris 1972: 51–2).

9 Cicero, *De oratore* (55 BC), Budé, 2.4.20–21; *Orator* (46 BC), Loeb, 68.228–229; and *Tusculan Disputations* (45 BC), Loeb, 2.23.56–57 and 2.16.37–2.17.41.

10 Propertius's interest was spurred by the fact that in Sparta women and men mingled freely in public, and especially on the sports field, where they were naked – Degas did a famous painting on the subject (London, National Gallery) – whereas in Rome women were chaperoned. On the erotic dimension of Greek sport, see Guttmann (1996), Scanlon (2002), and McClelland (2002b).

11 Reis (1994) cites some 60 passages of various lengths, drawn from all part of Horace's work, in which the poet makes significant references to sport. Some of these texts will de discussed in later chapters.

12 In one of his *Satires* (Loeb, 1.5.48–49) Horace specifically says that for health reasons he and Virgil abstained from playing vigorous ball games.

13 Virgil (70–19 BC) was the protégé of Augustus's friend (and virtual culture minister) Maecenas, and through him became an intimate of the emperor. The poet had read parts of the *Aeneid* to Augustus, who encouraged him to continue working on it. The poem was still incomplete at Virgil's premature death, but Augustus authorized its publication and entrusted two of the poet's friends to make such emendations as seemed necessary (Suetonius, 'Virgil', in *Lives of Illustrious Men*, Loeb, 31–41). We may take it that everything in the poem that speaks of sport and athletics met with the emperor's approval. This was an area in which he had decided views and in which he would later establish definite policies with specific goals in mind (see Chapter 4).

14 In the *Georgics* (Loeb, 1.507–14), the rush towards war is compared to a chariot whose driver has lost control of the horses.

15 'Greek athletics … never became part of the social scene in the western Roman world as did [gladiators, wild-beast hunts, and chariot-racing]' (Harris 1972: 50). More recent research (Newby 2002, 2005) has shown this traditional opinion to be wrong-headed. See Lovatt (2004) for a detailed comparison of *Aeneid* 5 with the Olympic program and the games in *Iliad* 23 and in Statius's *Thebaid* 6.

16 Despite the narrative similarity between the *Aeneid* and the *Iliad*, Cairns (1989) argues that the Latin poem owes more to the *Odyssey*.

17 On the function of the *Aeneid* 5 games in this policy, see Lovatt (2004).

18 A reconstruction of the Circus Maximus with its elevated imperial box is reproduced in McKay (1970: pl. 26); McKay also comments briefly on the resemblance of this site to the Circus (139–40).

19 This document was originally published in Latin in the form of bronze tablets, but survived only in a copy, with an accompanying Greek translation, inscribed in stone in a temple in Ancyra (mod. Ankara) It is also referred to as the *Res gestae divi Augusti*, the accomplishments of the deified Augustus, or the *Index rerum a se gestarum*, record of his own accomplishments.

20 Seneca's views on these subjects have been studied in greater detail by Cagniart (2000). His correspondence is referred to by a number of different titles – *Moral Epistles*, *Letters to Lucilius* (or some combination of the two) – but will be called here simply *Letters*.

21 Harris (1972: 69) takes the two terms together as denoting an equivalent of the British military practice of 'marking time at the double', or quick marching on the spot.

22 See in particular Golvin (1988), Facchini (1990), and Bomgardner (2000) for the amphitheatres, Humphrey (1986) on the circuses. The dimensions of these formerly vast structures reflected not only the need to accommodate large numbers of spectators but also the imperial power they symbolized.

23 Meijer (2004a) points out that films dealing with gladiators usually pay little attention to chronology and thus portray their fights inaccurately.

24 Almost nothing is known of Flaccus's life except that he died perhaps prematurely before 93. Like Apollonius of Rhodes' earlier Greek poem of the same name (third century BC), his *Argonautica* is the story of Jason's search for and capture of the golden fleece. Apollonius's contemporary Theocritus also described the boxing match in his *Dioskouroi*, the story of Castor and Pollux. On the gloves used in this fight, see Lee (1997).

25 The poem was published in 92 and is part of the cycle of myths related to Oedipus and his descendants. On the mythology and archaeology of the Nemean Games, see Miller (2004).

26   The armed combat succinctly evokes gladiatorial fights, in that the participants 'nudo subeant concurrere ferro', submit to engaging with bare iron (*Thebaid* 6.911).

27   Harris (1972), Thuillier (1996a), and Lovatt (2004) have commented on *Thebaid* 6. Virgil (*Georgics*, Loeb, 3.19–20) boasted that he would achieve fame by bringing the Olympic and Nemean games to Rome (in a literary sense), but it was left to Statius to actually do so.

28   ' ... histrionalis favor et gladiatorum equorumque studia ... Quos alios adulescentulorum sermones excipimus, si quando auditoria intravimus?'.

29   Grodde (1997) analyzes these passages in some detail.

30   The popular view of Roman spectacle entertainments propagated in films and novels such as *Quo vadis?*, *Ben Hur*, and *Gladiator* derives mainly from Suetonius and from the successor volume to his *Twelve Caesars*, the largely anonymous *Lives of the Later Caesars*. See also Wyke 1997.

31   A couple of centuries later, a highly placed Roman official, Symmachus, states that it is an absolute priority to have gladiators in a show celebrating an election (*Letters*, Budé, 2.46).

32   He has lifted the phrase and the idea almost literally from Plato, *Laws*, 8.830a.

33   The notion that there is a fit between certain sports and certain physical types was adumbrated by Aristotle (*Rhetoric*, Loeb, 1361b) and expounded more fully by Philostratos, *On Gymnastics*, in Miller (1991: 25–7, 31–2, 39). In the Renaissance it was picked up by Bardi (1580) and applied to the physical requirements of the different positions on a *calcio* team.

34   For a description of *harpastum* and other ball games mentioned here, see Chapter 3.

35   An excerpt from the *Exhortation for Medicine* and the full text of the pamphlet on ball playing can be read in Miller (2004: 173–6, 121–4).

36   On *episkyros* see Crowther (1997), McClelland (2002a) and Elmer (forthcoming).

37   Partial translations are in Robinson (1955) and Sweet (1987).

38   He was able to obtain some Scottish dogs that astounded the public when they appeared on the day of the rehearsal ('praelusionis die').

39   The identification of Sidonius' game with *harpastum* is made by Thuillier (1996: 89–90); see also McClelland (2002a: 411).

40   *Etymologies* is generally thought to have been published around 600. In some editions the title is given as *Origins*.

3 Sport in the forgotten centuries (2)

1   'Between the fifth and ninth centuries figurative art, especially human representation, was attacked on all sides' (Huyghe 1968: 84).

2   Legends connect this boy with the future King Arthur, Merlin the Magician, and, anachronistically, with the son of the emperor Constantine II. In the early twelfth century Geoffrey of Monmouth repeats the story in his *History of the Kings of Britain* (Geoffrey 1985: 5.140), but states only that they were playing, without mentioning ball. In the *Estoire* [history] *de Merlin* (1230, quoted in Merdrignac 2002: 299) the game has become *soule à la crosse*, a game in which the ball was propelled by a heavy cudgel with a curved end that players would also use to hit their opponents (see Chapter 4).

3   The Latin original reads,

> 'Corpore fuit amplo atque robusto, statura eminenti. ... Exercebatur assidue equitando ac venando; ... quia vix ulla in terris natio invenitur quae in haec arte Francis possit aequari. Delectabatur etiam vaporibus aquarum naturaliter calentium, frequenti natatu corpus exercens; cuius adeo peritus fuit ut nullus ei

juste valeat anteferri. … Turbam invitavit, ita ut nonnumquam centum vel eo amplius homines una lavarentur'.

(Eginhard 1967: 66–8)

4 Flannery and Leech (2004) provide the most recent, most complete, and best reproduced collection of these illuminations and other depictions, as far as ball games are concerned. For the tournament and other knightly sports, see Barber and Barker (1989).

5 The floor mosaics at Zliten that are the most detailed source for understanding gladiatorial fights and other Roman spectacles are similarly a frame around a set of panels whose decorative content is thematically unrelated to the border (Aurigemma 1926).

6 These are reminiscent of Virgil's *lusus Troiae*.

7 Although Chrétien's account is short on precise detail and long on brutal effects – in the joust both knights are knocked right off their horses onto the ground, Erec's sword slices through his adversary's helmet and cuts into his skull – it probably is the closest thing we have to a description of a Roman gladiatorial combat. Medieval novels of knightly adventures are like modern action movies. The protagonists suffer blows and wounds that ought to incapacitate them, but they carry on afterwards as if nothing unusual had occurred.

8 In *Perceval* two sisters get into a violent quarrel as to which of two knights, to whom they are attracted, is better.

9 On William Marshall see Painter (1933) and Duby (1984).

10 Contemporary English biographies, such as the Chandos Herald's life of the Black Prince and the anonymous account of the accomplishments of Henry V make no allusion to their subjects' athletic prowess.

11 The importance of jousting in the fourteenth century as a means of establishing a knight's prowess and right to consideration is evident in another text (*Hugues Capet* 1997). In this epic biography of the first king of France – Hugues ruled from 987 to 996 – the would-be monarch boasts to his uncle of his success in jousting and tourneying, and is advised to continue this activity, because he will be very highly honoured everywhere ('vous serez honorez partout moult hautement' (ll. 106–10, 575–80) – all quite anachronistically, since jousting and tourneying did not yet exist in Hugues' time.

12 Boucicaut practiced mounting a horse fully armed, running and walking long distances to increase his breathing ('pour accoustumer a avoir longue aleine'), and throwing the hammer to strengthen his arms and hands. As a result, no other nobleman could equal his athletic exploits: jumping on a horse fully armed without using the stirrup; from the ground, leaping onto the shoulders of a mounted man using only the man's sleeve for support; vaulting over a warhorse's neck, again from the ground; climbing up between two narrow walls by simply pressing his arms and legs against them; and climbing the underside of ladder using only his hands (Boucicaut 1985: 24–5). A late thirteenth-century verse romance, *Le roman de Silence* (Heldris 1972) possibly provided Boucicaut with a model. At 11 years of age the hero can outdo all his contemporaries in wrestling ('palaistre'), jousting, and swordplay.

13 Froissart (1963) chronicles other jousting tournaments as well, though in less detail. The most complete tableau of all such events that took place in the fourteenth and fifteenth centuries, as well as the historical sources that report them, can be found in Barber and Barker (1989).

14 For other tournament mishaps, missed targets, and the like, see Anglo (1988).

15 Loosely translatable as 'playing football, field hockey, handball, and other games'.

16 In a sense Bayard was the last representative – at least before Don Quijote – of Medieval chivalry. His ignominious death in battle from a harquebus shot can almost be said to have put an end to the French Middle Ages.

17 Brantôme (1864: 4.159–61) describes a chivalric competition of 1559/60 in which two of the highest members of the French aristocracy, the duc de Nemours and François de Guise, ran at the ring, i.e. tried to catch a ring with their lances while galloping at high speed. The duke was dressed as a 'femme bourgeoise' and carried a big bunch of keys that clanged together at the rhythm of the horse, while his opponent was costumed as an Egyptian woman and carried a monkey in his left arm in lieu of a baby. The whole spectacle amused the spectators and caused them to laugh. Duncan-Jones (1991: 201–12) describes tournaments in England in 1580/1 in which the jousting was relegated to a less important status, behind the costumes and décor.

18 Molinet's point of departure is the homonymy between the French word for Ghent – Gand – and the glove – *gant* – used when playing *jeu de paume*. Charles' poem is also in Gillmeister (1997: 130–1, with an English translation) and Molinet's in Gillmeister (2007), also with a translation.

19 On the *giuoco della pugna*, see Heywood (1969/1904); *calcio* designates soccer-football in modern Italian, but from the fifteenth through the eighteenth centuries the word referred to a game in which an inflatable ball could be hit with the hand, kicked, or even carried.

20 See Heywood (1969/1904), Davis (1994), and Rizzi (1995) for studies based on archival materials in Italy, Carter (1992) for England, and Mehl (1990) for France.

21 Kurt Lindner (Crescenzi 1957/1305: 10) notes that from the beginning of the fourteenth century the nature of European hunting literature changed owing to the increasing importance of personal experience as a guarantee of veracity. This was a major trend in European thought that had its roots in Abelard's twelfth-century principle that the universal can only be derived from the individual and that was firmly established in the early fourteenth century by William of Ockham, who refused 'to stretch knowledge beyond the bounds of ascertainable experience' (Leff 1958: 109 and 280). Turned around, this principle guarantees the validity of general rules that are derived out of experience. For a broader treatment of this subject, see Chapter 7.

22 See Innamorati (1965) for an anthology of early Italian hunting texts, beginning with Frederick II.

23 It was translated into English c. 1400 by a cousin of King Henry IV, under the title *Master of Game*, and passed off as an original.

24 Liechtenauer's book is a significant exception to this rule.

25 Dürer's book lay neglected until the early nineteenth century, and was not printed until 1907–9 when Dörnhöffer reproduced it in the *Jahrbuch der kunsthistorischen Sammlungen des allerhöchsten Kaiserhauses* and then republished it in 1910 as a separate large folio volume that included the Codex Wallerstein and other materials. The wrestling drawings have been reprinted in *Chronik* (1978).

26 Both the spurious Ott illustrations and Auerswald's book are reproduced in *Chronik* (1978).

27 Rules for a 1465 tournament in Milan were published by Angelucci (1866) and in English translation by Joachim Rühl (2006); Rühl's article also includes rules drawn up in England in 1466 that were meant to apply throughout the realm. On German tournament league rules, see Rühl 2007; and on the techniques used for keeping track of the score, Rühl 2006. Research in this area has also been done by Greg Malszecki, but it remains largely unpublished.

28 For a full account of Renaissance physical education, at least as far as Italy was concerned, see Körbs (1938). Humanist books on education that advocate physical

training, especially the handling of weapons and horses, may owe something to the importance of sport in the biographies of famous Medieval heroes.

29 Marozzo himself says that he began the book in his 'prima giovinezza', first flush of youth, but has waited until his 'ultima eta', his last years, to finish it. Thimm (1968/1898) lists a 1517 edition of Marozzo's book (Venice: Marchio Sessa), but this remains a phantom no one has seen. It may be the result of Thimm's omitting the 'L' from the date of the title page of the 1567 re-edition (MDLXVII). The fact that the main body of Marozzo's 1536 text is in old-fashioned gothic typeface rather than roman might also suggest that the publisher was passing off unsold 1517 copies as something new by adding a new title page.

30 Manciolino explicitly condemns the wordiness of his predecessors in the field, a remark that can only refer to Marozzo and that may therefore demonstrate at least the circulation of his text, if not its actual publication, before 1531.

31 'Accompagnando sempre la mano con il piede & il piede con la mano' (1531: f. 5v°).

32 The principles of the module, proportion, and harmony go back to the first-century BC architect Vitruvius. They were first enunciated for the Renaissance by Altoni's fellow Florentine, Leon Battista Alberti (*Della pittura*, on painting [1956/1435] and *De re aedificatoria*, on the art of building [1988/1450]).

33 Altoni's sense that his work broke with that of his predecessors is clear already from his title: *Monomachia* is the ancient Greek word for a gladiatorial fight; its use here places Altoni within an ancient tradition.

34 For a full account of these books and all the many others published from the fifteenth through the seventeenth century, see Anglo (2000).

35 On this, see Chapter 7 below and McClelland (1984). After 1600 the images in Italian manuals tend to revert to the anecdotal, showing gory scenes in which fencers drive long rapiers through their adversaries' eyes and out the back of their head (e.g. Giganti 1606, Capoferro da Cagli 1610).

36 Barletta (1993: 247) affirms that in the fifteenth century there was a boom in the production of furniture and that these pieces were often decorated with scenes of jousting and other games.

37 The 'tennis' that is the subject of these books and others up to the nineteenth century is of the indoor variety, also called 'real' or 'royal' tennis.

38 These rules can be found in De Luze (1933: 246–51).

39 Bredekamp (1993) takes the opposite view. On the humanistic character of Bardi's *Discorso see Mommsen* (1942).

40 A much less interesting, but more widely known, manual of horse vaulting is Stokes (1652).

41 Duncan-Jones (1991: 23, 163–7) also reports that Sidney was an avid tennis player and almost fought a duel with the earl of Oxford over who had precedence on the court.

42 'Filopono', Italicized Greek for 'lover of hard labour', could be translated as 'workaholic'. It was the nickname that Stefano di Francesco Sterponi, professor of rhetoric at Pisa and then at Florence, bestowed on himself.

43 The real title of the 1617 text – it was reissued in 1618 – was a *Declaration to His Subjects, Concerning Lawfull Sports to be Used*. It acquired the *Book of Sports* label when James' son Charles I republished it 1633.

44 The most thorough study of Dover's Cotswold Games is in Rühl (1975). On the application of the term 'Olympic' to these games, see Burns (1985).

45 This theme will be explored more fully in the final chapter.

4 The sports, the athletes, the material setting

1 Cicero, *Laws*, Budé, 2.15.38: 'Iam ludi publici … sint corporum certationes cursu et pugillatu et luctatione curriculisque equorum usque ad certam victoriam'.

2 I have modified the Loeb translation slightly. The 46–5 games became incorporated into the annual calendar of Roman festivities, under the title of Caesar's Victory Games (*Ludi Victoriae Caesaris*) and were held every year from 20–30 July.

3 The last recorded races in Rome were organized by the Ostrogothic king Totila in 549. Olivová (1989: 86) asserts that 'the graphic evidence suggests that the Frankish court, especially during the reign of Charlemagne … was again the scene of chariot-racing at the beginning of the ninth century', but she offers no authority for that remark.

4 Thuillier (1996b: 48–50, 61–9, 100–13) gives larger measurements and thinks a race might have lasted a half hour.

5 For photographs of charioteer paraphernalia and of mosaics depicting races, see Landes (1990).

6 Horsmann (1998: 172–306) lists 223 known charioteers; of these, 30% were slaves, 10% were freedmen, and 2% were free-born. He was not able to reach any conclusion concerning the social status of the others.

7 See Mahoney 2001: 27–35 for inscriptions detailing the lives and winnings of several charioteers. Like Greek athletes, stage actors, and other performers, charioteers had a union – or at least an association – that protected their interests.

8 On the circus as a sacred space for the *ludi*, Clavel-Lévêque (1984).

9 That a sport requires a symbolic basis in order to survive is, I think, beyond dispute. The argument that chariot racing disappeared because no one would pay for it (e.g. Cameron 1973) puts the cart before the horse. No one would pay for it because it had become an exercise that lacked signification.

10 The belief that Greek games were not popular among the Romans seems largely based on a few remarks made by Cicero. Crowther (2001) demonstrates, however, that Cicero had a much more nuanced approach to Greek athletics and even in places looked on them quite favourably. On the basis of mosaics and other archaeological findings, Newby (2002, 2005) argues that Greek games were quite popular in Rome, at least by the second and third centuries. Ghiron-Bistagne (1992) has studied Greek athletic competitions in Roman France, where they were more common than once thought.

11 Although these games were called *ludi*, and not *certamina* or *agōnes*, Caldelli (1993) argues that the program was essentially Greek in nature.

12 For a description of the stadium's structure, see Caldelli 1993: 83–4; for a reconstruction of the building, Facchini 1990: 76–7.

13 For mosaics illustrating Greek-style athletic events, see Newby (2005: 178–9).

14 'La gladiature a été tenue en horreur par les Romains, ou par certains Romains, ou, pour nous exprimer plus rigoureusement, à moitié par tous les Romains', On the nineteenth century's distaste for gladiatorial games and its willingness to believe that the ancient Greek east shared this distaste, see Robert (1940), who effectively destroys this myth, and more recently Wiedemann (1992: 128–9).

15 Following the example of Theodosius I, the emperor Eugene gave Symmachus some Saxon prisoners to fight as gladiators in a show he was putting on in 399, but 29 of them succeeded in strangling themselves to death (Symmachus, *Letters*, Budé, 2.46).

16 This is the spectacle that Seneca criticizes as being harmful to the moral character of the spectators and as lacking any display of skill such as one can appreciate in a regular gladiatorial show (*Letters* 7; see Chapter 1).

17 For the gladiators' oath, Horace, *Satires*, Loeb, 2.7.58–9, Seneca, *Letters*, Loeb, 37, and Petronius, *Satyricon*, Budé, 15.117; also Barton (1993: 14–15).

18 *Cf.* Junckelmann (2000a: 31): 'Gladiatorial combat … can … be correctly considered a specifically Roman form of competitive sport' (also 2000b: 12–13). W. Backhaus defended the notion that gladiatorial fights could be considered sport on the grounds that we cannot judge earlier periods on the basis of our own sensibility, but have to take theirs into account (quoted in Weiler 1981: 258). Thuillier (1996b: 12–13) refuses the notion such fights might be sport, but admits that they did have a sporting dimension and that Romans did not perceive any fundamental difference between them and other athletic spectacles.

19 For the contradictory, inconsistent treatment accorded gladiators, exploited for the pleasure they give, admired for their bravery, attractive to women, but excluded from society, see Tertullian (*On Spectacles*, Loeb, 21–2) and Aigner (1988).

20 Wiedemann (1992: 160) suggests that as soon as barbarians were allowed to join the Roman army (in the late Empire) and thus be incorporated into the apparatus of the state, 'it was difficult to define the margins of the civilised world' and gladiatorial fights became semiotically redundant.

21 Meijer (2004a: 208–19) gives a very readable account of the metamorphoses of the Colosseum from the fifth through to the twentieth century.

22 The site of the amphitheatre at Pompeii, at the southeast corner of the city had another cost advantage: the existing walls could be used as support for the tiered seating on the southern and eastern sides. Employing the perimeter wall as an amphitheatre support continued as a method of construction into the early modern period (Berce 1982). Golvin (1988) has examined the geographical situation of over 180 amphitheatres.

23 E.g. the manufacture of Trimalchio's goblets that bear the images of gladiators.

24 It is worth noting that, when it comes to terminology, the Romans used the word *certamen*, the word that comes closest in Latin to our word 'sport' and that was theoretically reserved for Greek games, to denote chariot races (Ovid), gladiatorial fights (Cicero), and *venationes* (Cassiodorus).

25 On the competitiveness of traditional Roman exercises see Vegetius 19951.9 and 2.23.

26 See Lovatt (2004: 109) for a table that sets out in detail the differences between Homer's games (*Iliad* 23), the Olympics, the Roman *ludi*, Virgil's games, and the games in Statius (*Thebaid* 6).

27 The importance of baths to the Romans cannot be overestimated. Writing in fifth century Gaul, Sidonius (*Letters*, Loeb, 2.9) describes in considerable detail a makeshift sauna, hot-tub, and cold bath that he and his friends built at a country house whose proper baths were still under construction.

28 Thuillier (1996b: 87–91, suggests that though there were no organized ball games for spectators, professionals probably did demonstrations in the baths and *palaestrae*.

29 Properly speaking, *ludus* in Latin referred to the ceremonial, ritual games that involved chariot racing and the like, while *lusus* meant 'play'. However, over time the denotation of *ludus* broadened and *lusus* tended to disappear from usage.

30 Mercurialis's classification is based largely on references found in Martial's *Epigrams*.

31 Sidonius's editors – Warmington (Loeb), Loyen (Budé) – have overlooked this phrase, preferring instead to try to decipher 'per catastropham', which occurs with reference to ball game only in another of Sidonius' letters (2.9); it might mean a tackle that turns an opposing player over, or simply an off-balance swerve (to avoid the ball) from which the player cannot recover.

32 See also Thuillier (1996b) and Crowther (1997).

33 Although Vegetius makes no mention of ball games as part of a soldier's training, Galen (1967, 1991) makes it clear that small-ball games have military value (McClelland 2003a).

34 I.e. the hereditary, land-owning patrician class disappeared and the priestly caste – quantitatively insignificant in Rome – became so numerous under Christianity as to constitute a class of its own (in France it became the first of the three estates).

35 *Jeu de paume*, or just *paume*, involved hitting the ball with your hand off a vertical surface that had a projecting slanted roof called a penthouse. To translate it as 'handball' is misleading, since it corresponds neither to what North Americans think of as handball nor to what the term normally means in Europe. It eventually evolved into indoor or real/royal tennis. Morgan (1995) rejects the notion that *jeu de paume* originated in the cloisters.

36 In this, as we shall see, *soule* resembled the knightly tournament.

37 There is only one image from antiquity – a bas-relief on a sixth-century BC Athenian statue base – that shows ball-players using sticks (reproduced in Harris 1972: pl. 47; Miller 2004: fig. 259).

38 Gillmeister (1997) argues that violent ball games such as *soule* and football were peasant or lower-class imitations of the knightly tournament.

39 The *Cantigas de Santa María* are a collection of hymns to the Virgin Mary together with accounts in prose of the various miracles she performed. The miracle connected to this image specifies that the player who is the object of the Virgin's intervention has been given a ring by his 'amiga' and is fearful of damaging it when playing ball ('con miedo de torcer el anillo cuando le diese a la pelota').

40 What follows here is mostly based on Heywood (1969/1904) and Salvestrini (1934). Herlihy (1958) argues that Heywood's account of the bridges is inaccurate.

41 *Pome* is thus described in *Ammaestramenti* (c.1550), but a later Florentine contemporary, Giulio Dati (1824/1600), claims it is a game that begins with the teams throwing hard, apple-shaped objects at each other, and then turns into a kind of *en masse* wrestling.

42 Until 1605 the Sienese *palio* was run through the streets between two specified points. That distance was then measured and recomputed as a certain number of laps around the Piazza del Campo. That this move was made to accommodate spectators seems clear. Montaigne rented a window space to watch the Florentine *palio* in 1581 and complained that watching it was not much of a pleasure, because it took place through narrow streets and one did not see anything except the horses racing madly by (Montaigne 1983; McClelland 2003b).

43 Changing tactics and technology in the field of war and weaponry (Contamine 1984; Hall 1997) modified conceptions of what might be sport and who might play.

44 Gian Fernando Spagnuolo, Gian Antonio Napoletano, Nardo Veneziano, Vincenzo Flisco, 'Jaches et Verdelot Francesi' (Scaino 1555: 46–7, 246–7, 277). The third and fourth named are in the employ of the prince of Ferrara, Scaino's patron. Morgan (1995: 29) cites a certain Richard Stairs as a notable mid-fifteenth-century tennis player.

45 Visiting the French court in 1572, the earl of Lincoln reported back to lord Burleigh, Elizabeth I's chief minister, that the after-dinner entertainment consisted, among other things, of 'dyvars vantars [vaulters] and leapers of dyvars sortes, vearie excellent', although he does not mention Tuccaro by name (Nichols 1823: 1.304).

46 In his *Essais* Montaigne (1965: 412) condemns men of low birth who, unable to comport themselves with the bearing and decency that is proper to the nobility, try to substitute acrobat feats.

47 Despite its vastness, the palace Louis XIV constructed at Versailles after 1660 provided no spaces for the practice of athletics, except for an enclosed tennis court that was actually 500 metres from the palace itself. Interestingly the Escorial palace of Spain's dour Philip II (begun in 1557) made, as far as I know, no provision for sport.

48 Rabelais's hero Gargantua, influenced by ancient Greco-Roman ideals, goes there to play 'à la balle, à la paulme, à la pile trigone', i.e. a rugby-like game (see Ill. 8), outdoor

tennis, and three-cornered catch (Rabelais 1994/1534: 65). Braque was in the area of the present-day Place de l'Estrapade.

49 Francioni (1993: pl. 15) shows the wide, straight Via Tornabuoni blocked off, with spectators watching two four-man teams play *pallone*.

50 The names that Settimanni supplies all indicate that the players were of lower class origin and had some other form of principal employment. E.g. one was called 'il Biccherajo', meaning perhaps a bartender ('bicchiere' = drinking glass); another was a cook to a cardinal, a third a 'setajuolo' or silk-worker.

51 For old maps showing the place and shape of the *prato*, see Boffito and Mori (1973). The configuration of the streets in that area – Via Melegnano, Borgo Ognissanti, Il Prato, Viale Fratelli Rosselli, and Lungarno Amerigo Vespucci – still replicates the Prato's outline.

52 On the meaning and significance for *calcio* of the terms 'wall' and 'moat', see Chapter 7.

53 Bardi's insistence that each *calcio* player should have the physique and the skills appropriate to the demands of the position he is asked to play is pre-figured by Aristotle (*Rhetoric*, Loeb, 1361b), Epictetus (*Discourses*, Loeb, 3.1.5–6), and Philostratos (in Miller 1991). Bardi also feels the need to specify that boys and old men cannot tolerate the physical demands of the game. As well, those who are ugly or too thin or have some physical disability – including blindness – should not play for aesthetic reasons: they would look ridiculous out on the public square.

54 This subject has been amply and expertly rehearsed by Sydney Anglo (2000) and more recently by Serge Vaucelle (2004). See also Chapter 3 above.

5 Tournaments, jousting, and the game of death

1 In his *Cligès*, Chrétien (1957/1176) specifies that the tourney is to take place in the plains between Oxford and Wallingford, towns that are 20 kilometres apart. Medieval tournaments could cover quite large distances.

2 Del Corazza (1894/1438) similarly reports on jousts and tournaments frequently taking place within the confines of Florence during the first third of the fifteenth century.

3 This remark is not completely true for Italy, where both the Colosseum in 1332 and the arena in Verona in the late sixteenth century could still be used for jousting and other equestrian events (Tosi 1946; Boiteux 1982; Montaigne 1983). Malcolmson (1973) remarks that even in the eighteenth century no places had been set aside exclusively for sport and Goethe (1976: 1.60–1) marvels at the fact that the Veronese did not think to play their *pallone* game in the arena, which had been restored.

4 This was the length of the permanent jousting course Henri had had constructed in the grounds of the Tournelles palace (Sauval 1724: 2.683–5). The joust in which he was killed actually took place on a temporary course presumably of a similar length. Pictorial representations usually show jousting courses to be much shorter, but that is because the artist has had only a limited space available. The birds-eye view of the jousts in the Piazza Navona in Rome (Barber and Barker 1989: 203) shows the course to be about one-third the length of the square, which is in turn about 300 metres long.

5 There is an illustration of how the rider gradually lowered his lance into place in Pluvinel (1625) and reproduced in Barber and Barker (1989: 205).

6 My calculations and other quantitative data are based on Malszecki (1982/1981).

7 Even when rules were not formally enunciated, it is clear from descriptions such as the one furnished by La Marche (1883) that they were in place and recognized by the participating knights.

8 Most contemporary accounts state, however, that the tourney did not actually start until 17 or 21 June.

9 Henri's program of jousting and hand-to-hand fighting is very like that of a tournament in Vicenza in 1552 (Messeri 1894), indicating that these events were all simple variants of a basic structure.

10 One of the judges, the seigneur de Tavannes (1508–73), says in his memoirs that the event was organized 'à l'imitation des anciens tournois' (Tavannes 1838/1573: 225). Bourciez (1967/1886: 19) claims that Henri was besotted with reading Spanish novels and terribly nostalgic for the chivalric exploits of past times.

11 The 1443 tourney described by La Marche (1883) was also a *pas d'armes*, but the *tenans* numbered 13 and none of them had anything to prove.

12 'Several clear-headed persons … saying that the majesty of the King was such that he ought to be the judge of the contest and not a participant'. In 1548 Henri had had more sense. He cancelled a dangerous joust 'con deminino', a lance with a long hard metal point, because, according to the Mantuan ambassador, jousts of this type were not appropriate for princes of his rank (Truffi 1911: 225). In 1559 Henri may also have been motivated by his own enthusiasm for 'rough sports and exercises' (Baumgartner 1988: 49 and 103–4). Brantôme (1864–82: 3. 277 ff.) reports that the king could not sit still. If he was not hunting or riding, he was running at the ring or playing tennis – he was very good at playing the dangerous net position – or pall-mall or rough ball games. If it was cold and snowy, he would slide and do long jumps on the ice, build snow forts and have snowball fights – always in front of an audience of specially summoned female courtiers.

13 To be sure, this was not an ordinary tournament, but a more violent kind of encounter called a 'round table' in which the knights sought to prove their skills and strength ('vires suas attemptarent').

14 Francisco de Alcocer (1559: 286–301) paints an even more sombre picture. In tournaments on horseback and in jousting there is 'peligro probable de muerte', probable danger of death, though in the kind of jousts that are used in 'our Spain' this is not the case. He also adds that 100–200 people are killed by bulls every year in Spain.

15 It also became more complicated, more subject to damage, and harder to repair. La Marche (1883: 326–7 and 323–3) reports several delays and postponements owing to damaged armour during jousts in Burgundy in July–August 1443.

16 Throckmorton was the English ambassador to Paris and by his account the only foreign envoy actually present at the joust. Romier (1914: 2.380) reproduces the size and shape of the two splinters that were extracted from Henri's eye. As Throckmorton says, they were 'of a good bigness'.

17 In his description of the state of England in 1685, Macaulay (1856: 1.320) states that, 'Multitudes assembled to see gladiators hack each other to pieces with deadly weapons, and shouted with delight when one of the combatants lost a finger or an eye'.

18 'Apres que par une longue guerre cruelle & violente, les armes ont esté exercées & exploictées en divers endroitz avec effusion de sang humain & trespernicieux actes que la guerre produict, … les armes (maintenant esloignées de toute cruaulté & violence) se peuvent & doivent employer avec plaisir & utilité, par ceux qui desirent s'esprouver & exercer en tous vertueux & louables faictz & actes' (Du Bellay 1908–31: 6.72–3).

19 In *Romeo and Juliet* (3.1) Shakespeare mocks the nobleman's willingness to quarrel and duel no matter how slight the pretext.

20 The later prose versions of Geoffrey's chronicle differ in the details of this event, tending to specify that the sports took place in open spaces outside the city (*campos extra civitatem*). Some mention boxing (*cestibus*), others a tournament (*simulachrum prelii*

equestrem ludum), an unidentifiable contest (*celtibus*), javelin (*hasta*), throwing heavy stones (*ponderosorum lapidum iactu*), and chess (*scaccis*).

21   A thirteenth-century chronicle attributes the invention of tournaments to a certain Geoffroi de Preuilly, who was killed in 1062 (Parisse 1985: 176). Parisse, following Georges Duby, rejects the notion that they were 'invented', and sees them – as do indeed most historians now – as evolving out of the 'petites guerres' or 'guerres privées' of Carolingian times.

22   On the commitments of knighthood in the feudal system, in addition to Goetz (1993) see Duby (1984), Scaglione (1991), and Flori (1998).

23   'Play a game that was not worthy of his manly qualities and that was not an imitation of war'. The Latin text borrows the classical terminology of Roman sport: 'certare palaestra ... ludere'. Du Bellay was the author of a set of poems commissioned by the king to celebrate the 1559 tournament. It was intended as a 'souvenir program' to be available in time for the event, but had not been finished printing before Henri's accident (Du Bellay 1908–31: 6.1.37–74 and 78–97).

24   'Erec had no intention of capturing horses or knights, but only of jousting and of doing well, so that his prowess would be evident'.

25   England's Edward III (1327–77) was particularly fond of tourneying in strange outfits (Barber and Barker 1989: 32–6).

6 Sport in the service of the *res publica*

1   Even Joachim du Bellay's Hymne au Roy sur la prinse de Callais had devoted several lines to Guise's 'vertu valeureuse' and to his other victorious military exploits on behalf of Henri (Du Bellay 1908–31: 6.20–32).

2   In a 21 June letter Nicolas Throckmorton, then English ambassador to Paris, mentions that Mary and the Dauphin frequently displayed the arms of England quartered with their own on their personal escutcheons (Throckmorton 1863/1559: 324–5, 347).

3   'I was not very strong when it came to wielding weapons and striking blows', quoted in Ricciardi 1992: 167.

4   The monument was Luigi Pulci's 1,280-line poem, *La Giostra* (Pulci 1986/1471: 61–120; the interpretation of the motto is in stanza 64, p. 86. The subject of *La Giostra* is ostensibly an earlier joust, held in 1466 on the occasion of the marriage of Lorenzo's sister, but the transference to the 'coming of age' joust in 1469 was apparently obvious.

5   On the non-adaptability of jousts and tourneying to central Italian customs, see Szabó (1985); also Trexler (1980: 233–5) and Heidi Chrétien (1994: 44).

6   'Wir behaupten dagegen: der Krieg ist Nichts als eine Fortsetzung des politischen Verkehrs mit Einmischung anderer Mittel' (Von Clausewitz 1993: 357).

7   Du Bellay had actually obtained a copyright in 1557 for what was by far the longest poem, 'L'entreprise du roy-daulphin', in the volume described in Chapter 5 as the 'souvenir program' for the 1559 tournament.

8   Ginestet (1991) is the only full-length study of the *collegia iuvenum* and of their predecessors, the *iuventutes*.

9   The term paradigm and what it denotes are borrowed from Thomas S. Kuhn's landmark essay, *the Structure of Scientific Revolutions*: '"Paradigms" [are] ... universally recognized scientific achievements that for a time provide model problems and solutions to a community of practitioners' (Kuhn 1962: x).

10   As Nelis (2001: 193) points out, the connection between Aeneas's stipulation of a *nondinum* of purification followed by athletic contests is semiotically complex with relation to later Roman ritual practices. Francis Cairns (1989: 218–19) argues that,

'games … may have had even greater religious significance for the Romans [than for the Greeks]'.

11 Briggs (1975: 268–9) claims that *naumachiae* were popular events in Virgil's time, but the one organized by Caesar seems to have been unique at the time the *Aeneid* was written. The boat race also seems to be a surrogate for other sports and activities. The sailors' bodies are oiled like those of Greek athletes (5.135), the ships carve furrows into the water (5.142) and thus become the ploughs of traditional Roman farmers, and much of the vocabulary used to describe the boat race is, in fact, drawn from chariot racing (especially 5.144–6 but also elsewhere). Feldherr (1995) has analysed Virgil's debt to contemporary circus spectacles.

12 Briggs (1975: 282) has described the *lusus Troiae* as an 'exquisite team performance' that enunciated an Augustan ideal.

13 The history of the *lusus Troiae* is long and complex (Heller 1946), but it was apparently revived as an activity for upper-class Roman youths by the dictator Sulla (138–78 BC), according to Plutarch (*Cato the Younger*, Loeb, 3.1). Julius Caesar staged the game and Augustus put it on 'very frequently, with older and younger boys, since he believed that this exhibition showed off the natural qualities of the Roman people' (Suetonius, *Augustus*, Loeb, 43). It certainly required a superior degree of horsemanship.

14 Virgil achieves his meaning very succinctly, through an intricate syntax that is worth quoting:

Actiaque Iliacis celebramus litora ludis	The Actian shores we honour with Trojan games,
Exercent patrias oleo labente palaestras	My comrades, stripped for action, slippery with oil,
Nudati socii.	Practice the wrestling of the fatherland.

Although a *palaestra* (Gk. *palaistra*) was strictly speaking a wrestling school attached to a gymnasium, in Latin and by Virgil's time it could simply designate a place to exercise, or the exercises performed there.

15 According to legend, Aeneas' son Iulus (also called Ascanius) was the progenitor of the clan to which both Julius Caesar and Augustus himself belonged, hence making them descendants of Venus and at least partially divine.

16 The allusion to wrestling on yellow sand (*fulva luctantur harena*) may be an allusion to the yellow dust (*xanthē konis*) that Greek wrestlers covered themselves with, according to Philostratos, *Gymnastikos* 56 (Miller 1991). In addition, of course *(h)arena* also evokes the stadium and the amphitheatre, called 'arenas' precisely because of the sand that covered their floors. *Cf.* also *Aeneid* 7.160–5 where the youth of Latium, a potential ally of the Trojans and, historically, a privileged component of Rome, are seen riding horses, racing chariots, practicing archery and javelin, and challenging each other in foot races and boxing.

17 Philippe-Auguste's famous contemporary, William Marshal, was described by his thirteenth-century biographer as having the kind of physical build that would have made him suitable to be a Roman emperor ('de la faiture / Resemblout il asez haut home / Por estre e[m]perére de Rome' (William 1891–1901/1220: ll. 730–2).

18 The 1457 decree (reproduced in Flannery and Leech 2004: 259, pl. 262) is taken as evidence of the antiquity of golf, but in fact the word at that time designated a very rough game closer in style to football.

19 The race continued to be run until 1858 and was revived in 1902. The wooden obelisks were replaced by the present stone ones in 1608.

20 Curiously, Bardi omits from this list another sporting activity, fencing, in which the Italians in 1580 were the acknowledged masters of Europe.

7 Athletics within the social fabric

1 The Latin text reads as follows:

> ... iam pridem ex quo suffragia nulli
> vendimus, effudit curas; nam qui dabat olim
> imperium fasces legiones omnia, nunc se
> continet atque duas tantum res anxius optat,
> panem et circenses.

2 *Cf. Aeneid* 5, where failure on the part of some of the exiled Trojans to attend the sports festival leads to their exclusion from the future Roman nation. Ovid's description of the *ludi* and the *munera* as good places to pick up girls (*Amores*, Budé, 3.2) suggests a positive social cohesion of a different sort, but moralists like the Stoic Seneca (*Letters*, Loeb, 7.80) and the Christians Tertullian (*De spectaculis*, Loeb), Prudentius (*Against Symmachus*, Budé), and St Augustine (*Confessions*, Budé, 1.10.16, 3.8.16, 6.8.13) criticize the *ludi* as morally and intellectually deleterious. Stoic and Christian attitudes were not the same however. Cicero and Seneca may have deplored the brutality they witnessed, but neither of them appears to have gotten up from his seat and gone home.

3 In his Italian travel journal Goethe (1976/1786–7: 55–6) imagines in a very powerful way just how the shape of the amphitheatre transformed the ancient crowd:

> Thus the multi-headed, multi-opinioned, fickle beast, wandering hither and yon, sees itself united into a single noble body, destined to be a single unit, bound and consolidated into a single mass, invigorated as one single shape, being of one single mind.

4 Already in 56 BC Cicero had made it clear that the 'populus Romanus' could express its opinion as part of the crowd of spectators at chariot races and gladiatorial fights ('ludorum gladiatorumque consessu') (Cicero, *Pro Sestio*, Loeb, 50.106).

5 The notion that strenuous physical activity must display the kind of gracefulness that signifies one is in control of one's bodily movements was a stipulated element of Greek gymnastic training (Plato, *Laws* 7–8). It is interesting to note that the word *palaestra* has come to mean for Cicero not just any old wrestling school but one in which you learned to fight in a manner that was as attractive to the onlookers as it was effective against an opponent. The idea that any productive gesture must combine beauty and utility was central to Roman thought.

6 Isidore (1991/600: 16–26) groups the *certamina* under the general heading of *ludus gymnicus*, games practiced in the gymnasium or palaestra.

7 Briggs (1975) emphasizes the manner in which Virgil's treatment of the athletic events alters their Homeric nature and brings them in line with Augustus's moral and social ideals.

8 Sidonius is also at pains to point out that he and the students with whom he played needed the physical exercise to limber up after too many hours spent in sedentary occupations.

9 A mark was worth about two-thirds of a pound sterling. For a résumé and an analysis of Richard's innovative 1194 decree, see Barber and Barker (1989: 24–6).

10 Knights enhanced their appearance and the public's ability to identify them by wearing elaborate decorative headpieces on their helmets, see, *inter alia*, René d'Anjou (1986).

11 On the relation between sport and sex in general, see Guttmann (1996), Scanlon (2002), and Guttmann *et al.* (2002).

12 On the role of spectators at early modern sports spectacles, see Guttmann (1986: 35–52).

13 Later illustrations in the book showing the tournament itself also reveal that 'la foule du peuple' did not bother to turn up.

14 Pasquier (1586: f. 85v°), who saw Henri's accident 'with my own eyes' spoke of there being an infinite number of witnesses, an 'infinité de tesmoins'.

15 Football is first recognized in decrees by a specific designation from 1314 on, both in Latin and the French that was still the administrative language in England: 'pelotes de pee [pied], pila pediva, pila pedalis', and no longer simply 'ludus pilae', the term in general use since Isidore.

16 On this see also Heywood (1969/1904) and Davis (1994).

17 Athletics might also be used to publicly degrade already marginalized social groups – Jews, prostitutes, poor old men and boys – by forcing them to race naked on foot or on donkeys at times of public celebration such as Carnival or the patron saint's day (Montaigne 1983/1580–1, the April mural in the Palazzo Schifanoia in Ferrara). On Carnival violence and degradation visited on the vulnerable members of society, see Burke (1978: 184–8).

18 Elias and Dunning (1972: 188) list 23 royal edicts in Britain against football between the fourteenth and the early seventeenth century.

19 It is also true that *soule*, being a cross-country game, could be more easily played in winter, when the fields were not under cultivation.

20 I am grateful to George Eisen for giving me a copy of Simri's article, Ilana Zinguer for providing me with an initial summary of it, and Vincent Decaen for translating both articles into English.

21 The online *London Encyclopedia* estimates the population of London to have been as much as 50,000 in the year 200, to have dropped to 14,000 by 1100, but to have climbed to perhaps 25,000 in 1200. Paris reputedly had 80,000 inhabitants in the year 150, only 20,000 at the first millennium, but over the next 200 years increased more than exponentially to 120,000 (see www.absoluteastronomy.com).

22 There is a modern transcription of the text in Heywood (1969/1904: 175–6) and an English translation and analysis in McClelland (2002a: 415–16, n. 15). There is a further description of *pome* in the *Ammaestramenti* (58r°–v°) but it concerns only the one-on-one tactics to be used when trying to catch another player or avoid being caught by him.

23 Because of the nudity, the author of the game's description says it is now a country game, unfamiliar to city-dwellers.

24 When a list of more precise rules was added to Bardi's *Discorso* in the 1673 edition, the first of them stipulated that *calcio* had obligatorily to be played at Sta Croce (1580/1978: 1.131).

25 The maps and views of Florence executed after 1580 (Boffito and Mori 1973 and the collection displayed in the Museo di Firenze Com'Era) show a line of buildings erected on the southern part of the Prato; this suggests that the space had by then lost its sacred character.

8 Body and mind: after the renaissance

1 For the content and shape of some of the material in this chapter I am indebted to Jill Levenson, François Roudaut, and the late Sheldon Zitner. The sword fight that is the subject of the first part of this chapter may be thought to be not sport and therefore out of place in this book. To argue that, however, is to assume a continuity of mentalities from the sixteenth century to now, which – following Michel Foucault (1966) – I do not believe to be the case. There is certainly animosity between Tybalt and the Montague clan, but the fighting in which they indulge is not really different from the willing but mortal encounters of the young Neapolitan nobles described by Petrarch (1934: 5.6) as gladiators or of the seventeenth-century swordfighters that Macaulay (1856: 1.320) talks about.

2 The 'books of arithmetic' that Shakespeare and his contemporaries might have known, from Robert Record's *The Ground of Artes, Teachyng the Worke and Practice of Arithmetike* (1542) through Jacques Peletier du Mans' *L'Aritmetique* (1549) to Bernard Salignac's *Principles of Arithmeticke* (Eng. trans. 1616 but written in Latin sometime earlier) illustrate the resolutely commercial character of this branch of mathematics. Examples usually reflect the problems of small wholesalers. The culminating chapters of all three books are devoted to 'accoumptyng,' and even in their earlier chapters they frequently rely for examples on case studies drawn from small business.

3 According to the edition used, this is either the third or the fourth scene of Act 2.

4 A *minim* (= half-note) was in the sixteenth century the basic symbol of musical notation, the way the quarter-note is now.

5 George Silver (1599/1972: 514, 563) tells about a '*Signior Rocco*', an '*Italian* teacher of Defence … that would have hit anie Englishman with a thrust, just upon any button in his doublet'.

6 Romeo is able to out-fence Tybalt for reasons that have nothing to do with technique, but with moral character and justifiable motivation, in the same way that the noble amateur Orlando is able to out-wrestle the professional but villainous Charles (*As You Like it*, 1.2).

7 These words are also used to characterize the ideal general comportment of the courtier (Castiglione 1972/1528) and so integrate fencing into the wider notion of civility.

8 Among the books I have in mind as illustrating this propensity are Leon-Battista Alberti's *Della pittura* (1435) and *De re aedificatoria* (1450), Albrecht Dürer's *Unterweysung der Messung* (1515/1525), Thomas Sebillet's *Art poetique françoys* (1548), Pontus de Tyard's *Solitaire second, ou prose de la musique* (1555), Omer Talon's *Rhetorica* (1557), and Andrea Palladio's *Quattro libri dell'architettura* (1570).

Bibliography

Agrippa, Camillo (1553) *Trattato di scientia d'arme*, Rome: Antonio Blado; 2nd edn (1568) Venice: Antonio Pinargenti; excerpt in (1978) Bascetta: 2.185–207; (English trans.) Jherek Swanger, Union City, CA: Chivalry Bookshelf (forthcoming).

Aigner, Heribert (1988) 'Zur gesellschaftlichen Stellung von Henkern, Gladiatoren und Berufsathleten', in I. Weiler (ed.) *Soziale Randgruppen und Außenseiter im Altertum*, Graz: Leykam: 201–20.

Alberti, Leon-Battista (1913) *I primi tre libri della famiglia* [1434–44], F. C. Pellegrini (ed.) Florence: Sansoni.

—— (1956) *On Painting* [1435], (trans.) J. R. Spencer, New Haven, CT and London: Yale University Press.

—— (1969) *The Family in Renaissance Florence*, (trans.) R. N. Watkins, Columbia, SC: University of South Carolina Press.

—— (1988) *On the Art of Building* [1450], (trans.) J. Rykwert, N. Leach and R. Tavernor, Cambridge, MA and London: MIT Press.

Alcocer, Francisco de (1559) *Tratado del juego … y de las Aspuestas, Suertes, Torneos, Justas, juegos de Cañas, Toros, y Truhanes …*, Salamanca: Andrea de Portonariis.

Alfonso, X El Sabio (1979) *Cantigas de Santa María* [1250], edición facsimil del Códice T.I.1 de la Biblioteca de San Lorenzo el Real de El Escorial, Madrid: Edilán.

—— (1985) *Cantigas de Santa María* [1250], (modern Spanish trans.) J. Filgueira Valverde, Odres Nuevos, Madrid: Castalia.

Altoni, Francesco (c. 1538) *Monomachia ovvero arte di scherma*, MS, Florence: Biblioteca Nazionale.

Ammaestramenti (c.1550) *Ammaestramenti per fare diversi equilibri, forze e destrezze di mano*, MS, Florence: Biblioteca Medicea Laurenziana.

Angelucci, Angelo (1863) *Il tiro a segno in Italia dal XII al XVI secolo*, Turin: Baglione.

—— (1866) *Armilustre e torneo con armi da battaglia tenuti a Venezia addi XXVIII e XXX maggio MCCCCLVIII*, Turin: Cassone.

Anglo, Sydney (1988) 'How to Win at Tournaments: The Technique of Chivalric Combat', *The Antiquaries Journal* 68: 248–64.

—— (ed.) (1990) *Chivalry in the Renaissance*, Woodbridge: The Boydell Press.

—— (2000) *The Martial Arts of Renaissance Europe*, New Haven, CT and London: Yale University Press.

Arasse, Daniel (1996) *Le détail. Pour une histoire rapprochée de la peinture*, Paris: Flammarion; 1st edn (1992).

Ariès, Philippe and Jean-Cl. Margolin (eds) (1982) *Les jeux à la Renaissance*, Actes du XXIIIe Colloque International d'Etudes Humanistes, Tours 1980, Paris: Vrin.

Aristides, Aelius (1983) *Eis Rhōmēn* [Regarding Rome, 155], in *Die Romrede* (ed. and trans.) R. Klein, Darmstadt: Wissenschaftliche Buchgesellschaft.

Artusi, L. and S. Gabbrielli (1976) *Feste e giochi a Firenze*, Florence: Becocci.

—— (1986) *Calcio storico fiorentino ieri e oggi*, Florence: Comune di Firenze.

Ascham, Roger (1904) *Toxophilus, or the Schole of Shoting* [1545] and *The Scholemaster* [1570], in *English Works*, (ed.) W. A. Wright, Cambridge: Cambridge University Press: vii–xx, 1–119 and 171–302.

Auerbach, Erich (1957) *Mimesis: The Representation of Reality in Western Literature*, (trans.) W. Trask, Garden City, NY: Doubleday Anchor; orig. German edn (1946) Berne: Francke.

Auerswald, Fabian (1539) *Ringerkunst: Fünf und achtzig Stücke*, Wittemberg: Hans Lufft; facs. repr. in (1978) *Chronik* (unpaginated).

Augenti, Domenico (2001) *Spettacoli del colosseo nelle cronache degli antichi*, Rome: 'L'Erma' di Bretschneider.

Auguet, Roland (1970) *Cruauté et civilisation: Les jeux romains*, Paris: Flammarion.

Augustus (1923) *Monumentum Ancyranum* [14], (ed. and trans.) E. G. Hardy, Oxford: Clarendon.

Aurigemma, Salvatore (1926) *I mosaici di Zliten*, 'Africa Italiana' 2, Rome-Milan: Società Editrice d'Arte Illustrata.

Auton, Jean d' (1889–95) *Chroniques de Louis XII* [1515], (ed.) R. de Maulde la Clavière, 4 vols, Paris: Renouard.

Bacci, Andrea (1622) *De thermis*, Rome: Mascardi; orig. edn (1571) Venice: Vicenzo Valgrisio.

Baker, William (1982) *Sports in the Western World*, Totawa, NJ: Rowman and Littlefield.

Balsdon, J. V. P. D. (1969) *Life and Leisure in Ancient Rome*, London: Bodley Head.

Baluda, Giocondo (c. 1630) *Trattato del modo di volteggiare & saltare il cavallo di legno*, MS, University of Bologna Library; excerpt in (1978) Bascetta: 1.49–106.

Barber, Richard and Juliet Barker (1989) *Tournaments: Jousts, Chivalry, and Pageants in the Middle Ages*, New York, NY: Weidenfeld & Nicolson.

Bardi, Giovanni (1580) *Discorso sopra il giuoco del calcio fiorentino*, Florence: Giunti; repr. (1615) and (1673) and in (1688) Bini: 1–29; modern edn in (1978) Bascetta: 1.127–62.

Barletta, Chiara (1993) 'Iconografia del gioco nel quattrocento', in (1993) Malato: 1, 239–50 and 18 plates.

Barrow, R. H. (1949) *The Romans*, Harmondsworth: Penguin.

Barthes, Roland (1982) 'Effets de réel', in G. Genette and T. Todorov (eds) *Littérature et réalité*, Paris: Le Seuil: 81–90.

Bartlett, Robert (1993) *The Making of Europe: Conquest, Colonization and Cultural Change 950–1350*, Princeton, NJ: Princeton University Press.

Barton, Carlin (1993) *The Sorrows of the Ancient Romans: The Gladiator and the Monster*, Princeton, NJ: Princeton University Press.

Bascetta, Carlo (ed.) (1978) *Sport e giochi. Trattati e scritti dal XV al XVIII secolo*, 2 vols, Milan: Il Polifilo.

Baumgartner, Frederic J. (1988) *Henry II King of France 1547–1559*, Durham, NC and London: Duke University Press.

Baxandall, Michael (1985) *Painting and Experience in Fifteenth Century Italy*, Oxford and New York, NY: Oxford University Press; orig. edn (1972).

Beacham, Richard (1999) *Spectacle Entertainments of Early Imperial Rome*, New Haven, CT and London: Yale University Press.

—— (2005) 'The Emperor as Impresario: Producing the Pageantry of Power', in (2005) Galinsky: 151–74.

Bell, Sinclair and Glenys Davies (eds) (2004) *Games and Festivals in Classical Antiquity*, BAR International Series 1220, Oxford: Archaeopress.

Bercé, Yves-Marie (1982) 'Les courses de taureaux dans le sud-ouest aquitain', in (1980) Ariès and Margolin: 19–31.

Berry, Herbert (1991) *The Noble Science: A Study and Transcription of Sloane Ms. 2530, Papers of the Masters of Defence of London, Temp. Henry VIII to 1590*, Newark, DE: University of Delaware Press; London and Toronto: Associated University Presses.

Bili (1979) *Vie de Saint Malo évêque d'Alet* [c. 875], (ed. and trans.) G. Le Duc, Dublin: Institute for Advanced Studies.

Bini, Pietro (1688) *Memorie dal calcio fiorentino tratte da diverse scritture*, Florence: Nella Stamperia di S. A. S. alla Condotta.

Boccalini, Traiano (1910) *Ragguagli di Parnaso* [1612], (ed.) G. Rua, vol. 1, Bari: Laterza.

Boffito, G. and A. Mori (1973) *Piante e vedute di Firenze. Studio storico, topografico, cartografico*, Rome: Multigrafica Editrice; repr. of 1st edn (1926) Florence: Giuntina.

Bogeng, G. A. E. (1926) *Geschichte des Sports allen Völker und Zeiten*, Leipzig: Seemann.

Boiteux, Martine (1982) 'Chasse aux taureaux et jeux romains à la Renaissance', in (1980) Ariès and Margolin: 33–53 and seven plates.

Bomgardner, D. L. (2000) *The Story of the Roman Amphitheater*, London and New York, NY: Routledge.

Boucicaut (1985) *Le livre des faits du bon Messire Jehan Le Maingre, dit Bouciquaut* [1400], (ed.) Denis Lalande, Textes Littéraires Français 331, Geneva: Droz.

Bouissac, Paul (1973) *La mesure des gestes. Prolégomènes à la sémiotique gestuelle*, The Hague/Paris: Mouton.

Bourciez, Édouard (1967) *Les Moeurs polies et la littérature de cour sous Henri II*, Geneva: Slatkine; 1st edn (1886), Paris.

Brailsford, Dennis (1969) *Sport and Society, Elizabeth to Anne*, London: Routledge and Kegan Paul.

Brantôme, Pierre de Bourdeille, seigneur de (1864–82) *Oeuvres complètes* [before 1614] (ed.) L. Lalanne, 10 vols, Paris: Renouard.

Bredekamp, Horst (1993) *Florentiner Fussball. Die Renaissance der Spiele. Calcio as Fest der Medici*, Frankfurt and New York, NY: Campus Verlag.

Bretonneau, Guy (1628) *Paezographia, dialogus praecipuas loquendi formulas complectens*, Paris: J. Libert.

Briceño Jáuregui, Manuel (1986) *Los gladiadores de Roma: Estudio histórico, legal y moral*, Bogotá: Instituto Caro y Cuervo.

Briggs, Ward (1975) 'Augustan Athletics and the Games of *Aeneid* 5', *Stadion* 1(2): 267–83.

Burgener, Louis (1982) 'Les jeux et exercices physiques en Suisse aux XVe et XVIe siècles', in (1982) Ariès and Margolin: 109–17.

Burke, Peter (1978) *Popular Culture in Early Modern Europe*, London: Temple Smith.

Burns, Francis (1985) 'Robert Dover's Cotswold Olimpick Games: The Use of the Term Olimpick', *Olympic Review* 210: 230–6.

Cagniart, Pierre (2000) 'Seneca's Attitude Towards Sport and Athletics', *Ancient History Bulletin* 14: 162–70.

Caillois, Roger (1967) *Les jeux et les hommes: le masque et le vertige*, 'Idées', Paris: NRF-Gallimard; 1st edn (1958).

Cairns, Francis (1989) *Virgil's Augustan Epic*, Cambridge: Cambridge University Press.

Caldelli, Maria Letizia (1993) *L'Agon Capitolinus, storia e protagonisti dall'istituzione domiziana al IV secolo*, Rome: Istituto Italiano per la Storia Antica.

Cameron, Alan (1973) *Porphyrius the Charioteer*, Oxford: Clarendon.

—— (1976) *Circus Factions: Blues and Greens at Rome and Byzantium*, Oxford: Clarendon.

Capoferro da Cagli, Ridolfo (1610) *Gran simulacro dell'arte e dell'uso della scherma*, Siena: S. Marchetti and C. Turi; excerpt in (1978) Bascetta: 2.235–40. Eng. trans. J. Kirby, *Italian Rapier Combat*, London: Greenhill Books, 2004; and J. Swanger, *Great Representation of the Art and Use of Fencing*, www.drizzle.com/~celyn/jherek/EngCF.pdf.

Carcereri, Luigi (1926) *Cosimo Primo granduca*, Verona: Bettinelli.

Carew-Reid, Nicole (1995) *Les fêtes florentines du temps de Lorenzo il Magnifico*, Florence: Olschki.

Carter, John Marshall (1988) *Sports and Pastimes of the Middle Ages*, Lanham, MD: University Press of America.

—— (1992) *Medieval Games: Sports and Recreations in Feudal Society*, Westport, CT: Greenwood Press.

—— and Arnd Krüger (eds) (1990) *Ritual and Record: Sports Records and Quantification in Pre-Modern Societies*, New York, NY, Westport, CT and London: Greenwood Press.

Cassiodorus, Magnus Aurelius (1973) *Variarum Libri XII* [mid-sixth century], (ed.) Å. J. Fridh, Tournhout: Brepols; (English trans.) S. J. B. Barnish, (1992) *The Variae of Magnus Aurelius Cassiodorus Senator*, Liverpool: Liverpool University Press.

Castiglione, Baldassare (1972) *Il libro del cortegiano* [1528], (eds) E. Bonora and P. Zoccola, Milan: Mursia; (English trans.) Charles Singleton (1959), Garden City, NY: Doubleday Anchor.

Castle, Egerton (1969) *Schools and Masters of Fence from the Middle Ages to the Eighteenth Century*, York, PA: George Shumway; 1st edn (1885); 2nd edn (1892).

Catonze, Liborio (1999) *Vizi, costume e peccati nelle ville romane di Sicilia: il Casale di Piazza Armerina*, Palermo: Walter Farina.

Chanson de Roland (1924) *La chanson de Roland, Oxford Version* (ed.) T. Atkinson Jenkins, Boston, MA: Heath.

Charles IX (1857) *La chasse royale* [1573], (ed.) H. Chevreul, Paris: Potier.

Charles d'Orléans (1966) *Poésies*, 2 vols [1465], (ed.) P. Champion, Paris: Honoré Champion.

Chaucer, Geoffrey (1958) *Canterbury Tales* [1400], (ed.) A. C. Cawley, London: Dent; New York, NY: Dutton.

Chiabrera, Gabriello (1952) *Canzonette, rime varie, dialoghi* [c. 1625], (ed.) L. Neri, Turin: UTET.

Chick, Gary and John Loy (1996) 'Definitions', in (1996) Levinson and Christensen: 1.247–9.

Chrétien de Troyes (1942) *Yvain (le chevalier au lion)* [1173], (ed.) T. B. W. Reid, Manchester: Manchester University Press.

—— (1955) *Erec et Enide* [1160–70], (ed.) Mario Roques, Paris: Champion.

—— (1957) *Cligès* [1176], (ed.) A. Micha, Paris: Champion.

—— (1958) *Le chevalier de la charrette [Lancelot]* [1177–81], (ed.) Mario Roques, Paris: Champion.

——— (1959) *Le roman de Perceval ou le conte du Graal* [1180], (ed.) W. Roach, Geneva: Droz; Paris: Minard.

——— (1990) *The Complete Romances*, (trans.) David Staines, Bloomington and Indianapolis, IN: Indiana University Press.

Chrétien, Heidi L. (1994) *The Festival of San Giovanni: Imagery and Political Power in Renaissance Florence*, New York, NY: Peter Lang.

Chronik (1978) *Chronik alter Kampfkünste. Zeichnungen und Texte aus Schriften alter Meister entstanden 1443–1674*, Berlin: Weinmann.

Cimilotti, Hercole (1587) *Il superbo torneo fatto nella regia città di Pavia il carnevale de 1587*, Pavia: G. Bartoli.

Clare, Lucien (1983) *La quintaine, la course de bague et le jeu des têtes, étude historique et ethno-linguistique d'une famille de jeux équestres*, Paris: CNRS.

Clavel-Lévêque, Monique (1984) *L'empire en jeux. Espace symbolique et pratique sociale dans le monde romain*, Paris: CNRS.

Clephan, R. Coltman (1919) *The Tournament, its Periods and Phases*, London: Methuen; repr. (1967) New York, NY: Ungar.

Collart, Paul (1978) *Au Palatin*, Paris: Belles Lettres.

Contamine, Philippe (1984) *War in the Middle Ages*, (trans.) Michael Jones, Oxford: Blackwell.

Cordier, Mathurin (1585) *Colloquiorum scholasticorum … ad pueros Latine paulatim exercendos*, Paris: Gabriel Buon; 1st edn (1564) Lyon: Straton.

Crescenzi, Pietro di (1957) *Das Jagdbuch* [1305], in *Deutschen Übersetzungen des 14. und 15. Jahrhunderts* (ed.) K. Lindner, Berlin: Walter de Gruyter.

——— (1965) *Opus ruralium commodorum* [1305], Latin-Italian excerpt in (1965) Innamorati: 1.127–93.

Cripps-Day, Francis Henry (1918) *The History of the Tournament in England and France*, London: B. Quaritch; repr. (1982) New York, NY: AMS Press.

Crosby, Alfred (1997) *The Measure of Reality: Quantification and Western Society, 1250–1600*, Cambridge: Cambridge University Press.

Crowther, Nigel (1983) 'Greek Games in Republican Rome', *L'Antiquité classique* 52: 268–73.

——— (1997) 'The Ancient Greek Game of Episkyros', *Stadion* 23: 1–15.

——— (2001) 'Cicero's Attitude to Greek Athletics', *Nikephoros* 14: 63–81.

——— (2004) *Athletika: Studies on the Olympic Games and Greek Athletics*, Nikephoros Beihefte 11, Hildesheim: Weidmann.

Cuvelier (1990) *La chanson de Bertrand du Guesclin* [c. 1400], (ed.) J.-Cl. Faucon, Toulouse: Editions Universitaires du Sud.

D'Allemagne, Henri René (1880) *Sports et jeux d'adresse*, Paris: Hachette; 2nd edn (1904).

da Vinci, Leonardo (1952) *Scritti scelti* [c. 1500], (ed.) Anna Maria Brizio, Turin: UTET.

Dall'Agocchie, Giovanni (1572) *Dell'arte di scrimia*, Venice: G. Tamburino.

Dallington, Richard (1604) *The View of Fraunce*, London: Symon Stafford; facs. repr. (1936) London: Shakespeare Association.

Daremberg, Charles and Edmond Saglio (1877–1919) *Dictionnaire des antiquités grecques et romaines*, 5 vols, Paris: Hachette.

Dati, Giulio (1596) *Lamento di Parione*, Florence: Giunti.

——— (1824) *Disfida di caccia tra i Piacevoli e Piatelli* [c. 1600], (ed.) D. Moreni, Florence: Il Magheri.

Davis, Robert C. (1994) *The War of the Fists: Popular Culture and Public Violence in Late Renaissance Venice*, New York, NY and Oxford: Oxford University Press.

Del Corazza, Bartolommeo (1894) *Diario fiorentino 1405–1438* [c. 1438], (ed.) G. O. Corazzini, in *Archivio Storico Italiano*, 5th series, 14: 233–98.

Della Casa, Giovanni (1994) *Galateo* [1555], (trans.) K. Eisenbichler and K. Bartlett, Renaissance and Reformation Texts in Translation, Toronto: Centre for Reformation and Renaissance Studies.

De Luze, Albert (1933) *La magnifique histoire du jeu de paume*, Paris: Bossard; Bordeaux: Delmas.

Denholm-Young, Noël (1948) 'The Tournament in the Thirteenth Century', in (1948) Hunt: 240–68.

Dictionary (1975–97) *Dictionary of Medieval Latin from British Sources*, Oxford: British Academy.

Diem, Carl (1960) *Weltgeschichte des Sports und der Leibeserziehung*, Stuttgart: Cotta.

Digby, Everard (1587) *De art natandi libri duo, quorum Prior regulas ipsius artis, posterior verò praxin demonstrationemque continet*, London: Thomas Dawson.

—— (1595) *A Short introduction for to learne to swimme ...*, (trans.) Christofer Middleton, London: Edward White; republ. in (1983) Orme: 113–207.

Discorso (c. 1560) *Discorso del giuoco della pallacorda*, MS, Florence: Biblioteca Nazionale.

Dissennati, Carlo (1982) *Giostra del saracino*, Arezzo: Aretia Libri.

Duarte of Portugal (1944) *Livra da ensinança de bem cavalgar toda sela* [1434], (ed.) J. M. Piel, Lisbon: Livraria Bertrand; repr. (1986) Lisbon: Imprensa Nacional-Casa de Moeda.

Du Bellay, Joachim (1908–31) *Oeuvres poétiques* [1547–60], (ed.) H. Chamard, 6 vols, Paris: Société des Textes Français Modernes.

Duby, Georges (1973a) *Le dimanche de Bouvines: 27 juillet 1214*, Paris: Gallimard.

—— (1973b) *Guerriers et paysans, VIIe–XIIe siècles*, Paris: Gallimard.

—— (1980) *The Three Orders, Feudal Society Imagined*, (trans.) A. Goldhammer, Chicago, IL and London: University of Chicago Press.

—— (1984) *Guillaume le Maréchal, ou le meilleur chevalier du monde*, Paris: Fayard.

Du Cerceau, J.-A. (1988) *Les plus excellents bastiments de France* [1576–9], (ed.) David Thomson, (trans.) C. Ludet, Paris: L'Aventurine.

Du Choul, Guillaume (1555) *Discours ... des bains et antiques excercitations grecques et romaines*, Lyon: Roville.

Du Faur de Saint Jorry, Pierre (1592) *Agonisticon ... sive de re athletica ludisque veterum gymnicis ...*, Lyon: F. Fabre; 2nd edn (1595) Lyon: Soubron and Des Prés.

Duncan-Jones, Katherine (1991) *Sir Philip Sidney, Courtier Poet*, New Haven, CT and London: Yale University Press.

Dürer, Albrecht (1910) *Fechtbuch* (ed.) F. Dörnhöffer, Vienna: F. Tempsky; excerpt in (1978) *Chronik*: unpaginated.

Duret, L. and J.-P. Néraudau (1983) *Urbanisme et metamorphoses de la Rome antique*, Paris: Belles Lettres.

During, Bertrand (1984) *Des jeux aux sports. Repères et documents en histoire des activités physiques*, Paris: Vigot.

Eder, Walter (2005) 'Augustus and the Power of Tradition', in (2005) Galinsky: 13–32.

Eginhard (1967) *Vie de Charlemagne/Vita Karoli Magni Imperatoris* [c. 828], (ed. and trans.) Louis Halphen, 4th edn, Paris: Belles Lettres.

Eichberg, Henning (1978) *Leistung, Spannung, Geschwindigkeit: Sport und Tanz in gesellschaftlichen Wandel des 18./19. Jahrhunderts*, Stuttgart: Klett-Cotta.

Eisenstein, Elizabeth (1983) *The Printing Revolution in Early Modern Europe*, Cambridge: Cambridge University Press.

Elias, Norbert (1939) *Über den Prozess der Zivilisation*, 2 vols, Basel: Haus zum Falken; 2nd edn, 2 vols (1969), (1979) Frankfurt: Suhrkamp; (English trans.) (1978) E. Jephcott, New York, NY: Urizen Books.

—— (1969) *Die höfische Gesellschaft*, Darmstadt and Neuwied: Luchterhand; (English trans.) (1983) E. Jephcott, Oxford: Blackwell.

—— and Eric Dunning (1972) *Sport: Readings from a Sociological Perspective*, Toronto: University of Toronto Press.

Elliott, J. H. (1968) *Europe Divided 1559–1598*, London and Glasgow: Collins.

Elmer, David (forthcoming) '*epikoinos*: The Ball Game *episkuros* and *Iliad* 12.421–3', *Classical Philology*.

Elyot, Thomas (1962) *The Book Named the Governor* [1531], (ed.) S. E. Lehmberg, London and New York, NY: Dent.

Erasmus, Desiderius (1965) 'Sport' ['De lusu' 1522], in *Colloquies*, (trans.) C. R. Thompson, Chicago, IL and London: University of Chicago Press: 22–30.

Estienne, Henri (1896) *La precellence du langage françois* [1579], (ed.) E. Huguet, Paris: Armand Colin.

Facchini, Sandra (1990) *I luoghi dello sport nella Roma antica e moderna*, Rome: Istituto Poligrafico e Zecca dello Stato.

Febvre, Lucien and Henri-Jean Martin (1971) *L'apparition du livre*, Paris: Albin Michel; 1st edn (1958).

Feldherr, Andrew (1995) 'Ships of State: *Aeneid* 5 and Augustan Circus Spectacles', *Classical Antiquity* 14(2): 245–65.

Ferguson, Niall (1999) *The Pity of War*, New York, NY: Basic Books; 1st edn (1998) London: Allen Lane.

Ferrari, Gian-Battista (1688) 'Florentinum Harpastum', in (1688) Bini: 33.

Filopono (Stefano di Francesco Sterponi) (c. 1518) [Il giuoco del calcio] untitled Latin letter to Francesco Onesti, in *Epistulae et orationes*, MS, Florence: Biblioteca Riccardiana, ff. 98v0–100ro; modern edn (1898) as *Il giuoco del calcio – Lettera del Filopono a Francesco Onesti*, (ed.) C. Nardini, Florence: Carnesecchi.

Fiore dei Liberi (1902) *Flos duellatorum in armis, sine armis, equester, pedester* [1410], publ. as *Il fior di battaglia*, (ed.) F. Novati, Bergamo: Istituto Italiano d'Arti Grafiche; repr. with intro. (1982) R. Nostini, Pisa: Giardini; excerpt in (1978) Bascetta: 2.125–44.

Fitzstephen, William (1908) *Descriptio Nobilissimae Civitatis Londoniae* [1174] in John Stow, *A Survey of London* [1603], (ed.) C. L. Kingsford, 2 vols, Oxford: Clarendon: 219–29; (English trans.) (1961) in *English Historical Documents 1042–1189*, (ed. and trans.) D. C. Douglas and G. W. Greenaway, 2nd edn, London: Eyre and Spottiswoode: 956–62.

Flannery, Michael and Richard Leech (2004) *Golf Through the Ages: Six Hundred Years of Golfing Art*, Fairfield, Iowa, IA: Golf Links Press.

Fleckenstein, Josef (ed.) (1985) *Das ritterliche Turnier im Mittelalter. Beiträge zu einer vergleichenden Formen- und Verhaltensgeschichte des Rittertums*, Göttingen: Vandenhoeck & Ruprecht.

Flori, Jean (1998) *Chevaliers et chevalerie au Moyen-âge*, Paris: Hachette Littératures.

Fontaine, Marie Madeleine (1991) *Le condottiere Pietro del Monte: philosophe et écrivain de la Renaissance, 1457–1509*, Geneva and Paris: Slatkine.

—— (1999) 'La représentation du corps à la Renaissance dans la littérature française (1530–1560)', doctoral thesis, Université de Paris IV-Sorbonne.

—— *et al.* (eds) (1990) *Le corps à la Renaissance*, Paris: Aux Amateurs de Livres.

Forbet L'Aisné (1599) *L'utilité qui provient du jeu de la paume au corps et à l'esprit, traduict du grec de Galien…*, Paris: Thomas Sevestre; republ. (1623) Paris: Ch. Hulpeau.

Forgeng, Jeffrey (2003) *The Medieval Art of Swordsmanship. A Facsimile and Translation of Europe's Oldest Personal Combat Treatise, Royal Armouries MS I.33*, Union City, CA: Chivalry Bookshelf.

Foucault, Michel (1966) *Les mots et les choses*, Paris: Gallimard.

Francioni, Stefania (1993) 'Iconografia del gioco nel cinquecento', in (1993) Malato: 1, 251–68 and 22 plates.

Frederick II (1955) *The Art of Falconry [De arte venandi cum avibus*, 1250], (eds and trans.) C. A. Wood and F. M. Fyfe, Boston, MA: Branford; London: Geoffrey Cumberlege, Oxford University Press; orig. edn, Palo Alto, CA: Stanford University Press.

Frère, Henri (1940) 'Le témoignage de Stace sur la σφαιρομαχια', *Mélanges de philologie, de littérature et d'histoire anciennes offerts à Alfred Ernout*, Paris: Klincksieck: 41–58.

Frescobaldi, Giovanni (1973–5) 'La palla al calcio' [c. 1460], in Antonio Lanza (ed.) *Lirici toscani del '400*, 2 vols, Rome: Bulzoni: 1.601–07.

Friedländer, Ludwig (1908–13) *Roman Life and Manners Under the Early Empire*, (trans.) A. B. Gough, 4 vols, London: George Routledge; New York, NY: E. P. Dutton; orig. German edn (1862–71) Leipzig: Hirzel.

Froissart, Jean (1902) *The Chronicle* [c. 1400], (trans.) John Bourchier [1523–5], 6 vols, London: David Nutt.

—— (1963) *Les chroniques* [c. 1400], in *Historiens et chroniqueurs du Moyen-Age*, (eds) A. Pauphilet and E. Pognon, Bibliothèque de la Pléiade, Paris: NRF-Gallimard: 367–944.

Gaiani, Giovanni Battista (1619) *Discorso del tornear a piedi*, Genoa; G. Pavoni.

Galen, Claudius (1951) *A Translation of Galen's Hygiene (De Sanitate Tuenda)* [c. 200], (trans.) R. M. Green, Springfield, IL: Charles C. Thomas.

—— (1967) *Scripta minora* [c. 200], (ed.) J. Marquardt, Amsterdam: Hakkert; orig. edn (1884) Leipzig: Teubner.

—— (1991) 'On Exercise with the Small Ball' [c. 200], in (1991) Miller: 116–19.

Galinsky, Karl (ed.) (2005) *The Cambridge Companion to the Age of Augustus*, Cambridge: Cambridge University Press.

Gardiner, E. Norman (1910) *Greek Athletic Sports and Festivals*, London: Macmillan; repr., Dubuque, IO: Brown Reprint Library.

—— (1930) *Athletics of the Ancient World*, Oxford: Clarendon.

Garzoni, Tommaso (1585) *La piazza universale di tutte le professioni del mondo, e nobili et ignobili*, Venice: Somascho.

Gaston Phoebus (1998) *The Hunting Book of Gaston Phoebus* [1387–9], (eds and trans.) M. Thomas *et al.*, London: Harvey Miller.

Geoffrey of Monmouth (1985–91) *The Historia Regum Britannie* [1136], (eds) N. Wright and J. Crick, (trans.) N. Wright, 5 vols, Cambridge: D. S. Brewer.

Ghiron-Bistagne, Paulette (1992) 'Les concours grecs en occident, et notamment à Nîmes', in *Spectacula–II: Le théâtre grec et ses spectacles*, (eds) C. Landes and V. Kramerovskis, Lattes: Musée Archéologique Henri Prades: 223–32.

Giganti, Nicoletto (1606) *Scola, overo teatro nelquale sono rappresentate diverse maniere, e modi di parare, e di ferir di spada…*, Venice: G.-A. and G. de Franceschi; excerpt in (1978) Bascetta: 2.215–19.

Gillmeister, Heiner (1997) *Tennis: a Cultural History*, London and Washington, DC: Leicester University Press.

—— (2007) 'The Tennis Metaphor in Renaissance and Stuart Political Poems', in (2007) McClelland and Merrilees.

Ginestet, Pierre (1991) *Les organisations de la jeunesse dans l'Occident romain*, Brussels: Latomus.

Giovannini, Luigi (1906) *Notizie storiche sul giuoco del ponte di Pisa. Giuoco di massa et schudo*, Florence: Biblioteca di Cultura Liberale.

Goethe, Johann Wolfgang (1976) *Italienische Reise* [1786–7], (ed.) Christoph Michel, 2 vols, Frankfurt; Insel.

Goetz, Hans Werner (1993) *Life in the Middle Ages*, (trans.) A. Wimmer, (ed.) S. Rowan, Notre Dame, IN: University of Notre Dame Press; orig. German edn (1986) Munich: Beck.

Golvin, Jean-Claude (1988) *L'amphithéâtre romain. Essai sur la théorisation de sa forme et de ses fonctions*, 2 vols, Paris: Diffusion de Boccard.

Gori, Pietro (1926) *Le feste fiorentine attraverso i secoli*, Florence: Bemporad.

Gosselin, Guillaume (1579) *Declaration de deux doubtes qui se trouvent en comptant le jeu de la paume...*, N.p.: n.a.

Grant, Michael (1967) *Gladiators*, London: Weidenfeld and Nicolson; New York, NY: Delacorte.

Grassi, Giacomo di (1570) *Ragione di addoprar sicuramente l'arme sia da offesa come da difesa...*, Venice: G. de' Cavalli; Venice: G. Ziletti.

—— (1594) *His true Arte of Defence, plainlie teaching by infallible Demonstrations, apt Figures and perfect Rules...*, (trans.) I. G., London: I. I.; facs. repr. in (1972) Jackson: 1–184.

Gregory of Tours (1884) *Opera* [594], (ed.) W. Arndt and Br. Krusch, *Monumenta Germaniae Historica, Scriptores Rerum Merovingicarum*, Hanover: n.a.

—— (1922) *Liber in Gloria confessorum* [594], in *Auswahl aus den Werken des Gregor von Tours*, (ed.) H. Morf, Heidelberg: Carl Winter.

—— (1927) *History of the Franks* [594], (trans.) O. M. Dalton, 2 vols, Oxford: Clarendon.

Greimas, A. J. (1987) *On Meaning: Selected Writings in Semiotic Theory*, (trans.) P. J. Perron and F. Collins, Minneapolis, MN: University of Minnesota Press.

Grodde, Olaf (1997) *Sport bei Quintilian*, Nikephoros Beihefte 3, Hildesheim: Weidmann.

Gunn, Steven (1990) 'Chivalry and the Politics of the Early Tudor Court', in (1990) Anglo: 107–28).

Guttmann, Allen (1978) *From Ritual to Record: The Nature of Modern Sports*, New York, NY: Columbia University Press.

—— (1986) *Sports Spectators*, New York, NY: Columbia University Press.

—— (1996) *The Erotic in Sports*, New York, NY: Columbia University Press.

—— (2000) Review of W. Decker, *Sport in der griechische Antike* and of a German translation of J.-P. Thuillier, *Le sport dans la Rome antique*, *Journal of Sport History* 27(1): 151–2.

—— (2004) *Sports: the First Five Millennia*, Amherst, MA: University of Massachusetts Press.

—— *et al.* (2002) 'Forum: The Athletic, the Aesthetic, and the Erotic', *Journal of Sport History* 29(3): 379–412.

Hale, J. R. (1977) *Florence and the Medici: The Pattern of Control*, London: Thames and Hudson.

Hall, Bert (1997) *Weapons and Warfare in Renaissance Europe*, Baltimore, MD and London: The Johns Hopkins University Press.

Hamilton, David (1998) *Golf, Scotland's Game*, Kilmalcolm: The Partick Press.

Hardie, Philip (1986) *Virgil's Aeneid: Cosmos and Imperium*, Oxford: Clarendon.

Harris H. A. (1964) *Greek Athletes and Athletics*, London: Hutchison.

—— (1972) *Sport in Greece and Rome*, Ithaca, NY: Cornell University Press.

Haskins, Charles Homer (1929) 'The Latin Literature of Sport', in *Studies in Mediaeval Culture*, Oxford: Clarendon: 105–23.

Haton, Claude (2001) *Mémoires 1553–1582*, (ed.) Laurent Bourquin, 3 vols, Paris: CTHS.

Heldris de Cornuälle (1972) *Le roman de Silence* [after 1250], (ed.) Lewis Thorpe, Cambridge: Heffer.

Heller, John L. (1946) 'Labyrinth or Troy Town', *The Classical Journal* 42(3): 123–39.

Hen, Ytzhak (1995) *Culture and Religion in Merovingian Gaul*, Leiden: Brill.

Henderson, Robert William (1947) *Ball, Bat, and Bishop: The Origin of Ball Games*, New York, NY: Rockport Press; repr. (1974) Detroit, MI: Gale Research.

Herlihy, David (1958) *Pisa in the Early Renaissance: A Study in Urban Growth*, New Haven, CT: Yale University Press.

Hershkowitz, Debra (1998) *Valerius Flaccus' Argonautica: Abbreviated Voyages in Silver Latin Epic*, Oxford: Clarendon.

Heywood, William (1969) *Palio and Ponte: The Sports of Central Italy from the Age of Dante to the XXth Century*, New York, NY: Hacker Art Books; orig. edn (1904) London: Methuen.

Hole, Christina (1949) *English Sports and Pastimes*, London: Batsford.

Honour, Hugh (1977) *Neo-classicism*, Harmondsworth: Penguin; orig. edn (1968).

Hopkins, Keith (1983) *Death and Renewal*, Sociological Studies in Roman History, vol. 2, Cambridge: Cambridge University Press.

—— and Mary Beard (2005) *The Colosseum*, London: Profile Books.

Horsmann, Gerhard (1998) *Die Wagenlenker der römischen Kaiserzeit. Untersuchungen zu ihren sozialen Stellung*, Stuttgart: Franz Steiner.

Hugues Capet (1997) *Huges Capet, chanson de geste du XIVe siècle*, (ed.) N. Laborderie, Paris: Champion.

Huizinga, Johan (1962) *Homo ludens, a Study of the Play Element in Culture*, Boston, MA: Beacon Press; orig. Dutch edn (1939) Amsterdam: Pantheon.

Humphrey, John (1986) *Roman Circuses. Arenas for Chariot Racing*, London: Batsford.

Hunt, R. W. (1948) *Studies in Medieval History Presented to Frederick Maurice Powicke*, (eds) R. W. Hunt, W. A. Pantin and R. W. Southern, Oxford: Clarendon.

Huyghe, René (1968) *Larousse Encyclopedia of Byzantine and Medieval Art*, New York, NY: Prometheus Press.

Innamorati, Giulio (ed.) (1965) *Arte della caccia. Testi di falconeria, uccellagione e altre cacce. Dal secolo XIII agli inizi del seicento*, 2 vols, Milan: Il Polifilo.

Isidore (1991) *Etymologiarum sive Originum Libri XX* [600], (ed.) W. M. Lindsay, Oxford: Clarendon; 1st edn (1911).

Isidori Frasca, Rosella (1980) *Ludi nell'antica Roma*, Attività Motorie 3, Bologna: Pàtron.

Jackson, James L. (ed.) (1972) *Three Elizabethan Fencing Manuals*, Delmar, NY: Scholars' Facsimiles and Reprints.

Jackson, William Henry (1985) 'Das Turnier in der deutschen Dichtung des Mittelalters', in (1985) Fleckenstein: 257–95.

Jacobelli, Luciana (2003) *Gladiators at Pompeii*, Los Angeles, CA: J. Paul Getty Museum.

Jacquot, Jean (ed.) (1956–75) *Les fêtes de la Renaissance*, 3 vols, Paris: CNRS.

Jakobson, Roman and Morris Halle (1956) *Fundamentals of Language*, The Hague: Mouton.

James [VI and] I (1982) *A Declaration Concerning Lawfull Sports to be Used* [1617], in *Minor Prose Works*, (eds) James Craigie and Alexander Law, Edinburgh: Scottish Texts Society: 101–9 and 217–40.

—— (1996) 'Basilikon Doron, or His Majesty's Instructions to his Dearest Son, Henry the Prince' [1599], in *The True Law of Free Monarchies and Basilikon Doron*, (eds) D. Fischlin and

M. Fortier, Tudor and Stuart Texts, Toronto: Centre for Reformation and Renaissance Studies.

Jameson, Fredric (1987) 'Foreword', in (1987) Greimas: vi–xxii.

Jenkyns, Richard (1980) *The Victorians and Ancient Greece*, Cambridge, MA: Harvard University Press.

Jennison, George (1937) *Animals for Show and Pleasure in Ancient Rome*, Manchester: Manchester University Press.

Josephus (1959) *The Jewish War* [100], (trans.) G. A. Williamson, Harmondsworth: Penguin.

Joubert, Laurent (1582) 'De gymnasiis et generibus exercitationum apud antiques', in *Opera Latina*, Lyon: S. Michel.

Journal (1854) *Journal d'un bourgeois de Paris sous le règne de François Ier (1515–36)*, (ed.) L. Lalanne, Paris: Renouard.

Journal (1975) *Journal d'un bourgeois de Paris (1405–1449)*, (ed.) A. Tuetey, Geneva: Slatkine Reprints; orig. edn (1881), Paris; also published as *Journal d'un bourgeois de Paris sous les règnes de Charles VI et Charles VII*, (ed.) A. Mary, (1929) Paris: Jonquières.

Junckelmann, Marcus (2000a) '*Familia gladiatoria*: The Heroes of the Amphitheatre', in (2000) Köhne and Ewigleben: 31–74.

—— (2000b) *Das Spiel mit dem Tod: So kämpften Roms Gladiatoren*, Mainz: Philipp von Zabern.

Jusserand, J.-J. (1901) Les *sports et jeux d'exercice dans l'ancienne France*, Paris: Plon-Nourrit.

Kaeuper, Richard (1999) *Chivalry and Violence in Medieval Europe*, Oxford: Oxford University Press.

Keegan, John (1998) *The First World War*, London: Hutchison.

Kidd, Bruce (1996) *The Struggle for Canadian Sport*, Toronto, Buffalo, NY and London: University of Toronto Press.

King, Anthony (1990) *Roman Gaul and Germany*, London: British Museum.

Klein, Robert (1970) *La forme et l'intelligible*, Paris: NRF-Gallimard.

Köhne, Eckhart and Cornelia Ewigleben (2000) *Gladiators and Caesars: The Power of Spectacle in Ancient Rome*, Berkeley, CA: University of California Press; orig. German edn (2000) Mainz: Philipp von Zabern.

Körbs, Werner (1938) *Vom Sinn der Leibesübungen zur Zeit der italienischen Renaissance*, Berlin: Weidmann; facs. repr. (1988) Hildesheim: Weidmann.

Krüger, Arnd and John McClelland (eds) (1984) *Die Anfänge des modernen Sports in der Renaissance*, Beiträge und Quellen zu Sport und Gesellschaft 2, London: Arena Publications.

Kuhn, Roger (1962) *The Structure of Scientific Revolutions*, Chicago, IL: University of Chicago Press.

Kustrin, Orestis and J. A. Mangan (2003) 'Lasting Legacy? Spartan Life as a Germanic Educational Ideal: Karl Ottfried Müller and *Die Dorier*', in (2003) Mangan: 28–45.

Kyle, Donald G. (1998) *Spectacles of Death in Ancient Rome*, London and New York, NY: Routledge.

—— (2003) 'From the Battlefield to the Arena: Gladiators, Militarism and the Roman Republic', in (2003) Mangan: 10–27.

Ladner, Gerhard (1966) 'The Impact of Christianity', in *The Transformation of the Roman World*, (ed.) Lynn White, Jr., Berkeley and Los Angeles, CA: University of California Press.

La Marche, Olivier de (1883) *Mémoires* [c. 1500], (eds) H. Beaune and J. d'Arbaumont, Société de l'Histoire de France, Paris: Renouard.

Landes, Christian (ed.) (1990) *Le cirque et les courses de chars: Rome-Byzance*, Lattes: Imago Lattes.

Landucci, Luca (1883) *Diario fiorentino dal 1450 al 1516* [c. 1517], Florence: Sansoni; (English trans.) (1927) A. de R. Jervis, London: Dent; New York, NY: E. P. Dutton.

Lassels, Richard (1670) *The Voyage of Italy*, Paris: Du Moutier.

La villa (1999) *La villa di Massenzio sulla via Appia: Il Circo*, (eds) G. Ioppolo and G. Pisani Sartorio, I Monumenti Romani IX, Rome: Istituto Nazionale di Studi Romani.

Lee, Hugh M. (1984) 'Women's Athletics and the Bikini Mosaic from Piazza Armerina', *Stadion* 10: 45–76.

—— (1997) 'The Later Greek Boxing Gloves and the "Roman" Caestus: A Centennial Reevaluation of Jüthner's "Über Antike Turngeräthe"', *Nikephoros* 10: 161–78.

Lee, Maurice Jr. (1990) *Great Britain's Solomon: James VI and I in His Three Kingdoms*, Urbana and Chicago, IL: University of Illinois Press.

Leff, Gordon (1958) *Medieval Thought: St Augustine to Ockham*, Harmondsworth: Penguin.

Levinson, David and Karen Christensen (eds) (1996) *Encyclopedia of World Sport*, 3 vols, Santa Barbara-Denver-Oxford: ABC-Clio.

Liechtenauer, Johann (1965) *Kunst des Fechtens* [c. 1389], (ed.) M. Wierschin, Munich: Beck.

—— (1985) *Kunst des langen Schwertes* [c. 1389], (ed.) H. P. Hils, Frankfurt: Lang.

Lockyer, Roger (1998) *James VI and I*, London and New York, NY: Longman.

Lovatt, Helen (2004) 'Epic Games and Real Games in Virgil's *Aeneid* 5 and Statius *Thebaid* 6', in (2004) Bell and Davies: 107–14.

Loyal Serviteur (2001) *La très joyeuse et très plaisante histoire du gentil seigneur de Bayart* [1525], Paris: Paléo.

Lukas, Gerhard (1982) *Der Sport im alten Rom*, Berlin: Sportverlag.

Macaulay, Thomas Babington (1856) *History of England from the Accession of James II*, 3 vols, New York, NY: Harper.

Madden, D. H. (1897) *The Diary of Master William Silence. A Study of Shakespeare and of Elizabethan Sport*, London, New York, NY and Bombay: Longmans Green.

Magoun, Francis P. (1938) *History of Football from the Beginnings to 1871*, Kölner Anglistische Arbeiten 31, Bochum-Langendreer: Heinrich Pöppinghaus; facs. repr., New York, NY and London: Johnson Reprint Corporation.

Mahoney, Anne (2001) *Roman Sports and Spectacles, A Sourcebook*, Newburyport, MA: Focus Publishing.

Malato, Enrico (ed.) (1993) *Passare il tempo. La letteratura del gioco e del intrattenimento dal XII al XVI secolo*. Atti del Convegno di Pienza 1991, 2 vols, Rome: Salerno.

Malcolmson, Robert (1973) *Popular Recreations in English Society 1700–1850*, Cambridge: Cambridge University Press.

Mallett, Michael (1974) *Mercenaries and Their Masters: Warfare in Renaissance Italy*, London: Bodley Head.

Malszecki, Greg (1982) 'The Physics and Aesthetics of Jousting', *Proceedings of the 5th Canadian Symposium on Sport and Physical Education* [1981], Toronto: School of Physical and Health Education: 87–94.

—— (1985) 'What's the Score on Jousting in Renaissance England?', unpubl. paper delivered at the annual meeting of the North American Society for Sport History.

Manciolino, Antonio (1531) *Opera nova, dove sono tutti li documenti e vantaggi che si ponno havere nel mestier de l'armi d'ogni sorte*, Venice: Niccolò d'Aristotile.

Mandell, Richard (1984) *Sport, a Cultural History*, New York, NY: Columbia University Press.

Mangan, J. A. (ed.) (2003) 'Militarism, Sport, Europe: War without Weapons', *European Sports History Review* 5.

Marozzo, Achille (1536) *Opera nova chiamata duello, o vero fiore dell'armi de singulari abattimenti*, Modena: Antonio Bergola (title pages of extant copies not always identical).

Marrou, Henri-Irénée (1981) *Histoire de l'éducation dans l'Antiquité*, 7th edn, 2 vols, Paris: Le Seuil; orig. edn (1948).

Masi, Bartolomeo (1906) *Ricordanze (1478–1526)*, (ed.) G.O. Corazzini, Florence: Sansoni.

Matthews, Victor (1990) 'Suram dare: A Gesture in Roman Ball Playing', *Nikephoros* 3: 185–7.

Matthieu, Pierre (1631) *Histoire de France soubs les règnes de François I...Louys XIII*, 2 vols, Paris: Vve N. Buon.

Maurin, Jean (1984) 'Les barbares aux arènes', *Ktéma* 9: 103–11.

McClelland, John (1984) 'Leibesübungen in der Renaissance und die Freien Künste', in (1984) Krüger and McClelland: 85–110.

—— (1990) 'The Numbers of Reason: Luck, Logic, and Art in Renaissance Conceptions of Sport', in (1990) Carter and Krüger: 53–64.

—— (1997a) 'Le tournoi de juin 1559 et les deux François de Guise', in *Le mécénat et l'influence des Guises*, (ed.) Y. Bellenger, Paris: Champion: 177–85.

—— (1997b) 'Un siècle de sport et de politique en Europe: 1469–1572', in *La comune eredità dello sport in Europa, Atti del 10 Seminario Europeo di Storia dello Sport*, (eds) A. Krüger and A. Teja, Rome: CONI-Scuola dello Sport: 21–5.

—— (1998) 'Sport', in *Encyclopedia of Semiotics*, (ed.) Paul Bouissac, New York, NY and Oxford: Oxford University Press.

—— (2002a) 'From Word to Deed: The Possibility of Reconstituting Late Ancient and Early Modern Athletic Practice from Written Documents', in *Actas – V Congreso de Historia del Deporte en Europa*, (eds) Teresa González Aja *et al.*, Madrid: Universidad Politécnica: 407–16.

—— (2002b) 'Eros and Sport: A Humanist's Perspective', in (2002) Guttmann *et al.*: 395–406.

—— (2003a) 'Ball Games, from the Roman Gentleman to the Renaissance Warrior', in *Militarism, Sport, Europe: War without Weapons*, (ed.) J. A. Mangan, *European Sports History Review* 5: 46–64.

—— (2003b) 'Montaigne and the Sports of Italy', *Renaissance and Reformation / Renaissance et Réforme* 27: 41–51.

—— (2003c) 'Theatres of Empowerment: Renaissance Spectator Sports and Their Ancient and Medieval Antecedents', in *Texte et représentation: les arts du spectacle (XVIe–XVIIIe siècles*, (ed.) B. Bolduc, *Texte: Revue de critique et de théorie littéraire* 33/34: 57–82.

—— (2004) 'Idéologies du sport: Moyen-Age et Renaissance', in *Sport et idéologie/Sport and Ideology*, (eds) Jean-François Loudcher *et al.*, 2 vols, Besançon: Comité Européen de l'Histoire du Sport, 2: 353–61.

—— (2006) Review Essay: 'The History of Golf: Reading Pictures, Viewing Texts', *Journal of Sport History* 32(3).

—— and Brian Merrilees (eds) (2007) *Athletes and Athletics in the Early Modern Era/Le sport et les athlètes au seuil de l'ère moderne*, Essays and Studies, Toronto: Centre for Reformation and Renaissance Studies.

McKitterick, Rosamond (1995) *The Frankish Kings and Culture in the Early Middle Ages*, Aldershot: Variorum.

Mehl, Erwin (1928) 'Das älteste Werk über das Bodenturnen: Archange Tuccaro: "Trois dialogues de l'exercice de sauter, et voltiger en l'air", Paris 1599', *Die Leibesübungen* 4, 2: 33–41.

—— (1930a) 'Das Petauron – ein Federbrett', *Die Leibesübungen* 6, 7: 178–80.

—— (1930b) 'Hieronymus Mercurialis, ein alter Streiter für die Leibesübungen. Zu seinem 400. Geburtstag', *Die Leibesübungen* 6, 19: 561–70.

—— (1937) 'Antonio Scaino "Trattato del giuoco della pall" (Venedig 1555). Das erste Ballspielbuch der Neuzeit – eine turngeschichtliche Urkunde aus der Wende vom Humanismus zum Hofmannsvorbild', *Erziehung* 56, 19/20: 437–45 and *Erziehung* 56, 21: 490–6.

Mehl, Jean-Michel (1982) 'Le pouvoir civil et les jeux sportifs dans la France médiévale', *Sport und Kultur/Sport et civilisation* XXXV/5/B: 15–16.

—— (1990) *Les jeux au royaume de France du XIIIe au début du XVIe siècle*, Paris: Fayard.

—— (ed.) (1993) *Jeux, sports et divertissements au Moyen Age et à l'âge classique*, Paris: Editions du Comité des travaux historiques et scientifiques.

Meijer, Fik (2004a) *The Gladiators, History's Most Deadly Sport*, (trans.) Liz Waters, London: Souvenir Press; orig. edn (2003) Amsterdam: Athenaeum – Polak & Van Gennep.

—— (2004b) *Wagenrennen: Spektakelshows in Rome en Constantinopel*, Amsterdam: Athenaeum – Polak & Van Gennep.

Menestrier, Claude François (1669) *Traité des tournois, joustes, carrousels et autres spectacles publics*, Lyon: Jacques Muguet; facs. repr. (1975) Roanne: Horwath.

Mercurialis, Hieronymus (1672) *De arte gymnastica libri sex* [1569], Amsterdam: Andres Frisius; facs. repr. (undated) Ilkley: Scolar Press.

Merdrignac, Bernard (2002) *Le sport au Moyen Age*, Rennes: Presses de l'Université de Rennes.

Messeri, Antonio (ed.) (1894) *Una giostra per amore in Vicenza nell'anno MDLII*, Florence: Salvadore Landi.

Miller, Stephen (1991) *Arete: Greek Sports from Ancient Sources*, 2nd edn (expanded), Berkeley, Los Angeles, CA and Oxford: University of California Press.

—— (2004) *Ancient Greek Athletics*, New Haven, CT and London: Yale University Press.

Molinet, Jean (1936–9) *Les faictz et dictz* [1505], (ed.) N. Dupire, 3 vols, Paris: Société des Anciens Textes Français.

Mommsen, Theodor E. (1942) 'Football in Renaissance Florence', *Yale University Library Gazette* 16: 14–19.

Montaigne, Michel de (1958) 'Travel Journal' [1580–1], in *The Complete Works of Montaigne*, (trans.) Donald Frame, Stanford, CA: Stanford University Press.

—— (1965) *Essais* [1580–92], (eds) P. Villey and V. L. Saulnier, Paris: Presses Universitaires de France.

—— (1983) *Journal de voyage* [1580–1], (ed.) F. Garavini, Paris: Gallimard.

Morgan, Roger (1995) *Tennis, the Development of the European Ball Game*, Oxford: Ronaldson.

Muhlberger, Steven (2002) *Jousts and Tournaments: Charny and the Rules of Chivalric Sport in Fourteenth-Century France*, Union City, CA: Chivalry Bookshelf.

Mulcaster, Richard (1994) *Positions Concerning the Training Up of Children* [1581], (ed.) W. Barker, Toronto, Buffalo, NY and London: University of Toronto Press.

Nardone, Davide (1989) *I gladiatori romani*, Rome: E.I.L.E.S.

Nelis, Damien (2001) *Vergil's Aeneid and the Argonautica of Apollonius Rhodius*, ARCA – Classical and Medieval Texts, Papers, and Monographs 39, Leeds: Francis Cairns.

Nennius (1985) *The Historia Brittonum* [830]. *3 The 'Vatican' Recension*, (ed.) D. N. Dumville, Cambridge: D. S. Brewer.

Newby, Zahra (2002) 'Greek Athletics as Roman Spectacle: The Mosaics from Ostia and Rome', *Papers from the British School at Rome* 70: 177–203.

—— (2005) *Greek Athletics in the Roman World: Victory and Virtue*, Oxford: Oxford University Press.

Nichols, John (1823) *The Progresses and Public Processions of Queen Elizabeth*, 3 vols, London: John Nichols and Son.

Nithard (1926) *Histoire des fils de Louis le Pieux* [843], (ed.) Ph. Lauer, Paris: Champion; (English trans.) B. W. Scholz and B. Rogers in *Carolingian Chronicles: Royal Frankish Annals and Nithard's Histories*, Ann Arbor, MI: University of Michigan Press.

Olivová, Věra (1989) 'Chariot Racing in the Ancient World', *Nikephoros* 2: 65–88.

Orme, Nicholas (1983) *Early British Swimming 55 BC–AD 1719*, Exeter: University of Exeter Press.

Painter, Sidney (1933) *William Marshall, Knight-errant, Baron, and Regent of England*, Baltimore, MD: Johns Hopkins University Press.

Panvinio, Onofrio (1600) *De ludis circensibus* [1568], Venice: G.-B. Ciotto.

Paris, Matthew (1880) *Chronica maiora* [1258] (ed.) H. R. Luard, 5 vols, London: Longman.

Parisse, Michel (1985) 'Le tournoi en France, des origines à la fin du XIIIe siècle', in (1985) Fleckenstein: 175–211.

Parker, Kenneth L. (1988) *The English Sabbath, a Study of Doctrines and Disciplines from the Reformation to the Civil War*, Cambridge: Cambridge University Press.

Pasquier, Estienne (1586) *Les Lettres*, Paris: L'Angelier.

Pauernfeindt, Andreas (1538) *La noble science des joueurs despee*, Antwerp: Vorstermann; trans. of (1516) *Ergrundung ritterlicher Kunst der Fechterey*, Vienna: Hier-Vietor.

Pauly, August Friedrich von *et al.* (1893–1972) *Paulys Realencyclopädie der classischen Altertumswissenschaft*, 34 vols, Stuttgart: Druckenmüller.

Percival, John (1997) 'Desperately Seeking Sidonius: The Realities of Life in Fifth-Century Gaul', *Latomus* 56: 279–92.

Petrarch (1934) *Le familiari* [before 1374], (ed.) V. Rossi, 4 vols, Florence: Sansone.

—— (1975) *Rerum familiarum libri I–VIII* [before 1374], (trans.) A. Bernardo, Albany, NY: State University of New York Press.

Piganiol, André (1923) *Recherches sur les jeux romains*, Strasbourg: Istra.

Plass, Paul (1995) *The Game of Death in Ancient Rome: Arena Sport and Political Suicide*, Madison, WI: University of Wisconsin Press.

Pluvinel, Antoine de (1625) *L'Instruction du roy en l'exercice de monter à cheval*, Paris: Michel Nivelle.

Poema (1963) *Poema de mio Cid* [1140], (ed.) R. Menéndez Pidal, 10th edn, Madrid: Espasa Calpe; (English trans.) (1959) W. S. Merwin, *Poem of the Cid*, New York, NY: New American Library.

Poliziano, Angelo (1976) *Stanze per la giostra* [1475], in *Poesie italiane*, (ed.) M. Luzi and S. Orlando, Milan: Rizzoli.

Pollux, Julius (1967) *Onomasticon* [190], (ed.) E. Bethe, Stuttgart: Teubner; 1st edn (1931); (partial English trans.) in (1991) Miller: 119–20.

Pulci, Luigi (1986) *La giostra* [1471], in *Opere minori*, (ed.) P. Orvieto, Milan: Mursia: 59–120.

Rabelais, François (1994) *Pantagruel* [1532] and *Gargantua* [1534] in *Oeuvres complètes*, (eds) M. Huchon and F. Moureau, Bibliothèque de la Pléiade, Paris: NRF-Gallimard: 209–337 and 1–153.

Récits (1887) Récits d'un bourgeois de Valenciennes (XIVe siècle), (ed.) F. Kervyn de Lettenhove, Louvain: Lefever.

Reis, Martin (1994) Sport bei Horaz, Nikephoros Beihefte 2, Hildesheim: Weidmann.

René d'Anjou (1986) *Le livre des tournois du roi René* [1460], intro. F. Avril, mod. French adaptation E. Pognon, Paris: Herscher.

Reynolds, L. D. and N. G. Wilson (1974) *Scribes and Scholars: a Guide to the Transmission of Greek and Latin Literature*, 2nd edn, Oxford: Clarendon.

Ricci, Bartolomeo (1978) [*Lettera sopra la pallamaglio*, c. 1553], (untitled Latin orig. with facing Italian trans.) in (1978) Bascetta: 2.261–9.

Ricciardi, Lucia (1992) *Col senno, col tesoro e colla lancia: Riti e giochi cavallereschi nella Firenze del Magnifico Lorenzo*, Florence: Le Lettere.

Rivkind, Isaac (1933) 'A Responsum from R. Moses Provençalo on Ball Games', *Tarbiz* 4(4): 366–76 [in Hebrew].

Rizzi, Alessandra (1995) *Ludus/ludere. Giocare in Italia alla fine del medio evo*, Treviso/Roma: Fondazione Benetton-Viella.

Robert, Louis (1940) *Les gladiateurs dans l'Orient grec*, Paris: Bibliothèque de l'Ecole des Hautes Etudes; repr. (1971) Amsterdam: Hakkert.

Robinson, R. S. (1955) *Sources for the History of Greek Athletics in English Translation*, Cincinnati: n.a.

Rochon, André (1963) *La Jeunesse de Laurent de Médicis (1449–1478)*, Paris: Belles Lettres.

Romier, Lucien (1914) *Les origines politiques des Guerres de Religion*, 2 vols, Paris: Librairie Académique Perrin.

Ronsard, Pierre de (1914–75) *Oeuvres complètes*, (eds) P. Laumonier, I. Silver and R. Lebègue, 20 vols, Paris: Société des Textes Français Modernes.

Roos, Paavo (1989) Review of Sturzebecker (1985) in *Nikephoros* 2: 259–66.

Rouéché, Charlotte (1993) *Performers and Partisans at Aphrodisias in the Roman and late Roman Periods*, London: Society for the Promotion of Roman Studies.

Rühl, Joachim (1975) *Die Olympische Spiele Robert Dovers*, Heidelberg: Carl Winter-Universitätsverlag.

—— (2001) 'Regulations for the Joust in Fifteenth-Century Europe: Francesco Sforza Visconti (1465) and John Tiptoft (1466)', *International Journal for the History of Sport* 18: 193–208.

—— (2006) 'Hommes et femmes dans les tournois du Moyen Age', *CLIO, Histoire, Femmes et Sociétés* 23: 17–45.

—— (2007) 'A Treasure-trove: One of the Four Originals of the Tournament Regulations of Heilbronn 1485', in (2007) McClelland and Merrilees.

Russell, Joycelyne G. (1969) *The Field of Cloth of Gold: Men and Manners in 1520*, London: Routledge and Kegan Paul.

Rymer, T. (ed.) (1830) *Foedera, Conventiones…*, Publication 11, vol. 32, London: Record Commission Publications.

Sainct-Didier, Henri de (1573) *Traicté contenant les secrets du premier livre sur l'espee seule*, Paris: Mettayer and Challenge; facs. repr. (1907) Paris: Société du livre d'art ancien et moderne.

Salvestrini, Virgilio (1934) *Antiche feste tradizionali pisane. Il gioco del mazza-scudo che precedette il gioco del ponte*, Pisa: Salvestrini.

Sansone, David (1988) *Greek Athletics and the Genesis of Sport*, Berkeley, Los Angeles, CA and London: University of California Press.

Sardo, Ranieri (1845) *Cronaca pisana dall'anno 962 sino al 1400* [c. 1400], (ed.) F. Bonaini, Archivio storico italiano 6(2): 73–244.

Sauval, Henri (1724) *Histoire et recherches des antiquités de la ville de Paris*, 3 vols, Paris: Moette et Chardon.

Savi, Fabrizio (1980) *I gladiatori. Storia, organizzazione, iconografia*, Rome: Gruppo Archeologico Romano.

Saviolo, Vincentio (1595) *His Practise. In two Bookes*, London: John Wolff; facs. repr. in (1972) Jackson: 185–488.

Scaglione, Aldo (1991) *Knights at Court: Courtliness, Chivalry, & Courtesy from Ottonian Germany to the Italian Renaissance*, Berkeley, Los Angeles, CA and Oxford: University of California Press.

Scaino, Antonio (1555) *Trattato del giuoco della palla*, Venice: Giolito de' Ferrari; modern edn (2000) (ed.) G. Nonni, Urbino: QuattroVenti; excerpt in (1978) Bascetta: 2.271–323; (English trans.) (1951) W. P. Kershaw, London: Strangeways Press; and (1984) P. A. Negretti, London: Racquetier Productions.

Scanlon, Thomas (2002) *Eros and Greek Sport*, London and New York, NY: Oxford University Press.

Scarborough, John (1971) 'Galen and the Gladiators', *Episteme* 5(2): 98–111.

Schiavone, Aldo (2000) *The End of the Past: Ancient Rome and the Modern West*, (trans.) M. J. Schneider, Cambridge, MA and London: Harvard University Press.

Schindler, Otto G. (2001) 'Zan Tabarino, "Spielmann des Kaisers": italienische Komödianten des Cinquecento zwischen den Höfen von Wien und Paris', *Römische Historische Mitteilungen* 43: 411–544.

Schmidt, Sandra (2006) 'Luftspringen und Kopfübern – Bewegung als Wissenschaft und Kunst in der Frühen Neuzeit', doctoral thesis, Berlin, Freie Universität.

—— (2007) 'Trois dialogues de l'exercice de sauter et voltiger en l'air – Strategies of ennoblement of a bodily practice in the 16th century', in McClelland and Merrilees (2007).

Segar, William (1590) *The Book of Honor and Armes*, London: Richard Jhones; facs. repr. (1975) (ed.) D. Bornstein, Delmar, NY: Scholars' Facsimiles and Reprints.

Semenza, Gregory M. Colón (2003) *Sport, Politics, and Literature in the English Renaissance*, Newark, DE: University of Delaware Press.

Sermini, Gentile (1968) 'Il giuoco della pugna' [1425], in *Novelle*, (ed.) G. Vettori, 2 vols, Rome: Avanzini and Torraca: 1.193–7.

Serres, Jean de (1598) *Recueil des choses memorables avenues en France sous le regne de Henri II*, 2nd edn, n.a., unpaginated; 1st edn (1595).

Shelton, Jo-Ann (1988) *As the Romans Did: A Source Book in Roman Social History*, Oxford and New York, NY: Oxford University Press.

Sidney, Sir Philip (1962) *The Poems of Sir Philip Sidney*, (ed.) W. A. Ringler, Oxford: Clarendon.

—— (1963) *The Prose Works*, (ed.) A. Feuillerat, 4 vols, Cambridge: Cambridge University Press; orig. edn (1912).

Silver, George (1599) *Paradoxes of Defence…*, London: Edward Blount; facs. repr. in (1972) Jackson: 489–570.

—— (1898) *Bref Instructions upon my Pradoxes* [sic] *of Defence* [1599], British Library Sloan ms. 376; (ed.) C. G. R. Matthey, in *The Works of George Silver*, London: G. Bell; facs. repr. in (1972) Jackson: 571–634.

Simonsohn, Schlomo (1977) *History of the Jews in the Duchy of Mantua*, Publications of the Diaspora Research Institute 17, Jerusalem: Kiryath Sepher.

Simri, Uriel (1973) 'The Responsa of Rabbi Moses Provençalo (1560) about the Game of Tennis on Sabbath', in *Proceedings of the First International Seminar on the History of Physical Education and Sport*, Netanya: Wingate Institute: 19–25 and 51–2 [in Hebrew]; (English trans.) Vincent Decaen in (2007) McClelland and Merrilees.

Statius (1988) *Silvae IV*, (ed. and trans.) K. M. Coleman, Oxford: Clarendon.

Stokes, William (1652) *The Vaulting Master: or, the Art of Vaulting. Reduced to a Method, comprized under certaine Rules...*, Oxford: Richard Davis.

Stone, Lily C. (1960) *English Sports and Recreations*, Folger Booklets on Tudor and Stuart Civilization, Washington, DC: Folger Shakespeare Library.

Strutt, Joseph (1969) *The Sports and Pastimes of the People of England* [1801], Bath: Firecrest.

Sturzebecker, Russell (1985) *Athletic-Cultural Sites in the Greco-Roman World*, West Chester, PA: R. L. Sturzebecker.

Suetonius (1967) *Peri Blasphēmiōn. Peri Paidiōn (Extraits byzantins)*, (ed.) J. Taillardat, Paris: Belles Lettres.

Swaddling, Judith (1999) *The Ancient Olympic Games*, 2nd edn, London: British Museum.

Sweet, Waldo (1987) *Sport and Recreation in Ancient Greece*, Oxford: Oxford University Press.

Szabó, Thomas (1985) 'Das Turnier in Italien', in (1985) Fleckenstein: 344–70.

Talhoffer, Hans (1887) *Fechtbuch aus dem Jahre 1467*, (ed.) G. Hergsell, Prague: Calve.

—— (2000) *Medieval Combat. A Fifteenth-Century Illustrated Manual of Swordfighting and Close-Quarter Combat*, (ed. and trans.) Mark Rector, London: Greenhill Books; Mechanicsburg, PA: Stackpole Books.

Tavannes, Gaspard de Saulx, seigneur de (1838) *Mémoires* [c. 1573], in Michaud et Poujoulat, *Nouvelle Collection des mémoires pour servir à l'histoire de France*, Paris: Chez l'Éditeur du Commentaire Analytique du Code Civil, 8.1–504.

Tenagli, Michelangelo (1538–66) *Ricordi*, MS, Florence: Biblioteca Riccardiana.

Terry, David (2003) 'Boxing: Some Early British History', *Annual of CESH* 4: 41–8,

Thibault, Girard (1628) *Académie de l'espée...ou se demonstrent par reigles mathematiques...*, Leiden: Elzevier.

Thimm, Carl (1968) *A Complete Bibliography of Fencing and Duelling...*, New York, NY: Benjamin Blom; facs. repr. of orig. ed. of 1898.

Thomas, Keith (1983) *Man and the Natural World: A History of the Modern Sensibility*, New York, NY: Pantheon; also as *Man and the Natural World: Changing Attitudes in England 1500–1800*, London: Allen Lane, Penguin Books.

Throckmorton, Nicholas (1863) [Letters to Lord Cecil, the Lords of the Council, and Elizabeth I, 15 May–8 July 1559], in *Calendar of State Papers, Foreign Series, of the Reign of Elizabeth*, (ed.) J. Stevenson, vol. 1, London: Longman, Green, Longman, Roberts & Green: 255–365.

Thuillier, Jean-Paul (1987) '"Auriga/Agitator": de simples synonymes?', *Revue de philologie, de littérature et d'histoire* 61: 233–7.

—— (1996a) 'Stace, *Thébaïde* 6: les jeux funèbres et les réalités sportives', *Nikephoros* 9: 151–67.

—— (1996b) *Le sport dans la Rome antique*, Paris: Errance.

Tosi, Mario (1946) *Il torneo di Belvedere in Vaticano e i tornei in Italia nel cinquecento*, Rome: Storia e Letteratura.

Treadgold, Warren (1997) *A History of the Byzantine State and Society*, Stanford, CA: Stanford University Press.

Trexler, Richard (1980) *Public Life in Renaissance Florence*, New York, NY: Academic Press.

Truffi, Riccardo (1911) *Giostre e cantori di giostre. Studi e ricerche di storia e letteratura*, Rocca S. Casciano: Licinio Cappelli.

Tuccaro, Arcangelo (1599) *Trois dialogues de l'exercice de sauter et voltiger en l'air*, Paris: Claude de Monstr'oeil; re-issued Tours: Georges Griveau, 1616.

Tuchman, Barbara (1978) *A Distant Mirror: The Calamitous 14th Century*, New York, NY: Knopf.

Turner, Frank (1981) *The Greek Heritage in Victorian Britain*, New Haven, CT and London: Yale University Press.

Ueberhorst, Horst (1972–89) *Geschichte der Leibesübungen*, 6 vols in 7 parts, Berlin, Munich and Frankfurt: Bartels and Wernitz.

Ulmann, Jacques (1977) *De la gymnastique aux sports modernes*, Paris: Vrin; 1st edn (1965) Paris: Presses Universitaires de France.

Vadi, Filippo (2001) *L'arte cavalleresca del combattimento* [1482–7], (eds) M. Rubboli and L. Cesari, Rimini: Il Cerchio.

Vanoyeke, Violaine (1992) *La naissance des Jeux Olympiques et le sport dans l'Antiquité*, Paris: Belles Lettres.

Varchi, Benedetto (1838–41) *Storia fiorentina* [1565], (ed.) Lelio Arbib, Florence: Società Editrice delle Storie del Nardi e del Varchi.

Vaucelle, Serge (2004) 'L'art de jouer à la cour: Transformation des jeux d'exercice dans l'éducation de la noblesse française au début de l'ère moderne', doctoral thesis, Paris: Ecole des Hautes Etudes en Sciences Sociales.

Vegetius (1995) *Epitoma rei militaris* [fourth century], (ed.) Alf Önnerfors, Stuttgart and Leipzig: Teubner.

Vegio, Maffeo (1933–6) *De educatione liberorum* [1444], (eds) M. W. Fanning and A. S Sullivan, 2 vols, Washington, DC: Catholic University of America.

Vergerio, Pier Paolo (2002) *The Character and Studies Befitting a Free-Born Youth* [c.1400], in *Humanist Educational Treatises*, (ed. and trans.) Craig W. Kallendorf, The I Tatti Renaissance Library, Cambridge, MA and London: Harvard University Press: 3–74.

Vesley, Mark (1998) 'Gladiatorial Training for Girls in the *Collegia Iuvenum* of the Roman Empire', *Echos du Monde Classique/Classical Views* 42: 85–93.

Vieilleville, Francois de (1757) *Mémoires* [1571], 5 vols, Paris: Guérin and Delatour.

Vigarello, Georges (2000) *Passion sport: Histoire d'une culture*, Paris: Textuel.

—— (2002) *Du jeu ancien au show sportif: la naissance d'un mythe*, Paris: Le Seuil.

Villalobos, Simon de (1605) *Modo de pelear a la gineta*, Valladolid: Andres de Merchán.

Ville, Georges (1979) 'Religion et politique: comment ont pris fin les combats de gladiateurs', *Annales ESC* 34: 651–71.

—— (1981) *La gladiature en occident des origines à la mort de Domitien*, Rome: Ecole Française de Rome.

Vives, Juan Luis (1913) *On Education. A Translation of the De tradendis disciplinis* [1531], (trans.) Foster Watson, Cambridge: Cambridge University Press.

—— (1970) *Tudor School-boy Life. Dialogues* [a trans. of *Latinae linguae exercitatio*, 1540], (trans.) Foster Watson, London: Frank Cass.

Von Clausewitz, Carl (1993) *Vom Kriege*, in *Kriegstheorie und Kriegsgeschichte: Carl von Clausewitz, Helmuth von Moltke*, (ed.) R. Stumpf, Frankfurt: Deutscher Klassiker Verlag.

Walbank, F. W. (1969) *The Awful Revolution: The Decline of the Roman Empire in the West*, Toronto: University of Toronto Press; 1st edn (1946).

Ward-Perkins, Bryan (1984) *From Classical Antiquity to the Middle Ages: Urban and Public Building in Northern and Central Italy AD 300–850*, Oxford: Oxford University Press.

Weiler, Ingomar (1981) *Der Sport bei der Völkern der alten Welt: Eine Einführung*, Darmstadt: Wissenschaftliche Buchgesellschaft.

West, Michael (1973) 'Spenser, Everard Digby, and the Renaissance Art of Swimming', *Renaissance Quarterly* 26(1): 11–22.

Whitfield, Christopher (ed.) (1962) *Robert Dover and the Cotswold Games. Annalia Dubrensia*, London: Sotheran

Wiedemann, Thomas (1992) *Emperors and Gladiators*, London and New York, NY: Routledge.

William the Marshall (1891–1901) *L'histoire de Guillaume le Maréchal* [c. 1220], (ed.) Paul Meyer, 3 vols, Société de l'Histoire de France, Paris: Renouard.

Willughby, Francis (2003) *Book of Games. A Seventeenth-Century Treatise on Sports, Games and Pastimes* [before 1672], (eds) D. Cram *et al.*, Aldershot and Burlington, VT: Ashgate.

Wilson, David M. (1985) *The Bayeux Tapestry. The Complete Tapestry in Colour*, London: Thames and Hudson.

Wistrand, Magnus (1992) *Entertainment and Violence in Ancient Rome: The Attitudes of Roman Writers of the First Century A. D.*, Göteborg: Acta Universitatis Gothoburgensis.

Wynman, Nicolas (1538) *Colymbetes, sive de arte natandi*, Augsburg: Henricus Steyner.

Young, David (1985) *The Olympic Myth of Greek Amateur Athletics*, Chicago, IL: Ares.

Zitner, S. P. (1969–70) 'Hamlet Duellist', *University of Toronto Quarterly* 39: 1–18.

Index